FORGOTTEN
FIFTEENTH

FORGOTTEN FIFTEENTH

THE DARING AIRMEN WHO CRIPPLED HITLER'S WAR MACHINE

BARRETT TILLMAN

REGNERY
HISTORY

Regnery History™ is a trademark of Salem Communications Holding Corporation; Regnery® is a registered trademark of Salem Communications Holding Corporation

First paperback edition published 2015: ISBN 978-1-62157-404-0

Originally published in hardcover, 2014: ISBN 978-1-62157-208-4, cataloging information below

Library of Congress Cataloging-in-Publication Data

Tillman, Barrett.
 Forgotten Fifteenth : the daring airmen who crippled Hitler's war machine / Barrett Tillman.
     pages cm
 Includes bibliographical references and index.
 1. United States. Army Air Forces. Air Force, 15th. 2. World War, 1939-1945--Aerial operations, American. 3. World War, 1939-1945--Campaigns--Mediterranean Region. I. Title.
 D790.2215th .T55 2014
 940.54'4973--dc23
                              2014001772

Published in the United States by
Regnery History
An imprint of Regnery Publishing
A Salem Communications Company
300 New Jersey Avenue NW
Washington, DC 20001
www.RegneryHistory.com

Manufactured in the United States of America

10 9 8 7 6 5 4 3 2

Books are available in quantity for promotional or premium use. For information on discounts and terms, please visit our website: www.Regnery.com.

*Dedicated to the members of the
U.S. Army Air Forces who served in the
Mediterranean Theater of operations
during the Second World War.*

CONTENTS

PREFACE ix

PROLOGUE xi

CHAPTER ONE: Up from the Desert 1
November 1943–January 1944

CHAPTER TWO: The Winter War 27
January–March 1944

CHAPTER THREE: Italian Spring 55
March–June 1944

CHAPTER FOUR: East to Ploesti 81
April–June 1944

CHAPTER FIVE: Mediterranean Summer 115
July–September 1944

CHAPTER SIX: Other Players 149
1944–1945

CHAPTER SEVEN: Air Supremacy 183
September–December 1944

CHAPTER EIGHT: Mission Accomplished 215
January–May 1945

CHAPTER NINE: Legacy 247
May 1945 and beyond

ACKNOWLEDGMENTS 273

APPENDIX 277

NOTES 287

BIBLIOGRAPHY 311

INDEX 315

PREFACE

In early 2012 a World War II veteran of the Eighth Air Force, which had been based in Britain, asked if I were writing another book. When I told him the subject, he almost scoffed. "The Fifteenth? They were down there in Italy. Why write about them?"

I bit my lip then replied, "Because they helped win the war."

Probably no one knows how many books have been published about the "Mighty Eighth," but there have been dozens, even excluding unit histories. This, however, is the first full-length history of the "Forgotten Fifteenth," which conducted the southern half of the Allied strategic bombing campaign in Europe. After nearly seventy years, the Fifteenth's story is long, long overdue for a telling.

And what a story it is.

During a hard-fought, four-month campaign in the spring and summer of 1944, the Fifteenth shut down the Axis powers' main source of oil. The cost was high—nearly 240 aircraft lost and their crews killed or captured—but the effort was ultimately worthwhile. The near-total destruction of the Ploesti complex in Romania had far-reaching consequences for the German war machine.

Yet in its eighteen months of operations—from November 1943 to V-E Day in May 1945—the Fifteenth accomplished more than turning off Hitler's Balkan oil tap. The five bombardment wings struck other petroleum targets throughout the southern and central Reich, ruined enemy communications, and constantly hammered sources of production. Not all were in Germany, as Fifteenth airmen operated in the airspace of a dozen other Axis or occupied nations.

Even more than writing an operational history, I want to tell the story of "the Forgotten Fifteenth" as an institution. That would be impossible without a bottom-up perspective, from the flight lines on Foggia airfields to headquarters in Bari. I gained an education in researching this book, often drawing upon interviews conducted decades ago.

I have ensured that every Fifteenth Air Force flying group—if not every unit—is mentioned in this book. The veteran contributors represent eight of the Fifteenth's bomb groups and four fighter groups plus three Luftwaffe units. Coverage of the famed Red Tails of the 332nd Fighter Group is proportionate to their role among the other twenty-nine groups of the Mediterranean strategic air force.

Aviation purists note that Germany's famous Messerschmitt "Me 109" fighter actually was the Bf 109, for *Bayerische Flugzeugwerke* or Bavarian Aircraft Factory. The "Me" designation was adopted in 1938 and applied to new designs from that date. I have used both the "Bf" and "Me" designations where appropriate.

Barrett Tillman
March 2013

PROLOGUE

The bombers crossed the Alps at Brenner Pass, northbound for Munich. At 4,500 feet elevation, Brenner was among the lowest of the alpine passes, its late spring verdancy spanning the border between Italy and Austria.

Some four hundred miles north of their Italian bases, the bombers were well along the route toward Innsbruck and into southern Germany. By the time they crossed the pass, they were established at cruise speed, making 180 to 210 mph four miles above the gap in the spine of Europe.

A few airmen reflected that Brenner Pass was accustomed to conflict; they thought the Carthaginian genius Hannibal's surviving war elephants may have used the same passage into Italy twenty-two centuries before.

Some fliers had made the trip more than twenty times, but they seldom failed to take in the gorgeous scenery. The Alps often defied description: the crystalline clarity of the high whiteness was unlike anything most fliers had ever seen. Even those who had trained in the American West had little to compare to it: the Sierra Nevada had more peaks topping thirteen thousand feet but covered less than one-third the area of the Alps. Craggy mountains, snow-capped much of the year, towered on either side of the green valley. It was a view that few Europeans—let alone Americans—had ever seen. Not until the post-war boom in commercial aviation would large numbers of air travelers see Brenner's beauty from above.

The young Americans looking down on the scene, however, took only passing note. Most were under twenty-five years old; probably none were over forty. The purpose of their flight was far removed from sightseeing. Each of the five hundred bombers bore four or five tons of high explosives, destined for the armories that supplied the Wehrmacht.

The visitors flew in miserable conditions. Five miles above sea level, they sucked bottled oxygen through rubber hoses and masks, leaving their mouths and throats dry and raspy. The cold penetrated their electrically heated suits, gloves, and boots. The temperature at that altitude hovered around thirty degrees below zero Fahrenheit. Frostbite was a frequent cause of casualties. Waist gunners flexed their legs and bent their knees; most stood at their windows for the entire six-hour mission. The tubes in which the men relieved themselves froze, and many bombers had no chemical toilets. Some crews resorted to cardboard boxes.

The Liberators and Flying Fortresses cruised at twenty-three to twenty-seven thousand feet, where contrails formed—hot engine exhausts condensed in the super-chilled air to produce the telltale "cons." Above them, escorting fighters also produced the long white tendrils that made visual identification so easy for the defenders.

Innsbruck lay just ahead; Munich seventy miles beyond.

Ahead, above, and on the flanks roamed formations of escorting fighters: single-engine Mustangs and twin-engine Lightnings in their weaving patterns to avoid outrunning the bombers.

All too soon, intercoms and radios sparked into life.

"Heads up! Here they come!"

"Bandits, twelve o'clock!"

On the periphery of the bomber stream, fighters bearing black crosses and white stars tangled in frantic, churning combat. Four-plane flights broke into two-plane sections, then often into singles. Loners were vulnerable; intelligent pilots sought friends. The most eager sought victims.

Some of the defenders inevitably broke through.

By twelve-plane *Staffeln* and thirty-six-plane *Gruppen*, the Messerschmitts and Focke-Wulfs slammed into the ordered ranks. Bombers' noses and top turrets opened fire, twin .50 calibers chattering away, sending tracers curling outbound, crisscrossing streams of German 20mm cannon shells. Inevitably both sides scored hits. A Messerschmitt, caught in the crossfire of a bomber formation, cartwheeled out of control, spiraling crazily through space as it tumbled to destruction.

The other fighters came straight in, with a combined closing speed of more than 400 miles per hour. Ambitious young Teutons pressed their attacks to minimum range, gauging the distance in their Revi gun sights. The aim point was the cockpit of the nearest bomber, seeking to kill the two pilots on the flight deck. Gouges of aluminum and sprinkles of shattered glass tinkled through the high, frigid air, and a four-engine giant dropped out of formation. Other fighters jumped on it, eager to complete the kill.

Inside the bombers, waist gunners took fleeting shots at gray-green silhouettes flashing through the formation. The single handheld Brownings thumped out their authoritative basso at thirteen rounds per second. In extended combat, empty brass cartridges fell in piles around the gunners' booted feet. Teenaged airmen reverted to their basic gunnery classes in Utah or Texas: "A fighter's not a duck or pheasant. You're flying at 200 mph so aim behind him to hit him!"

Almost unnoticed at first, black-brown explosions erupted in the air ahead. Nearing the target, radar-controlled flak batteries had tracked the *Indianers* and gained a firing solution. When the first shells burst, Luftwaffe gun crews made immediate corrections, refining the geometry using the target height and speed. With both figures verified, the antiaircraft crews did not need to track the moving targets. They put round after round into a cube of airspace, knowing that the *Viermots* had to fly through the area. From there on it was three-dimensional mathematics. How many planes could penetrate a given piece of sky without colliding with a projectile bearing enough explosive to destroy one or more aircraft?

Avoiding the worst of the flak zone, the defending fighters disengaged, awaiting events. As long as they could avoid the American escorts, the FWs and Me's could reposition for a shot at the bombers turning southward for home.

Home was Foggia, near the Adriatic coast of Italy, the base of the Fifteenth U.S. Army Air Force. At that moment it was a long, long way off.

CHAPTER ONE

UP FROM THE DESERT

NOVEMBER 1943–JANUARY 1944

The general's name was James Harold Doolittle, and he might have been the finest airman who ever lived. Short, stocky, and balding, the former boxer and gymnast exuded confident competence. He combined an unexcelled cockpit reputation with a searching intellect that had won him flying trophies and academic honors—and a powerful will to succeed.

A noted air racer, Doolittle had won every event worth entering in the 1920s and 1930s and earned one of the first doctorates in aeronautics. As a lieutenant colonel he achieved even greater fame and lasting glory as leader of the Tokyo raid in April 1942, leading sixteen army B-25s in an unprecedented operation. The Mitchell bombers took off from the aircraft carrier *Hornet* far from the Japanese coast, struck six cities, and got away clean. One plane diverted to Russia and though the others ran out of fuel, the Doolittle raid sent

American morale soaring when the nation needed a boost as never before.

Upon return home, Doolittle received the Medal of Honor and promotion to brigadier general. That summer he assumed command of the U.S. Twelfth Air Force, preparing for the Allied invasion of North Africa. There he gained a second star before year's end. Consequently, in March 1943 Doolittle rose to lead the North African Strategic Air Force (NASAF), including British units. Despite his seniority, he continued flying combat, including the first U.S. air raid on Rome in June. He also flew a few sorties in a Spitfire, learning the fabled British fighter's capabilities, and confided that if he had encountered some German aircraft, he would not have been disappointed.[1]

In twelve months of operating in North Africa, Doolittle had acquired vital knowledge and experience. He matured quickly as an air commander, combining bomber, fighter, reconnaissance, and troop carrier units into an efficient, increasingly capable entity. The NASAF included ten British bomber squadrons, providing a joint command that boded well for Doolittle's future.

Now, on the first day of November 1943, Major General Doolittle assumed his third command in the Mediterranean Theater. From his sun-bleached headquarters in Tunis, he prepared to take the air war to the European mainland.

Anglo-American forces had landed in Italy during early September—the British across the Messina Strait from Sicily and the Americans at Salerno, farther up the west coast. A slogging ground campaign ensued, grinding to a halt against prepared positions that Germany called the Gustav Line. Italy has some of the finest defensive terrain in Europe, and Field Marshal Albert Kesselring made full use of it. That winter the campaign bogged down in mountain fighting barely eighty miles north of Foggia. Meanwhile, Allied forces had occupied Taranto in the heel of the Italian boot and Bari across the peninsula on the east coast, further securing southern Italy.

Against the background of the Italian campaign, the Fifteenth Air Force was created on short notice. With an eye on the muddy Foggia plain, on October 9 Army Air Forces commander Henry H. Arnold had proposed that the Joint Chiefs of Staff authorize the Fifteenth immediately. As Arnold noted, "It was to be equipped with groups already in Italy, supplemented by fifteen more from the States."[2]

Approval came fast. On October 22 General George C. Marshall, the army chief of staff, notified theater commander Dwight Eisenhower that the Fifteenth would stand up in ten days. The Allied command structure placed Doolittle under a British Theater commander, Field Marshal Sir Henry Maitland Wilson. Meanwhile, the Fifteenth's operations would be conducted under a longtime colleague of Doolittle's, Lieutenant General Carl Spaatz, overall commander of U.S. Strategic Air Forces. Spaatz lacked Doolittle's achievements and intellect, but it was a relationship based on long experience and mutual regard.

All was not sweetness and light among the Americans, however. Recalling his first meeting with Eisenhower in late 1942, Doolittle conceded that the supreme commander "took an immediate dislike to me; he had little or no use for me."[3]

There were two reasons for Eisenhower's disdain: Doolittle's characteristic bluntness was seldom popular at court, and despite his rank and the Medal of Honor, he remained a reserve officer. Eisenhower seemed to dismiss Doolittle as a glorified throttle jockey, though the aviator would have been justified in casting the West Pointer as a glorified desk jockey. Apparently Eisenhower, the consummate service politician, never grasped that Jimmy Doolittle knew more about aviation than most other people knew about anything.

When Doolittle established the Fifteenth Air Force, he escaped Eisenhower's hostility, as Ike had moved to England to prepare for the invasion of northern Europe. By then some of his frost had begun melting, as Doolittle had written his wife, "Think I am gradually selling myself to General Eisenhower but have a long way to go yet before he will be willing to admit his original estimate was wrong."[4]

The Germans had bloodied the American army in Tunisia in 1943. But with the conquest of Sicily that summer, the Allies were poised to take the European mainland. In support of that goal, Spaatz gave the Fifteenth Air Force four missions:

(1) Achieve air superiority by destroying the Luftwaffe in the air and on the ground.

(2) Participate in Operation Pointblank, the Anglo-American Combined Bomber Offensive (CBO) against Axis industry, including aircraft factories and airfields, ball-bearing plants, oil refineries, armament production, and submarine bases.

(3) Support ground forces in the Mediterranean Theater by attacking enemy transport in Italy and over the Brenner Pass into Austria. (The tactical Twelfth Air Force would provide direct air support to Allied armies.)

(4) Attack Axis forces and facilities in the Balkans.[5]

A longer-term goal was the buildup of air strength to support the Allied invasion of southern France, scheduled for the summer of 1944 after the Normandy landings.

The original CBO directive of January 1943 was amended by the Allied Combined Chiefs of Staff in May, who ordered "a joint United States–British air offensive to accomplish the progressive destruction of the German military, industrial and economic system, and the undermining of the morale of the German people to a point where their capacity for armed resistance is fatally weakened. This is construed as meaning so weakened as to permit initiation of final combined operations on the Continent." Some airmen believed that the last sentence was added to ensure that strategic airpower supported the overall Allied war effort—especially on the ground. Consequently, the Americans would target German war production by day, while the Royal Air Force continued attacking cities and, therefore, German morale, by night.[6]

FOGGIA

Barely 150 miles east-southeast of Rome and twenty miles inland, Foggia was an obvious choice for concentrating the new air force. The locale placed heavy bombers within reach of every likely target in the theater: Zagreb was 230 miles away, Sofia barely four hundred. Budapest, Vienna, Athens, and Munich lay within a five-hundred-mile arc; Regensburg, Bucharest, Ploesti, and Prague within six hundred miles; Blechhammer within 670; Marseilles within 730; and Berlin within nine hundred. The German capital remained out of the Fifteenth's range almost until the end of the war, but the most vital target—Romania's rich oil fields—was within reach. Hundreds of American bombers would crash in the Balkans before the war was won.

On October 30, two days before establishing the Fifteenth, Doolittle attended the Ninety-ninth Bomb Group's hundredth mission barbeque and beer party at Oudna Airfield just outside Tunis. The group had made its record in only seven months, and rain failed to dampen the fliers' enthusiasm. Good spirits always trailed in "General Jimmy's" slipstream.

Doolittle knew that his time in Tunis would be brief. He was to move his headquarters to Italy in thirty days—no small task given the complexity of the move. His staff included Major Bruce Johnson, a longtime aide who had attached himself to Doolittle's command by volunteering to deliver priority mail to Twelfth Air Force headquarters in Algiers. Once there he announced his intention to stay.

Jimmy Doolittle appreciated that kind of nerve. In the mid-1930s he had gamed the system by convincing the army and Shell Oil that each supported developing high-cost, high-octane fuel when neither would have done so independently. In 1942 he employed a left-hand, right-hand strategy to gain approval from General "Hap" Arnold and his chief of staff to lead the Tokyo mission. Neither officer realized he had been conned until too late to change.

Doolittle wanted the move from Tunisia to Italy—430 miles— accomplished in one day to sustain the pace of air operations. Bruce

Johnson was up to the task. He flew to Italy to scout locations around Foggia.

The British had captured the Foggia airfields in October, displacing the Italian Loyalists and German forces. Johnson's reconnaissance was not encouraging, however, as the Allies had been bombing for months. "There wasn't one damn thing left in Foggia that wasn't blown to hell or too small," he reported.[7]

Looking farther afield, the intrepid Johnson struck pay dirt in Bari, seventy miles down the coast from Foggia. He was impressed with the headquarters of the Italian Air Force, now largely aligned with the Allies and occupied by the British. The building was "large and plush and was ideal for our purposes." Johnson practiced international relations by pulling Doolittle's rank on the Brits while charming the Italian general, who was delighted to share space with so famous an aviator. But before the Americans arrived, their new allies ransacked the building, swiping almost anything worth keeping. That did it: Johnson decided that the locals were more trouble than they were worth and bodily ejected them. He never saw the Italian general again.[8]

Dating from the third century BC with a population of two hundred thousand, Bari was a mixture of antiquity and Mussolini. "Il Duce" had rewarded the city with an arena called "Bambino Stadium" for delivering the most babies (and future *soldati*) of any Italian city in a prescribed period.[9]

Heavily bombed during the Italians' and Germans' tenancy, Bari's facilities received priority treatment for reconstruction. Aviation engineer battalions immediately moved in to repair and improve runways and buildings.

Besides Foggia itself, twenty other fields surrounded the area. Some were exclusively for bombers and some for fighters, but some served both types of aircraft throughout the Fifteenth's existence. Additionally, fighter and medium bomber groups of the Twelfth Air Force lived cheek by jowl with some Fifteenth units.

The original Fifteenth Air Force staff was large by 1943 standards, with more than two hundred officers, some fifty civilian experts, and hundreds of enlisted men. Cramming fifteen or more subordinate offices into the building was like working a three-dimensional puzzle, but Johnson and company did it.

Outside Bari, the new air force took shape. As Arnold had proposed, the new command consolidated the heavy bomb groups of Doolittle's Twelfth Air Force and Louis H. Brereton's Ninth, which was moving to Britain as a tactical air force. The Fifteenth thus received parts of two bomb wings and three fighter groups totaling 930 aircraft and twenty thousand men. There were originally 210 B-17s and ninety B-24s, but that ratio would be reversed in the coming year.[10]

BOMBERS

Originally, the Fifteenth nominally comprised two medium bomb wings with five groups of B-25s or B-26s, which almost immediately returned to XII Bomber Command. In fact, two of the B-25 groups never flew a mission in the Fifteenth, while the others reverted to the Twelfth in January. Considering their brief tenure, the medium bombers probably were assigned to provide Doolittle with experienced wing organizations.[11]

Until the Foggia bases were available, the Fifteenth continued operating from Tunisia. The first three bomb groups—one with Boeing B-17 Flying Fortresses and two with Consolidated B-24 Liberators—landed in Italy during November, followed by three more Fortress groups and a Liberator outfit in December.

Brigadier General Joseph H. Atkinson's Fifth Bomb Wing was the Fifteenth's only B-17 unit, eventually comprising six groups. Of those, the Second was by far the most senior. It had received the first Flying Fortresses in 1937 and worked hard at exorcising the many gremlins from the new bomber's silvery art-deco airframe. The Second made headlines with a series of long-distance flights, including the spectacular interception of an Italian cruise liner nearly eight hundred miles off the east coast in 1938. The lead navigator had been an up-and-coming airman named Curtis LeMay. By November 1943 the group had logged some eighty missions.

Brigadier General Carlyle H. Ridenour's Forty-seventh Wing introduced the B-24 to the Fifteenth, originally with the Ninety-eighth, 376th, and 450th Groups. The first two—the "Pyramiders" and "Liberandos"—were seasoned, having accomplished the spectacular low-level mission against the oil fields of Ploesti, Romania, in August 1943. The 376th would become known for a bomber that disappeared in April 1943 and was discovered in the Sahara in 1958—the *Lady Be Good*. The 450th subsequently went by the name "Cottontails" for its white rudder markings.

There was a healthy and approximately friendly rivalry between B-17 and B-24 crews. Both carried similar bomb loads with ten-man crews. The "Lib" cruised 30 mph faster than the "Fort" and had marginally better range. The Boeing, however, was easier to fly. It was said that you could recognize a B-24 pilot by his overdeveloped left bicep because he often flew with his right hand on the throttles.

The '17 took more punishment and could fly higher but seldom did. It took a lot of fuel to get to thirty-five thousand feet, and most Fortresses flew between twenty-five and twenty-seven thousand. Liberator crews called the Fortress "the Hollywood bomber" (Clark Gable had flown one in 1938's *Test Pilot*), while B-17 men said the Liberator was the crate the Fortress came in.

Conventional wisdom held that there were only four things wrong with a B-17—its Wright "Cyclone" engines. When pilots shut down after landing, sure as gravity, oil would start pooling beneath each one. Actually, there was nothing inherently wrong with the engines, but in the frantic industrial rush to expand the military, quality control inevitably slipped. Aircraft engines were built by automobile manufacturers unaccustomed to aviation tolerances.

Aficionados insisted they could tell an engine's quality by its sound. That was true up to a point. The Liberator's Pratt & Whitneys ran with a feline purr while the Fort motored along with the distinctive Wright rattle. Both power plants performed well—each was rated at 1,200 horsepower—but Wrights never acquired the P&W mystique.

A fully loaded B-24J weighed fifty-five thousand pounds at take-off with 2,750 gallons of high-octane gasoline—eight and a half tons of fuel—to deliver two and a half tons of ordnance. A typical bomb load was ten five-hundred-pounders or five thousand-pounders. To put bombs on target, each Liberator or Fortress required two pilots, a navigator, a bombardier, a flight engineer, a radioman, and four or five gunners.

The B-24's production success was largely the fruit of a management genius named Charles E. Sorensen. The main Liberator factory was Ford's plant at Willow Run, Michigan. The 3.5-million-square-foot factory employed thirty thousand men and women, who delivered the first bomber in May 1942. Thirty-seven months later, in June 1945, the plant's 8,685th B-24 rolled off the assembly line: 47 percent of all Liberators produced, including components for other factories. With three shifts, that was 234 bombers a month; eight a day. It took three hours to build a 36,500-pound, four-engine airplane.[12]

Ford became so efficient that an aircraft of 1,250,000 parts (including 313,000 rivets) was produced in 17,350 man hours—down from 201,826 man hours before the war. The comparable figure was 24,800 hours at Consolidated's San Diego plant, or 36 percent more.[13]

North American and Douglas also built Liberators. Their 1,763 aircraft amounted to less than 10 percent of the total. From 1943, Boeing was increasingly committed to the huge B-29 Superfortress, relying on subcontractors to deliver sufficient B-17s. Thus, Douglas and Lockheed-Vega produced 5,750 Fortresses—nearly half the total.

The crews of both bombers had much in common. Both the B-17 and B-24 waist positions were unnecessarily cramped because the original designs placed the left and right gunners back to back. Only in late production blocks were the waist windows offset, alleviating the crowding.

Crews scoured the interiors of new aircraft, looking for penciled notes from female workers, "Rosie the Riveters," giving their name, address, and, sometimes, bra size. Experienced fliers learned to look under control panels. "It sure worked because a lot of guys wrote to them," recalled one flier. "To this day I don't know if any marriages occurred, but there were lots of letters anyhow."[14]

FROM THE GROUND UP

An air force is built from the ground up, and the Fifteenth was no exception. With its level terrain and nearby rock quarries for runway construction, the Foggia plain appeared well suited for a complex of airfields, but logistic support lagged. The aviation engineer units had to wait their turn for badly strained shipping space, and sometimes personnel arrived without all their heavy equipment. The thousand men in an engineer battalion needed a wide assortment of gear: trucks, bulldozers, rock crushers, compacters, and much more.

As the official Army Air Forces chronicle notes, however, "The job had been underestimated ... by higher commanders who were eager to get the strategic air force over Germany by the southern route." Because of "the unexpectedly vile weather" and the pressing schedule, the early bases were composed of pierced steel matting rather than cement for proper all-weather runways. Foggia, in fact, absorbed most of the pierced steel planking in the Mediterranean. The original deadline for completion of October 31 proved overly optimistic. The combined efforts of the Twenty-first Engineer Aviation Regiment and two independent battalions were required to get five bomber bases and a fighter base marginally operational, but they could not receive bombers until December.[15]

While Foggia's winter wheat germinated in the moist earth, most of the area became a quagmire. At Lecce, for instance, the loose soil became saturated with rain, and available drainage prevented the field's use until February. By the time the early Foggia runways were finished, other construction was three months behind schedule.

One group history notes, "It was soon discovered that Italy is no more immune to winter rains than North Africa, and the field at Foggia Main was a semi-quagmire. But this condition was of no aid in digging foxholes, for a few inches beneath the mud was a layer of rock that defied penetration. To add to the disconcertion, the field was overcrowded with all types of allied aircraft."[16]

Meanwhile, the underappreciated, overworked engineers toiled prodigiously, fighting shortages of personnel, equipment, and supplies and Foggia's cloying, clogging clay. The AAF's official history records, "The winter of 1943–44 in the Heel was a nightmare of buckling runways, frenzied repairs, mud, water—and neglect of other construction."[17] That neglect meant "dismal" living conditions for the engineers until they caught up on airfield construction. Only then did they turn their attention to improving their own facilities.[18]

Another group history describes Foggia weather as "very harsh. The summers were hot and dusty. The winters were cold and wet. Buildings were few, and airplane maintenance crews worked in the open. The men lived in tents using homemade gasoline stoves for heat. The men constantly had to struggle through mud and water, snow and ice, or choking dust, depending on the season."[19]

Living in the mud of Italy's farmland was rugged. Aircrews slept in tents and often ate their chow outdoors. Sick call brought bouts of coughing from colds and stomach upsets stemming from nerves. Jim Peters Sr., a flight engineer, had transferred from the infantry to the AAF and recalled his flying days with the Ninety-ninth Bomb Group at Tortarella: "On the north end of the runway our pilots had to clear a fifteen-foot dirt railroad embankment and some telephone poles.

With a full load of fuel and bombs we held our breath as our B-17s struggled to get off the steel plank runway. One morning after a particularly nasty crack up I heard the engineers blowing up the left over bombs."[20]

THE AIR CAMPAIGN

The Army Air Forces was part of the U.S. Army. Unlike Britain, Germany, Italy, and a few other nations, the United States kept its main air arm subordinate to the army. An independent air force remained a cherished goal for American airmen, but it would have to await the postwar political battles on the Potomac front.

There was a lot of feuding between the ground forces and the air force, much of it over personnel. By necessity the air force was heavy with officers: one for every six noncommissioned officers and enlisted men. An infantry or armored division, by contrast, typically had one officer for twenty-three men. Small wonder, then, that the army chief of staff, George C. Marshall, and others were concerned about the dramatic expansion of the AAF. Every heavy bomber crew contained four potential platoon leaders (often one company commander) and six squad leaders—not counting the enormous maintenance and support force essential to keep aircraft flying.

Before the war, the air force's strategic doctrine had assumed the successful deployment of long-range, self-defending bombers capable of precision accuracy. By the time the Fifteenth went operational in November 1943, that optimistic theory had been battered into bloody reality. The AAF had pinned its hopes on the ability of bombers to defend themselves because there were no long-range fighters. The technological tail, in other words, was wagging the doctrinal dog. A series of Eighth Air Force missions deep into Germany came perilously close to ending daylight bombing when, on August 17, 1943, sixty bombers were lost attacking Schweinfurt and Regensburg, a

16-percent loss rate. That disaster was followed in October by "Schweinfurt II," with 20-percent losses. Luftwaffe defenses were so effective that, with an average loss per mission of 4 percent, it was statistically impossible for a heavy bomber crew to survive a tour of twenty-five missions.

Originally faced with a less lethal defense, the southern air campaign suffered far fewer losses. But on the same day as the disastrous double strike in Germany—also the day that Sicily fell—American air units in the Mediterranean Theater lost sixteen planes operationally and five in combat.[21] Regardless of the locale, as long as the bombers penetrated hostile airspace, a price would be paid.

The Army Air Forces badly needed to prove itself, while learning its trade as it went along. Even when the "heavies" reached their targets in sufficient numbers, bombing accuracy often was poor. For twelve months in 1942–1943, the Eighth pounded German submarine bases in France and Germany, losing some 120 bombers—nearly a 5-percent attrition—with almost nothing to show for it. Yet the AAF continued bombing massive U-boat pens of reinforced concrete for months after conceding that the targets could not be destroyed. The Fifteenth launched a few missions against sub pens in Marseille without notable effect. Clearly heavy bombardment needed to knock out some vital targets if the enormous effort, expense, and losses were to be justified.

EARLY MISSIONS

On the day that Doolittle formed the Fifteenth, his B-17s bombed the harbor of La Spezia in northwestern Italy and a bridge at Vezzano, almost on the Austrian border. Meanwhile, B-25 Mitchells went after rail yards at Ancona and Rimini, 180 to 230 miles up the coast. No heavy bombers were lost—a good start but no reason for optimism.

The second day of operations brought the Fifteenth's first strategic mission: bombing the Messerschmitt fighter factory at Wiener Neustadt, south of Vienna. It was an important target, producing one-third of all Bf 109s delivered that year. Ninth Air Force B-24s had attacked the plant five times since August with indifferent results. But on November 2, four B-17 groups staging through incomplete Italian bases were joined by Liberators of the Ninety-eighth and 376th Groups—139 bombers in all. The Ninety-eighth was temporarily under Lieutenant Colonel Julian Bleyer (who the day before had succeeded the legendary John R. "Killer" Kane of Ploesti fame), while the experienced Colonel Keith Compton led the 376th.

It was a long mission from Tunisia, one of the longest yet. The B-24s flew some 850 miles to the target, about half that distance over the Tyrrhenian and Adriatic Seas.

During the outbound leg, a 376th Liberator lost the use of three superchargers, forcing Lieutenant Benjamin Konsynski's *Flame McGoon* to lose formation. Nevertheless, the crew pressed ahead and bombed solo, being harassed by Bf 109s defending their Austrian nest. Coming off the target, the pilots shoved up the power and nudged the nose down, accelerating away from the continuing threat. But in the fast, shallow descent, the big bomber gained speed rapidly. By the time *Flame McGoon* caught up with the other "Liberandos," it was steaming along like the proverbial bat out of hell. As Konsynski recalled, "We caught our formation and we were going so fast we flew right through it and out in front, so we had to cut our throttles all the way back to get back into formation." On the emergency field at Bari, British mechanics counted nearly 180 holes in the Liberator's tough hide.[22]

After aborts and early losses, 112 bombers loosed 327 tons of ordnance on the target, doing a thorough wrecking job on a fighter assembly building and two hangars, badly damaging another assembly shop plus other firms' facilities while holing runways.

Doolittle's operations officer, Brigadier General Charles F. Born, hailed the mission as "the outstanding event" of the new command's first four months. Wiener Neustadt production was reduced by 73 percent from the previous month, continuing to decline in December—probably a net loss of about 325 fighters. The Germans proved extremely resilient, however, and the Fifteenth would return to Wiener Neustadt often.[23]

In the air, bomber gunners claimed fifty-six interceptors shot down in a twenty-minute gunfight. Both sides overclaimed, but the Germans were far closer to the mark. The Luftwaffe wrote off eight Messerschmitts in exchange for fifteen *Viermots* credited versus eleven Americans downed. A sevenfold exaggeration in bomber gunner claims was not unusual. With perhaps dozens of gunners simultaneously shooting at multiple targets in a fast, dynamic combat, errors were inevitable.

Crews of the six missing Forts and five Liberators represented sixty-eight fliers killed and forty-one captured. The 6.5-percent attrition could not be sustained for long. Despite the successful bombing, at that rate the Fifteenth would be extinct in fifteen missions.

A Fortress pilot flying his fiftieth mission on the Wiener Neustadt raid, First Lieutenant Richard Eggers, ensured that his crew had jumped before he released the controls. The doomed Second Group Fortress dropped into a spin, but Eggers got out. "In the movies," he said, "you count to three and pull the ripcord. That's what I did and it worked." Eggers's downing was less wrenching than many. He landed in a tree, "hanging a few feet from the ground as safe as a baby in a cradle." When found by soldiers and civilians, he had no choice but to surrender. "Errol Flynn I am not, and accepted their invitation to lunch in a nearby town."

Eggers's copilot was Flight Officer Donald Elder. The policeman who captured him showed him the dog tags of two dead crewmembers and a pair of baby shoes carried by tail gunner Sergeant Thomas

Zelasko. Later a Luftwaffe sergeant told Elder that his friends were buried in a small town near the crash site. "I asked him what kind of burial they had, and he said it was not a military one but they did get a decent burial...." Eggers, Elder, and the other six fliers survived the war as prisoners.[24]

✪ ✪ ✪

Bombers flew in both directions on November 2. That evening the Luftwaffe launched a large air raid against Bari's port—a hundred Junkers 88 bombers. Surprise was complete, the attack devastating.

Among the thirty ships in Bari harbor was the transport *John Harvey*, loaded with tons of secret mustard-gas bombs kept in case the Axis resorted to chemical warfare. She spilled liquid sulfur into the harbor as she went down, and an explosion released a cloud of mustard gas over the town. Hundreds of sailors, medical staff, and civilians were blinded and burned by the poison, and scores died. The Americans and British tried at first to keep the existence of the chemical weapons a secret, for fear of provoking the Germans, but they eventually had to acknowledge the obvious.

Allied naval casualties at Bari were placed at a thousand dead with perhaps as many civilians killed. Seventeen ships were destroyed, and others sustained serious damage. The port and town were so badly damaged that the facility was not reopened until February 1944.[25]

Explosions from ammunition-laden ships blew out several windows in Doolittle's new headquarters. The next day he delivered pointed monologues to commanders of the area radar stations, night fighter squadrons, and antiaircraft batteries.

AT WAR WITH THE WEATHER

The Joint Chiefs had agreed to set up the Fifteenth in part because an Italian base would bring southern targets into the range of air attack but also because of Italy's weather. The sunny Mediterranean climate, they presumed, would offer more flying days than the Eighth could extract from soggy Britain, and so was seen as an Allied force multiplier. Those expectations proved to be mistaken. Lacking favorable weather, radar bombing capability, and enough long-range fighters, Doolittle's command did what it could for the rest of the year. After the Wiener Neustadt attack, the Fifteenth logged only six comparable missions before year's end. Weather beyond Italy limited the command to "local" strikes against communications networks, rail marshalling yards, and airfields in Italy, France, Greece, and Bulgaria, and even those missions were costly. An attack on the Innsbruck marshalling yard and the Augsburg Messerschmitt factory on December 19 cost a dozen bombers.[26]

THE POLITICAL FRONT

In late November, while the Fifteenth was logging its first missions, the Cairo Conference sharpened Allied grand strategy as President Franklin Roosevelt and Prime Minister Winston Churchill agreed how to conduct the European war. Then they proceeded to Tehran to consult with the Soviet Union's Joseph Stalin.

In Cairo, General Arnold claimed, "many knotty and controversial problems [were] solved." That was one interpretation. Though the Combined Chiefs approved creation of the U.S. Strategic and Tactical Air Forces (USSTAF), the British officers added they did "not agree in principle with the American decision."[27]

En route home on December 9, Arnold stopped at Bari to brief Spaatz, Doolittle, and the Twelfth Air Force commander, Major General John K. Cannon. Eisenhower had been named supreme commander for the 1944 invasion of northern France, and he wanted his desert airmen with him in England. That included Doolittle, but mainly it meant Spaatz. Consequently, Major General Ira C. Eaker, who had built the Eighth Air Force from the ground up, would replace Spaatz as Mediterranean air commander. Doolittle was selected to relieve him in London—a situation to Doolittle's liking if not Eaker's. The high-level shuffling was interpreted by some as service politics, most notably in Eaker's circle.

In February 1942, Eaker had arrived in Britain with a six-man staff, establishing his headquarters in a former girls' school. By the time he left to command the Mediterranean Allied Air Forces in January 1944, the "Mighty Eighth" had grown to twenty-seven bomb groups and ten fighter groups—two-thirds of its ultimate strength.

Eaker recalled years later, "Eisenhower—because of his experience in leading the forces in North Africa and the invasion of Sicily and Italy—he was going back to take the Supreme Allied Command. So [General Jacob] Devers, the U.S. senior in Britain, and I were sent down to take his place and Spaatz' place in the Mediterranean. General Eisenhower had nothing against me as an individual. I do know that General Marshall opposed it. General Arnold, I think, was on the other side. He wanted Spaatz to go back to England and command ... all our strategic air operations."

Eaker remained commander of the Mediterranean Allied Air Forces until April 1945, when he became Hap Arnold's deputy in Washington.[28]

FIGHTERS

The Fifteenth's first three fighter groups flew Lockheed's exotic-looking, twin-boomed P-38 Lightning, which in 1939 became the first American production aircraft capable of 400 mph. With exceptional performance, the wartime '38 was dubbed the "Fork-tailed Devil" (supposedly by the Germans—*der Gabelschwanz Teufel*—but the moniker more likely originated in Lockheed's PR shop).

Colonel Robert Richard's First Group traced its heritage to 1918. Its heroes included champion balloon buster Frank Luke of the Twenty-seventh Squadron and the Ninety-fourth's ace of aces, Eddie Rickenbacker, both Medal of Honor recipients. Many second-generation fighter pilots tried hard to live up to the group's reputation, and inevitably some pushed too hard. The group diarist wrote the epitaph of one youngster after a December mission over Spezia: "He tried to become a hero and instead lost everything."[29]

The Fourteenth Group found the Lightning a demanding aircraft, losing nearly twenty planes and several pilots before leaving for Britain in August 1942. One squadron remained in Iceland, but the group lost another six pilots and at least eight more planes before leaving England for Algeria in November.[30]

The Fourteenth's initiation into the aerial combat big leagues was rough, pitting its pilots against Luftwaffe professionals at the top of their game. In about ten weeks the group lost thirty-two of its fifty-four pilots and was reduced to seven operational Lightnings by January 1943. Facing steady attrition, many of the group's pilots became fatalistic. During an inspection trip, Hap Arnold asked Captain Ralph J. Watson how long he could continue flying. "Doc" Watson replied, "Until I'm shot down, General."[31]

As P-38 production lagged, the Fourteenth was pulled out of combat to re-form with a new squadron in May. Its new commander was Lieutenant Colonel Oliver B. "Obie" Taylor, a former sailor barely four years out of West Point. The group moved to Triolo on December 12, and in the next two weeks its pilots claimed thirteen victories against four losses.

Taylor logged some four hundred hours in the P-38, and he developed a deep appreciation of the aircraft's demands and its capabilities. "It required at least twice as much flying time," he wrote, "perhaps more, to achieve the level of skill which was necessary to realize the full capability of the ship, compared with what it took with a single-engine fighter. In fact, my observation was that you never stopped learning about handling the plane, no matter how much time you logged in it. Naturally, this was something of a problem with green pilots, since you could not develop the desired competence in the usual sixty to eighty hours. Only after about 150 or 200 hours could a man hope to be an expert, but when he reached that point he could be unbeatable in the '38."[32]

Lieutenant Colonel George McNichol's Eighty-second Fighter Group had vacated Tunisia for Lecce, Italy, in early October 1943, arriving two months before the First and Fourteenth. On Christmas Day, while on escort to the rail yard at Udine, Italy, the Eighty-second was attacked from above and behind. Leading the high squadron was Major Hugh Muse, on his last scheduled mission. The Luftwaffe pilots were experienced and lethal—Oberleutnant Otto Schultz, a squadron commander, had sixty kills since 1940.

The fight began at twenty-five thousand feet and wound its way down, penetrating a cloud layer at eight thousand feet and continuing to the ground. The Ninety-fifth Squadron reported, "The P-38s upon reaching the deck experienced ice conditions on windshields and gun sights interfering materially with operation." The contest lasted forty minutes, several eternities in air combat. Six pilots were missing—three survived in captivity—and two more crash-landed in Italy. Despite the confirmation of only one kill by the Ninety-sixth Squadron, the two German units involved—Jagdgeschwader 51 and 53—wrote off four 109s. The Germans claimed nine, only one more than actual American losses.[33]

Missions like Wiener Neustadt had shown that unescorted bombers were as vulnerable in the Fifteenth Air Force as in the Eighth. Doolittle insisted on more fighters, and a fourth "pursuit" unit—the 325th Fighter Group, known as the Checkertail "Clan"—was sent to Italy from the Twelfth Air Force in December. To the desert veterans, the new base at Celone, with its dry, grassy plain, was "the best bivouac area the personnel had enjoyed since coming overseas."[34]

✪ ✪ ✪

In every military endeavor, leadership counts more than hardware. The 325th's commander was tall, skinny, redheaded Lieutenant Colonel Robert L. Baseler, who enjoyed verbal sparring with enlisted men. In

Tunisia, however, he had ribbed his crew chief once too often, insisting that Sergeant Clem Eckert laughed like the ventriloquist Edgar Bergen's puppet Mortimer Snerd. The CO's P-40 Warhawk bore the name *Stud* on the left side, and Eckert retaliated by painting *Mortimer Snerd* on the right. Colonel Baseler ordered the sergeant to remove the offending moniker, but Eckert was obstinate. A compromise of sorts was reached when the group transitioned to Thunderbolts. Baseler's new mount became *Big Stud*, minus the secondary name.

The group's checkerboard emblem was the result of Baseler's childhood admiration of the flamboyant German ace Werner Voss, who, it was said, had painted a checkerboard pattern on his Fokker in the Great War. Baseler had adopted a similar emblem for his fighters, only to discover later that Voss's trademark had actually been a mustached face painted on his cowling.

Puckishly independent, Baseler was the kind of commander who prefers asking forgiveness rather than permission. When the Allies had closed in on Sardinia, Baseler—then a mere major—took it upon himself to demand the island's surrender. His P-40 pilots dropped a note to the local commandant, saying in part, "We wish to advise you that this message is directed to you by the 'Checkerboard' Warhawk Fighter Group, without instruction from, or the knowledge of higher commands. In the event that you accept the offer, we shall forward it to the High Command for immediate action. We have taken it upon ourselves to make this suggestion because we have been operating regularly over your territory and you are familiar with the situation in which you find yourself." The Italian commander declined the Clan's generous offer, requiring American ground forces to seize the island in September.[35]

The 325th's new airplane was quite different from the other groups' P-38s. There was no Lockheed elegance in the big Republic P-47 Thunderbolt, with its huge two-thousand-horsepower radial engine and its shattering armament of eight .50 caliber machine guns. Its drawback was a relatively short range, even with drop tanks.

Upon moving to Italy, the group applied its old P-40 yellow and black tail markings to its P-47s. Bob Baseler and his three checker-tailed squadrons anticipated taking the fight to the enemy in the new year. Before then, however, a new aerial threat emerged.

When Mussolini returned from internal exile in September 1943, his armed forces were split along political and geographic lines. The air force, concentrated in the industrial north, largely sided with the Fascist regime, while those units in the south could only join the Allies.

The erstwhile Regia Aeronautica was divided. The northern portion became the pro-Mussolini Aeronautica Nazionale Repubblicana (ANR), while the southern Co-Belligerent Air Force entered temporary exile in North Africa, eventually receiving Allied aircraft. The ANR required three months to reorganize and re-equip, emerging in December with three fighter groups, two bomber groups, and a few transport units. Some of the Loyalist pilots were experienced, as half of Italy's two dozen double aces sided with the ANR.[36]

The Fifteenth clashed only rarely with the ANR, probably scoring fewer than fifty kills against Italian aircraft. Italy had always produced world-class airmen, and the World War II generation was stylish as well. When a fighter squadron landed at an American base in late 1943, P-38 pilots were astonished to see the Italians climb from their Macchis in dress uniforms, complete with capes and white gloves.

THE COMBINED BOMBING OFFENSIVE

While grand strategy and service politics played out, Doolittle's fliers continued fighting and dying. The Allied air chiefs continued the Combined Bombing Offensive, begun in June 1943 with the Americans attacking industrial targets by day and the Royal Air Force continuing its nocturnal campaign. The priorities were German aircraft factories, ball bearing plants, petroleum production, and civilian morale.

Doolittle's portion of the CBO included the Messerschmitt plant at Augsburg, which produced twin-engine fighters. On December 19 the target was blanketed by clouds, forcing the fifty bombers to unload eighty-six tons into the undercast. The defenders, nevertheless, were able to climb through the weather and hack down three Libs.

Three days after Christmas, the 376th Group left ten of eighteen Liberators around Vincenza marshalling yard. Things turned to hash from the beginning. Unable to rendezvous with another bomb group in the weather, the 376th's mission commander, Lieutenant Colonel Theodore Graff, opted to continue without fighter escort. Survivors surmised that Vincenza's reputation as a "milk run" influenced Graff's decision. But ten minutes from the target, forty or more Germans hit the "Liberandos," attacking three and four abreast. They were from the same two wings that had destroyed the Ninety-fifth Fighter Squadron on Christmas Day, and they were just as effective against bombers. Lieutenant James M. Collison's Liberator was perhaps the first hit: two engines shot out, controls damaged, intercom destroyed. Collison ordered a bailout. The rest of the 512th Squadron also was shot down: six B-24s in a matter of minutes.

Of ninety-nine fliers in the ten missing bombers, only one returned. Collison's flight engineer, Sergeant Arthur M. Leadingham, who had been picked up by Partisans, turned up safe three months later, though thirty-five pounds lighter. His ordeal included an infected leg, traveling by railroad with a Yugoslavian woman who spoke no English, and hiding in mountain villages. When he got back to Bari, he was told he was going home. "This was great news," he recalled, "because I don't believe I had much fight left in me."[37]

The Ninety-seventh Bomb Group arrived just before Christmas, nearly completing the Fifth Wing. The group's commander, Colonel Frank Armstrong, had become legendary among Eighth Air Force crews in Britain. He described the environment:

When bomber crews are operating five miles or more above the earth, they are not actually in man's element.... Men cannot live at 25,000 feet without oxygen and heat. A broken oxygen line is the immediate fore-runner of death unless an emergency bottle can be reached. I have known gunners to bail out over enemy territory at high altitude when their oxygen was shot away. Their decision was made quickly—seconds are precious when there is absolutely nothing to breathe. Cold is fierce and deadly at 44 below.... In the heat of combat at high altitude when a gun jams, gunners have a tendency to eliminate their gloves for "just a second" in an effort to make an adjustment. Before the gunner realizes what he is doing and replaces his hands inside the heated gloves, frostbite has done its dirty work. Long, weary days in a hospital is the reward. Gunners are aware of the penalty they will surely pay if they do not keep warm. On the other hand I have seen youngsters who would use their frozen hands as hammers to maul a jammed gun back to life.[38]

The AAF conducted a survey of more than eleven hundred B-17 crew casualties in 1944. The results were surprising. Ball turret gunners, exposed to the world while hanging beneath the aircraft, represented less than 6 percent of all aircrewmen killed or wounded. Curled up in their cramped cocoon (forty-four inches in diameter), sitting on steel behind two-inch laminated glass, they were well protected.

Especially vulnerable were bombardiers (17.6 percent of casualties) and navigators (12.2 percent), who rode in the nose, most exposed both to flak and fighters, especially when Luftwaffe squadrons began making head-on company front attacks. Similarly, tail gunners—inevitably the primary target of enemy fighters attacking from behind—took 12.5 percent of the killed and wounded.[39]

THE WEATHER WAR, CONTINUED

Despite the coalition's best-laid plans, the supposedly balmy Mediterranean climate offered no advantage over the fogbound British Isles. Most of Europe had cloud cover 85 percent of the year—310 days. Italy, presumably, was sunnier, but not by much. In its first two months of operations, the Fifteenth launched worthwhile heavy bomber missions on thirty days versus twenty-six by the Eighth (excluding harassment missions and leaflet drops). Italian-based B-25 and B-26 medium bombers flew more missions, but they could not achieve what Allied planners desired, and only ten of the Fifteenth's missions struck beyond Italy.[40]

Veterans of North Africa required some adjustment to the Italian climate. Tunisian summer temperatures ranged between sixty and 105 degrees Fahrenheit in 1943, with five days of rain or fog per month. November's range was a pleasant fifty-three to seventy-seven, with thirteen days of poor weather. In contrast, Foggia's temperatures in late 1943 ran from barely above freezing to seventy-five degrees, with twenty days of rain or fog in December.[41]

The Foggia plain was scenic but it could be hostile. Winter brought a blanket of snow little different from Britain's. Mostly living under canvas, men stuffed their "ticking" with straw for mattresses and often slept fully clothed. Aircrews often wore flight suits to bed, and some scrounged used parachutes since the silk or nylon provided extra warmth. Tents were heated by improvised stoves fueled with oil drained from the sumps of aircraft engines. Warm months brought dysentery and malaria.

At year end Doolittle had nine operational airfields, including the administrative base at Foggia itself. The satellite fields mostly lay within thirty-five miles northwest to southeast of Foggia. Most of two bomb wings were gathered around Foggia, including four B-17 groups of the Fifth Wing. Three Liberator outfits of the Forty-seventh Wing also were on hand in time to spend the holidays in Italy. The irony was not lost on the men—many observing their first Christmas outside America, dropping ordnance on their fellow men. Actually, the results were desultory, as B-26s and "heavies" attacked rail yards in northern Italy without notable effect. Some planes failed to find any targets through the weather.

In December 1943 the Fifteenth Air Force counted 4,500 officers and 26,880 men with 739 B-24s and 200 B-17s with 1,115 crews. The latter represented 35 percent of the force's total personnel of 31,380. Doolittle wielded a sizeable command, but it was still feeling its way while anticipating great events in the coming year.[42]

A DISTANT GOAL

In its first two months, the Fifteenth lost more than seventy aircraft including twenty-six Lightnings. But transfers affected inventory more than attrition did. With the departure of the B-25s in November, the Fifteenth numbered 564 aircraft, 5,000 officers, and 33,000 men. Jimmy Doolittle thus ended the year with 370 fewer aircraft than when he began.[43]

At year's end, for the Eighth and the Fifteenth, strategic bombardment remained a massive asset in search of an achievable mission. Some important targets had sustained heavy blows, but none was destroyed. Air commanders were beginning to grasp the unpleasant reality of strategic bombing: there was no magic bullet, no airborne stake to be driven through the monster's industrial heart. Each target would have to be struck again and again, until at length the Axis's pulse ceased.

On December 31, 1943, that goal was still a long way off.

THE WINTER WAR

JANUARY–MARCH 1944

On January 3, 1944, only two months after establishing the Fifteenth, Jimmy Doolittle turned the command over to Lieutenant General Nathan F. Twining. "General Jimmy" was headed for England to replace Ira Eaker as commander of the Eighth Air Force. Eaker was taking over the Mediterranean Allied Air Forces, a position he would retain almost until V-E Day. Doolittle, who had had a rocky start with the commander of the European Theater, later wrote, "I was pleased that I had finally sold myself to Ike."[1]

TWINING

Forty-six-year-old Nathan F. Twining, whose family had served its country since before the Revolution, had the military in his DNA.

His older brother was a naval officer and his younger brother a Marine Corps general. An uncle, also Nathan, had been an admiral.

A lifelong outdoorsman, Twining had enjoyed a rural Wisconsin upbringing. In 1916, as a young rifleman, he was drawn to the Oregon National Guard, which emphasized marksmanship. His unit was activated that year for the Punitive Expedition in pursuit of the Mexican bandit *jefe* Pancho Villa. The army failed to catch its man, but the expedition was not entirely fruitless, for it gave Corporal Twining his first exposure to aircraft.

The promising youngster received an appointment to West Point but missed the Great War, graduating a week before the 1918 armistice. He finished in the top 40 percent of his 311-man class, earning notice for football and hockey.

An infantry officer, Twining applied for pilot training four years running, and his persistence paid off. He pinned on his silver wings in 1924 and immediately became a flight instructor. Twining proved an inspiring teacher: he passed up Christmas leave to help a student overcome an injury, earning the man's lifelong loyalty. The subordinate, Elwood Quesada, who became a lieutenant general, recalled, "I never knew Nate to indulge in a self-serving act as a junior officer or a senior officer."[2]

During the 1930s Twining commanded two attack squadrons and survived Franklin Roosevelt's disastrous attempt to have the army take over civilian airmail flights. He continued his professional education with courses at the Air Corps Tactical School and the Command and General Staff College, where colleagues recognized him as a comer.

Known as an able staff officer, Nate Twining worked under Hap Arnold in the Army Air Corps's building period, 1940–1942. He was promoted to brigadier general in June 1942 and gained a combat command, leading the Thirteenth Air Force in the Southwest Pacific for most of 1943.

The veteran airman nearly lost his life early that year. Flying from Guadalcanal to New Caledonia, his B-17 ran out of fuel and was ditched in the ocean. Twining and thirteen others survived six days at sea before rescue. At year's end he took leave in the States and was unexpectedly tapped for the Fifteenth Air Force. Though he had clashed with Arnold during a pioneering flight to Alaska in 1934, the AAF chief appreciated his Pacific record. Twining asked to spend Christmas with his family, and Arnold "compromised" by allowing him to spend the morning at home. Then he boarded a transport plane for Italy.

The new commander arrived during a time of transition in the European air war. On January 1, 1944, the Eighth and Fifteenth were placed under Lieutenant General Carl Spaatz as commander of United States Strategic Air Forces in Europe (USSTAF). In turn, "Tooey" Spaatz reported to British air marshal Sir Charles Portal, air representative on the Combined Chiefs of Staff in Britain.

American air commanders now faced a two-front political war. They devoutly wished to avoid the control of Air Marshal Sir Trafford Leigh-Mallory, the accomplished political infighter and dagger man heading the Allied Expeditionary Air Forces in the forthcoming invasion of France. Similarly, they wanted to be relatively free of the U.S. Army Ground Forces, which meant Eisenhower. Yearning to demonstrate what strategic bombing could accomplish, the airmen hoped to keep the distraction of supporting the land war to a minimum.

When Twining relieved Doolittle, the Fifteenth organizational chart was filled in. Twining's chief of staff was Brigadier General Robert K. Taylor, an experienced administrator who had served briefly in England. Brigadier General Charles F. Born was Twining's "A-3," assistant chief of staff for operations and training. A former cavalryman and West Point assistant football coach, he arrived in a lateral move from XII Bomber Command.

A key player was Major Roy W. Nelson Jr., who had been weather officer of North African Coastal Command. A fast climber, he was less than four years out of West Point when he joined the original Fifteenth Air Force staff. Given the Joint Chiefs' expectation that the

Italian climate would permit more flying than Britain, Nelson's responsibilities were grave.

Meanwhile, Doolittle had built the Fifteenth to 37,700 men, including 1,100 crews for more than 900 heavy bombers. A heavy bomb group was eventually allocated 465 officers and about 1,800 men—a total of some 2,260, including nearly a thousand crewmen. Twining took that inheritance and built upon it, for building was necessary. Early in the new year, he obtained essential support infrastructure of two air depots and three air service groups with more to come.

Maintenance kept an air force moving. In Italy as elsewhere, combat squadrons and groups provided organic first- and second-echelon maintenance and repairs at the unit and base level. Service groups provided third-echelon aircraft maintenance plus material and engineering support to combat units. Fourth-echelon depot-level work—heavy maintenance and complete engine overhauls—was beyond the capacities of combat and service groups. Newly arrived aircraft often passed through depots to ensure compliance with recent requirements.

Combat missions were conducted by aircrews, but no flying was possible without the "wrench benders" on the flight line and in the hangar—the men who skinned their knuckles trying to dislodge a stubborn cotter pin, who had permanent grime under their fingernails from changing oil or greasing brake pads.

✪ ✪ ✪

With most of the airfield construction finished or nearing completion, airmen had more time for recreation. Bingo games became a popular indoor activity, safely out of Foggia's cloying mud if not free of chilling temperatures. In January the Fourteenth Fighter Group reported, "Italians are working on a permanent kitchen with cement foundation and brick walls. The 48th [Squadron] bar is being put up at one end of the long mess hall."[3]

Twining enjoyed opulent quarters in Bari: a four-story building overlooking the harbor and a carpeted office with a large, modern desk and draperies flanked by maps and organizational charts. But he was no rear-echelon commander. He took pains to encourage his command, preferring a personal touch when possible. He made the awarding of medals and commendations an opportunity to assess personnel, morale, and readiness. Nevertheless, Twining cut his airmen little slack. Surveying the units on hand and those en route, he wanted new bomb groups to fly a combat mission within ten days of arrival, men and aircraft permitting.

BOMBING CIVILIANS

Early in the new year, the Fifteenth was ordered to bomb Balkan cities, especially the capitals Bucharest, Romania, and Sofia, Bulgaria. The administrative and transportation centers of each city were legitimate targets, but their civilian population areas seemed another matter to some fliers.

Neutral until 1941, Bulgaria joined the Axis but retained diplomatic relations with Moscow until September 1944. The U.S. Joint Chiefs of Staff thought that hammering Sofia might inflict enough psychological and political damage to prompt Bulgaria's withdrawal from the Axis.[4]

The Twelfth Air Force had first sent B-25s against Sofia in November 1943, and the Fifteenth attacked rail yards through the end of the year. None of the missions inflicted substantial damage, raising doubts that the result was worth the effort. The early missions had disrupted the city's life and forced thousands to evacuate. But the government was no more responsive to civilian wishes than were other Axis regimes, and it remained in Germany's orbit.

Despite Bulgaria's stubborn resistance, Allied air commanders persisted in their effort to force its submission. On January 10 aircrews were briefed to bomb obviously non-military areas. The 301st Group noted, "Some airmen were not too happy about bombing civilians, but 'orders seem to be orders.'"

The 140 Fortress crews followed orders and strewed 418 tons of ordnance across the capital. A bombardier recorded, "We were ordered to string our bombs through the downtown, which we did. News reports said much damage and a panic among the people."[5] The Fifteenth's strike was followed by a Royal Air Force attack that night. Residential areas were destroyed, utilities were seriously interrupted, fires blazed out of control, and many civilian workers were unwilling to return for a week. Nevertheless, the city continued to function, so the bombers would return.

SUPPORTING SALERNO

On January 22, Twining's airmen were briefed for attacks on transport centers along Italy's north-south communications routes. Stalled around Salerno on the west coast, the Allies opted for a seaborne envelopment, going ashore at Anzio, seventy miles from Rome. The Second Group laid down an excellent bomb pattern on the Campoleone railway station, smothering rail lines, bridges, and a transformer station.

Free of flak and fighters, bomber crews coming off coastal targets gaped at the assemblage of sea power off Anzio: ninety ships plus landing craft embarking forty thousand Allied soldiers. The Twelfth Air Force flew interdiction missions, trying to prevent German reinforcements from reaching the beachhead. Lightnings searched at low level, strafing trains and vehicles.

Initially the landings met almost no resistance, but a ferocious German counterattack brought the Allied advance to a sudden halt. On February 17 the Fifteenth dropped nearly a thousand tons on German positions, also targeting enemy logistics in northern Italy and France. But the Army Air Forces had bigger tasks than supporting ground forces, and Twining's bombardiers would soon have more important targets in their crosshairs.

ESCORTS

Twining brought along a former Thirteenth Air Force subordinate, Brigadier General Dean Strother, to run fighter operations. Consequently, Strother established the 306th Fighter Wing at Fano with authority over the four existing groups.

The fighters' mission was to protect the bombers, and the Fifteenth generally adhered to the doctrine of close escort that Eaker had imposed when running the Eighth. With only four groups, however, Strother was limited in his immediate options and could not yet duplicate Doolittle's aggressive policy for British-based fighters.

There was more to the escort mission than simply running interference. The Fifteenth's intelligence shop analyzed German radio traffic and determined that interceptors tried to hit the heavies about fifteen minutes before they crossed the target. Consequently, on January 30 the Americans shifted tactics, putting fighters over half a dozen Luftwaffe fields around Udine in northeastern Italy.

Bob Baseler's 325th Group had flown thirty-seven previous missions in P-47s without much luck, clashing with German fighters only six times. The dry spell ended spectacularly on January 30, when the Fifteenth bombed enemy airfields around Udine. Baseler proposed a maximum effort with sixty planes, flying low over the Adriatic to avoid enemy radar, then climbing "on top" and dead reckoning above the clouds. His navigation was perfect: arriving ahead of the bombers, he caught gaggles of enemy aircraft swarming up to meet the B-17s. From a beautiful altitude perch, the Thunderbolts waded in.

The result was bedlam. For thirty-five minutes the Checkertails chased a variety of "bandits" amid a promiscuous barrage from German flak gunners. The opposition offered a smorgasbord of Axis aircraft: eight types of fighters, bombers, transports, and liaison planes.

Captain Herschel Green, a twenty-three-year-old Kentucky sharpshooter who had honed his aim in P-40s, perfected his technique in

Thunderbolts. Previously grounded with malaria, he shook off the bug and waded into a flock of trimotor Junkers 52s fleeing the area.

Green told rapt reporters, "When we spotted the Ju 52s beneath us, I was so anxious to get to them that I dove too fast and passed them over. I turned and came back to the first four. It was like climbing steps, shooting all the way. All four blew up in my face. I then chased a Macchi 202 at treetop level before catching him after a five-minute chase."[6]

Reforming his flight, Green caught a Dornier bomber, his sixth kill of the flight. His three wingmen claimed seven more. Herky Green became the Fifteenth's first ace and the first "ace in a day." There would only be two others.

In all, eighteen of Baseler's pilots claimed thirty-seven planes for the loss of two. The Eighty-second Group Lightnings, escorting Liberators, tangled with some aggressive Messerschmitts and claimed six. Major Charles Spencer, a squadron commander flying his last mission, downed a 109 but was last seen descending out of control. In contrast, Lieutenant Maurice Morrell scored on his first mission.

January 30 established a benchmark: forty-five shootdowns in one day remained the Fifteenth's record for the rest of the war.

BOMBER BOXES

Twining's command, though new, was maturing. Shortly after arriving, he had decided upon a smaller tactical formation than the Eighth, which had a far greater proportion of B-17 groups. The Liberator usually cruised five thousand feet lower than the Fortress, as the hefty B-24 became sluggish at higher altitudes. Whereas VIII Bomber Command employed a fifty-four-plane formation, the Fifteenth (which had no separate bomber command) favored forty planes in a six-box arrangement. Two twenty-plane components flew in trail, each comprising three squadron boxes. The center squadron with six planes, called "Able Box," was led by the mission commander with his deputy as a wingman. On either side were seven bombers: Baker Box to the right and Charlie to the left. The second element was similarly composed with Dog, Easy, and Fox Boxes.

Though suited to the B-24's characteristics, the six-box formation had unavoidable problems. It was necessarily wide, resulting in broad bomb patterns on the ground. In mid-1944, therefore, the Fifteenth adopted a diamond formation, tightening accuracy but exposing planes to more flak.[7]

The Fifteenth's bomb wings saw some technical changes as B-17G models began appearing in January. The ultimate expression of the Flying Fortress, the G featured a two-gun "chin" turret under the nose, usually operated by the bombardier. It offered a partial solution to the Fort's most vulnerable aspect—the Luftwaffe's head-on attacks, which B-17Fs could not adequately deflect. But it was no panacea, as the 301st Group was the first to lose a G model with four Fs during an attack on Piraeus, Greece, on January 11. Nevertheless, the F models soldiered on at least until July.

Whatever the bomber, aircrews endured nearly identical conditions in B-17s and B-24s. Waist gunners were the most stressed, as they spent nearly the entire mission standing in place. Said one gunner, "We sat in the radio compartment for takeoff and landing, but otherwise we had to stay at our waist position, constantly looking for enemy aircraft and calling out possible collisions with other bombers. It was a little better when Plexiglas windows became available, but still you stood up for six hours or more without much to do. At the end of the mission you felt stiff and sore, but you still had to clean your own gun and one of the others as well."[8]

CASSINO

In mid-February the Allied advance stalled when it ran into strong German defensive positions, including the ancient Benedictine abbey at Monte Cassino. Ninety miles west of Foggia, it occupied a strategic position, dominating the Rapido River and Route Six leading north to Rome.

Established in the sixth century by St. Benedict himself and the cradle of Western monasticism, Monte Cassino had been repeatedly sacked and rebuilt over the centuries. The most recent rebuilding had followed an earthquake in 1349. The German commander in Italy, Field Marshal Albert Kesselring, had notified the Allies and the Vatican that the abbey was not occupied, hoping to avoid damage to the historic site. British intelligence, however, misinterpreted enemy radio intercepts, and the Allied command approved bombing of "the world's most glorious monastery."[9]

The Americans dropped leaflets before the mission, warning local residents to evacuate. Then, on the morning of February 15, 142 Fortresses of the Second, Ninety-seventh, Ninety-ninth, and 301st Groups preceded eighty-seven medium bombers of the Twelfth Air Force.[10]

Many units excused men with religious concerns from flying the mission, as was done previously when Rome was bombed. It was a consistent AAF policy, as veterans of North Africa recalled, to avoid mosques in Muslim countries. Most fliers, however, shared the opinion of the Second Bomb Group's mission commander, twenty-five-year-old Major Bradford E. Evans, who had flown two missions to Rome and felt no reluctance in bombing Cassino, which was reported to be sheltering German troops.[11] Some devout airmen flew despite their reservations. Aerial gunner Dominic Licata of the Ninety-seventh Group said, "Of all the targets we hit, the one at Monte Cassino was the one that really got to me because I am a good Catholic. When they bombed that monastery, it gave me a funny feeling, but I guess the only thing you can say … is that it was war."[12]

Flying unusually low and encountering no flak or fighters, the B-17s attacked from fifteen thousand to eighteen thousand feet. They hit the monastery and surrounding countryside with 387 tons of bombs, razing the huge building in minutes. But some bombing was wildly erratic, striking friend and foe alike. Watching the process, two lieutenant generals grew wary. Ira Eaker and his former ETO colleague Jacob Devers were perched on a rooftop expecting to witness precision bombing from relatively low altitude. But watching the drop, Devers asked, "Are those bombs going to land over there?" The airman glanced at the target, up at the bombers, and computed the timing. Instinct and experience kicked in: "I'm afraid not." That stick of bombs struck well behind them, three miles short of the target.[13]

Other Allied soldiers experienced far worse, including the Fifth Army's commander, Lieutenant General Mark Clark. Far behind the lines, his command trailer was rattled by a succession of near misses.

The abbey was further wrecked by American artillery, but weather and command inefficiency prevented exploitation of the shock effect. After the bombing, the Germans occupied the site. The stone rubble afforded excellent defensive positions for Kesselring's tough paratroopers, trained for assault by some of the finest defensive troops on Earth.

Air attacks continued over the next month, with fighters strafing the rubble between bombing missions. On March 14 the Fifteenth responded to a request from the British to attack the town of Cassino before another ground assault. Following Twelfth Air Force Mitchells and Marauders, one wing each of B-17s and 24s trailed over the pockmarked battlefield. The mission was a fiasco. Loose formations, incorrect altitude, and an inexperienced lead bombardier resulted in more damage from friendly fire. This time, U.S. casualties were few, though a British general's trailer and mess tent were ruined.

Personally embarrassed, Eaker fired off a reprimand to Twining. He ordered that Twining or a staff member be present next time bombs were dropped near Allied troops and required the staff to have radio contact with bombers. Twining conducted his own investigation, citing poor air discipline, malfunctioning bomb racks, and smoke over the target area. Among other measures, he established a bombardier's school for remedial training, as some units had arrived without finishing the stateside syllabus.[14]

Despite their absolute air supremacy, it took forces from eight allied nations—Americans, British, French, New Zealanders, Poles, Ghurkas, Indians, and Loyalist Italians—to dislodge the Luftwaffe paratroopers from Monte Cassino. The defenders did not withdraw until mid-May.

BIG WEEK

Everyone recognized that 1944 would be the decisive year of the war. It would feature the Allied invasion of northern France, opening the western front demanded by the Soviets, and squeezing Germany in a geostrategic vise from three directions—the Russians from the east, the Anglo-Americans from north and south.

U.S. Army ground commanders sometimes accused the airmen of pursuing their own agenda and preferring to attack strategic targets in the enemy homeland rather than supporting field armies. In turn, the fliers noted—correctly—that, with no Allied presence in northern Europe, the air campaign was in effect the long-sought second front.

Spaatz, Doolittle, Eaker, and Twining knew that their time was limited. The Combined Bomber Offensive was scheduled to end around the first of April, when American strategic airpower would come under Eisenhower's command. At that point the heavies would be sent after transportation targets to choke off German communications throughout occupied Europe. Few knew the date of D-Day, but it was obvious that it would come in late spring or early summer. The strategic air forces, consequently, had about two months to work whatever explosive magic they could. They went for the Luftwaffe's—namely Hermann Göring's—jugular.

The campaign—officially named Operation Argument but known to history as Big Week—was aimed at Germany's aviation industry.

In late February the Eighth and Fifteenth sent aerial task forces numbering hundreds of bombers at a time on a six-day blitz against aircraft factories and related targets throughout Germany and Austria. Assisted by the RAF's Bomber Command, which conducted three major night operations, their goal was to inflict debilitating and lasting damage to Luftwaffe production and operating bases.

Doolittle and Twining had an unprecedented number of heavy bombers with growing numbers of escort fighters. But what they needed most was out of their control—a week of uninterrupted good weather.

In late February, the Fifteenth Air Force comprised three bomb wings with twelve groups (eight B-24s) and four fighter groups (three P-38s, one P-47). When the Eighth kicked off Big Week on Sunday, February 20, however, Twining's bombers were limited to supporting the Anzio beachhead, but the buildup continued with the arrival of the 461st Bomb Group at Torretta.

THE DEFENDERS

Arrayed against Twining's formations was Luftflotte (Air Fleet) Two in Italy with seven fighter groups (six with Bf 109s) from five wings plus a Fascist Italian group flying Macchi-Castoldi 205s. Meanwhile, Fighter Division Seven near Munich deployed elements of six single-seat and two twin-engine "destroyer" wings totalling a dozen Messerschmitt groups.

Some notable airmen led the Reich's southern air defenses. Lieutenant General Joachim-Friedrich Huth of Fighter Division Seven had lost a leg in World War I but was determined to continue flying. He succeeded, returning to the cockpit in the 1930s. At age forty-four he earned the Knight's Cross leading a Bf 110 wing in the Battle of Britain. Promoted to general, he commanded fighter divisions from 1942 onward. From his headquarters at Schleissheim he defended southern and central Germany with eight single-engine fighter groups and four twin-engine groups, plus fighter school units. Huth coordinated with his subordinate division to the east, in Austria.

Commanding the air defense center in Vienna was an exceptional man, Colonel Gotthard Handrick. Born in 1908, he joined the Luftwaffe and excelled at sports. He won the gold medal in the pentathlon at the Berlin Olympics in 1936 and a year later was leading a fighter group in Spain, where he shot down five Republican aircraft. He continued flying combat in World War II, commanding a group of Jagdgeschwader 26 until June 1940, when, as a major, he assumed command of the wing, remaining until August at the height of the Battle of Britain. Later he commanded two other fighter wings, and in early 1944 he was a vigorous thirty-six-year-old colonel serving as *Jagdfliegerführer Ostmark*. His domain was the airspace over all but western Austria.

An illustrious name headed Air Fleet Two in northern Italy. General Wolfram von Richthofen, a cousin of Germany's greatest World War I ace, had earned a doctorate in aeronautics in the 1920s. Having served in combat in Spain, Western Europe, the Balkans, the Mediterranean, and Russia, he combined enormous experience with an icy intellect. He deployed elements of five Luftwaffe fighter wings plus the Repubblica Sociale Italiana, still loyal to Mussolini.[15]

Among the Italians, motivation varied. Some airmen sought to defend national honor, some reveled in continuing to fly, most probably stuck to their friends. In any case, the newly operational Aeronautica Nazionale Repubblicana showed some of the late Regia's fiery competence. On January 3, defending targets in the Turin area, the First Group's Macchi-Castoldi 205s taught the Fourteenth Fighter Group a hard lesson, downing three Lightnings and probably another from the U.S. First Group without losses.

If some Italians approached aerial combat as a sport, many Allied airmen did not. P-38 pilots were likely to shoot parachuting enemies, the Republican Air Force reported. An Aeronautica Nazionale fighter pilot was murdered in his chute on March 11, and another met the same fate seven days later. Both times this "barbarity" was perpetrated by Lightning pilots "from close range," eliminating any doubt that it was intentional.[16]

BIG WEEK TUESDAY

On February 20, Argument's opening day, the Mighty Eighth put up a thousand bombers for the first time, but the Fifteenth was grounded by weather. The next day Doolittle launched some 850 heavies while Twining awaited events.

Then on Tuesday, the twenty-second, weather largely skunked Doolittle's plans (fewer than a hundred heavies reached their primary targets), but Twining sent B-17s to the Petershausen rail marshalling yard and B-24s against Regensburg's factories and an air depot at Zagreb. The first two represented a landmark: the Fifteenth's first penetration of German airspace.

The Forty-seventh Wing went to Regensburg, 550 miles from Foggia. The Eighth had been operating in homeland skies for a full year, but to aircrews of the Ninety-eighth, 376th, 449th, and 450th Bomb Groups, it was a major event. And inevitably, it drew opposition.

The 449th Group Liberator flown by First Lieutenant Wilson Jones took damage to an engine en route to the target. Jones then had to shut down another engine on the right side. According to his copilot, Otis Mitchell, "We realized number three was going to have to run as long as it could."[17]

Limping along with barely half power, the Liberator fell astern of the formation. In war's grim logic, it was better to sacrifice one plane than to lose others in a vain effort to protect it. Jones formed up with three other stragglers but took little consolation. They were even worse off and gradually lost altitude and drifted off.

With two healthy engines and the erratic number three, Jones's
ship cleared the Alps. Though the mountains were no serious imped-
iment to aircraft of the era, a bomber pilot called them "perilous
territory to cross when losing altitude."[18] Jones and Mitchell decided
to veer eastward, avoiding likely interception over northern Italy, and
proceeded down the Yugoslavian coast. All the while the blessed
number three engine kept running, despite leaking oil for several
hours. Multi-engine pilots were trained to handle an engine out on
both wings, but two engines on the same side could be unmanageable.
Mitchell explained, "Jones and I decided that we were staying with
the ship but agreed it was best to give the remainder of the crew the
option of bailing out. All decided to take their chances with the ship.
It was a good choice as the number three engine continued to run all
the way across the Adriatic."[19]

Thanks to good judgment and Pratt & Whitney, Jones and Mitchell reached Italy and plunked down at the first field they found—a
P-38 base. Examining their Liberator, they found holes ranging in size
from a half-inch to a washtub. Somehow the 449th did not receive
word from wing headquarters, and by the time Jones and company
returned to base, their clothes had been packed for shipment home
and another crew had occupied their tent. "They were not happy to
see us return," Mitchell recalled.

The Fifteenth claimed forty enemy planes downed at a cost of
sixteen bombers and two fighters. The losses could have been far
worse. The tallies of downed German planes, however, were typically
optimistic. The Jagdwaffe wrote off only fifteen fighters.[20]

BIG WEEK WEDNESDAY

The next day, weather again forced a stand-down in Britain, but
for once the Italian climate afforded partially clear skies. Though
several formations were thwarted by local weather, 102 bombers got
to Steyr, the massive Austrian industrial complex that included a major

ball bearing factory and a Messerschmitt airframe and engine plant that shipped components to Wiener Neustadt and Regensburg for final assembly.

The target complex was huge—170 acres and thirty thousand employees. Navigators and bombardiers were carefully briefed on landmarks and checkpoints leading to the target area, especially the river bends northeast of the city. From there, individual groups would find their assigned targets.

The P-38 escorts' fuel capacity required them to return before completing the northbound leg of the journey. Luftwaffe controllers, aware of the situation, concentrated an estimated one hundred fighters against the Libs. Bf 110s of Destroyer Wing One gauged the distance nicely, firing their underwing rockets from a thousand yards astern of the bombers, then closed in with their four 20mm cannon. They were repelled only when withdrawal-support Lightnings appeared.

Waist gunner Sergeant Harry Pribyla of the 454th Group likened the encounter to a stop-action movie as 109s flashed across his field of view. A Messerschmitt fired a lethal burst into a nearby bomber's left wing. "The B-24 went into a slow, lazy roll, and kept going. Nobody got out."[21]

The 449th, recently arrived at Grottaglie, in the Italian heel, had lost its original commander, Colonel Darr H. Alkire, on January 31 when he was shot down over Aviano. Eight of the crew had parachuted onto a Luftwaffe airdrome, where one was scooped up by a cheerful German speaking superb English; he had lived in Houston for seven years.[22] The 449th's new CO was thirty-three-year-old Colonel Thomas J. Gent Jr., only three weeks into his command. A lead-from-the-front airman, he would log forty-six missions until relieved.

One Liberator crashed on takeoff, killing all ten men onboard. Another fell to fighters near the target, as recalled by a gunner who reckoned Steyr "my most awesome raid: 24s, 17s, 109s, FWs, 110s, black flak, red flak, white flak, everything mixed and planes going down all around."[23]

Steyr cost seventeen bombers. The 376th and 450th Groups were especially hard hit, each losing eight Liberators. The bombing was excellent, however. Post-strike assessment indicated the destruction of one-fifth of the factory that delivered up to 15 percent of Germany's ball bearings.

BIG WEEK THURSDAY

On Thursday, February 24, the Eighth targeted ball bearing and aircraft factories at Steyr in weather that limited enemy response, but the Fifteenth had no such luck against a Bf 110 factory beyond the range of Twining's fighters. Gotthard Handrick's radar controllers concentrated three groups for large, aggressive attacks on the small force of eighty-seven Fortresses over Schweinfurt and Gotha. Unimpeded, four to six interceptors at a time swept in while some fired long-range rockets and even dropped aerial bombs. Then, from the west, Huth's Fighter Division Seven contributed a Bf 109 and a 110 group that slammed into the B-17s over the target.

Swarmed by perhaps 120 fighters, the Second Bomb Group was chopped to pieces, losing fourteen planes, including the entire trailing squadron. Four other B-17s and a P-38 also went down. The Fortresses were heavily outnumbered by enemy interceptors, but the group maintained its formation and bombed the target, receiving a Distinguished Unit Citation for the performance. The Ninety-ninth Group also bombed accurately, though crews counted thirty-one planes with flak holes upon return to Tortorella.

The mission inflicted a heavy blow on the Fifteenth—nearly 20-percent losses over the primary target, despite good withdrawal cover by 146 fighters. The defenders counted nineteen losses, a dozen of those to Eighty-second and Fourteenth Group Lightnings south of Steyr. It was becoming obvious that the Fifteenth badly needed long-range escort fighters capable of breaking up Luftwaffe groups before they concentrated against the bombers. Though two Mustang groups had recently gone operational in Britain, the Mediterranean would have to wait.

BIG WEEK FRIDAY

At the end of the week, the weather finally took a favorable turn for the Americans. Unusually clear skies permitted planners to select any European targets in range of Britain or Italy.

Spaatz's commands concentrated northern and southern task forces against Regensburg. The Fifteenth dispatched nearly four hundred bombers to targets in Germany, Austria, and Italy, but only 176 flew against the primary target, which once again was Regensburg. Mission planners timed the southern prong to arrive over the target one hour before the northern force, hoping to catch the defenders on the ground rearming and refuelling.

The 450th Group sent twenty-nine Liberators against the Messerschmitt complex, and the defenders struck early, beginning three hundred miles out. Two white-ruddered "Cottontails" were victims of the Luftwaffe's *Herrausschutz* tactic—forcing a bomber out of formation so it could be hounded to destruction individually. As if that weren't enough, on the journey home the group encountered impenetrable weather—a huge cloud bank that forced a descent almost to wave-top level over the Adriatic en route to Manduria. Pilots sweated their way home beneath lowering clouds.

Hardest hit was the 301st, which lost a dozen B-17s. One was piloted by First Lieutenant Chester Koch, who bailed out his surviving crew, then set the doomed ship on autopilot. He parachuted onto the 7,300-foot Mount Kasereck, near Salzburg, where he spent a bitterly cold night. The next morning, as Koch was making his way downhill, he encountered a German pilot. Master Sergeant Hermann Stahl had downed a B-17 before abandoning his shot-up Messerschmitt, losing a boot in the process. The two fliers reached an accord, the American offering the German one of his flying boots worn over regular shoes. Together they continued their snowy descent until met by a civilian *Volkssturm* unit.[24]

Colonel Herbert E. Rice's Second Group rang up another stellar mission, receiving an unprecedented two Distinguished Unit Citations in two days.

Bombing was judged better than good. The 449th's mission summary concluded, "The Prufening works were completely wiped out. Not a building was left standing. The destruction was complete as happened in any heavy bombardment attack of the war."[25]

Operating beyond the range of Lightnings and Thunderbolts, the Forts and Libs had to shoot their way in to the targets and then shoot their way out. Some waist gunners stood amid growing piles of .50 caliber brass cases. The loss rate nearly matched the bloodletting of the day before: thirty-three of 176, or almost 19 percent.

In all, the Fifteenth lost forty-three planes that Friday—one-fourth against Regensburg—including four P-38s. It was more than twice the loss of the previous day, contributing to a record monthly toll of 131 planes, nearly double January's figure. Meanwhile, the Luftwaffe quartermaster crossed off thirty-seven fighters, nearly as many as were lost to the Fifteenth in the previous three days.[26]

BIG WEEK: DEBRIEF

During Big Week, the Fifteenth launched about five hundred bomber sorties, as against 3,300 by the Eighth. In all, the Americans dropped nearly ten thousand tons of bombs (40 percent of them on aircraft factories). Using the visible destruction to roof areas, Allied intelligence officers determined that the bombing campaign had damaged or destroyed 75 percent of the buildings in the targeted plants.[27]

But aerial photos could not reveal what lay beneath the rubble or remaining cover. The machinery and tools used to produce aircraft and engines often survived with little or no serious damage, and Germany's unusually efficient dispersal plan usually diluted the damage. Over the previous year, Albert Speer, the Reich's thirty-eight-year-old organizational genius, had optimized the armament industry. Operation Argument, therefore, targeted a network that was still expanding, taking up previous slack. For instance, Hitler had not permitted women to work in armament plants until early 1943.[28]

Throughout most of the war, air commanders were reluctant to return to targets that had already extracted a heavy price. A "restrike" policy—bombing through the holes in factory roofs—might have achieved greater results, but aircraft, crews, maintenance, and the eternal weather problems often prevented optimum damage. The increasing dispersion and efficiency of Germany's industrial plant, moreover, allowed the Third Reich to accelerate its aircraft production through most of the war.

Nevertheless, the combination punch delivered by the Eighth and the Fifteenth achieved results. Between the missions of the twenty-second and the twenty-fifth of February, Regensburg's and Augsburg's Messerschmitt plants were considered "utterly destroyed," with nearly every building struck. Aircraft deliveries plummeted from 435 fighters in January to 135 in March, a drop entirely attributable to the bombing. Regensburg did not achieve normal production until June. Augsburg, however, was up to speed in just five weeks, and other factories took up much of the slack.[29]

Postwar analysis determined that Argument deprived the Luftwaffe of perhaps two months of production—some two thousand fighters destroyed in their nests, and more than three hundred downed in combat. The heaviest damage was done to factories producing twin-engine fighters, which posed a lesser threat to bombers. Though no one could appreciate it at the time, the attack on the Messerschmitt factory at Augusburg delayed completion of the Me 262 jet fighter, which did not appear until that summer.

In retrospect, Allied commanders failed to appreciate "the phe-
nomenal recuperability of the aircraft industry, especially its airframe
branch." They estimated the monthly production of German single-
engine fighters in the first half of 1944 at 655, whereas 1,580 were
actually delivered.[30]

Ball bearing production also proved exceptionally resilient, partly
because of its physical nature and Germany's astute policy of keeping
the "pipeline" full. Thanks to Speer's remarkably efficient dispersal
scheme after the Eighth's two Regensburg strikes in 1943 and imports
from Sweden, the "antifriction-bearing" industry survived and even
flourished.

Argument cost the Army Air Forces 226 bombers and twenty-eight
fighters, totaling some 2,600 airmen. The 6-percent bomber loss rate
was heavy (four was considered sustainable), but some planners had
anticipated losing more than a hundred bombers in one day. During
Big Week, the Fifteenth lost eighty-nine bombers (forty-two B-17s)
and nine fighters, two-thirds of the February toll of 131. The increasing pace of operations had naturally produced greater attrition, from
fifty-three planes (twenty-one fighters) in December to seventy (thirty-
four fighters) in January.[31]

In January 1944, the German Air Force had lost 307 day and night
fighters in the west and nearly three hundred pilots—a 12-percent
attrition. February losses remain uncertain, but they probably reached
355 day fighters with 225 aircrewmen over Germany. Disastrous
losses among German twin-engine fighter groups forced their withdrawal to the east.[32]

Big Week permitted the Fifteenth Air Force and the Luftwaffe to
take one another's measure. Twining's bombers proved that they could
inflict telling damage on vital targets, but they paid a price for every
success. Ambitious young Teutons in Messerschmitts and Focke-
Wulfs, with thousands of other Germans manning flak batteries,
exacted a toll that clearly was unsustainable even for the Americans.
The very foundation of U.S. airpower was called into question: Could

the self-defending bomber survive against determined fighter opposition?

WORSENING WEATHER

Not only did Twining have fewer aircraft than the Eighth, but his effort was degraded by worsening weather. For instance, the 456th Group went operational at Stornarella on February 10 but dropped no bombs on six of its first ten missions until March 8.[33] The 451st reported that Gioia "became a sea of mud and water as the weather continued to go from bad to downright unbearable. The steel matt runway had almost sunk out of sight."[34]

Individual units' problems fit the larger pattern. The Americans had anticipated more operating days in sunny Italy than in Great Britain, but nature decreed otherwise. In the first quarter of 1944, nearly 40 percent of the Fifteenth's bombing missions were marred by poor visibility around Foggia and over intended targets.[35]

Excluding aborted missions, the Eighth Air Force operated heavy bombers on 303 days in 1944. The figure for the Fifteenth was 251—a startling 20-percent discrepancy. But whatever the numbers, aircrews frequently flew in marginal or poor weather. Years later, many pilots reflected that instrument flying was the weakest part of their training.[36]

While veteran groups recovered from Big Week, reinforcements arrived. The 461st Group "Liberaiders" settled in at Toretta on a field constructed on private property. The "landlord" was a nobleman, Baron Pavoncelli, who occasionally visited his tenants. Some of the Americans spoke Italian, permitting a personal relationship, though the group's main translator, Lieutenant Philip J. Caroselli, was shot down a few weeks later.

A farmer, Baron Pavoncelli maintained a barn and stables and did not object when some tenants appropriated hay to stuff their cotton mattresses. Occasionally the baron loaned one of his horses to equine-minded officers, including the group commander. Redheaded Colonel Frederick Glantzberg took advantage of the offer, and sometimes locals doffed their caps to him with "Buon giorno, barba rosa."[37]

Glantzberg was a thirty-nine-year-old MIT graduate who had been flying since 1928. In 1932 then-lieutenant Glantzberg was struck in flight by a twenty-pound trailing antenna from another aircraft. Despite a fractured skull, Glantzenberg recovered from a graveyard spiral at just five hundred feet, aided by the rear-seat pilot. Surgeons removed four square inches of his skull, but he refused to have a plate installed. Amazingly, he not only remained on active duty, but continued flying for eleven thousand hours, including a full tour of fifty missions. He frequently nudged his troops with, "Let's not stand around on one foot."[38] His group logged its first missions in April, and the crews appreciated Glantzberg for his leadership in the air.

Colonel Marden Munn brought the 459th Group to Giulia in February. He had been an American Airlines pilot before joining the army, where he flew attack aircraft and bombers. Upon assuming command of the 459th he already had 2,200 hours of military time. Munn led his group on its first eleven missions and nearly one-fourth of the first ninety, "including the bad ones." In contrast, his successor, previously stationed in the Panama Canal Zone and Galapagos Islands, logged only eleven of 172 missions in the last nine months of the war. That man, a West Pointer, retired as a major general, Munn as a colonel.[39]

Senior air force officers, unlike many ground commanders of comparable rank, frequently had to expose themselves to enemy action. Casualties among infantry and armor colonels were rare in comparison with their airborne counterparts, but fliers had the option to sit out the rough ones. The fact that so few did, preferring to emulate the likes of Glantzberg and Munn, inspired their airmen who shared identical risks.

With more groups arriving that spring, the Fifteenth was emerging from accelerated adolescence into early maturity. Doolittle and Twining had been forced to bring the command along quickly—probably faster than any numbered air force. Nearly every level learned much of its trade on the job, and Eaker, who had built the Eighth under similar conditions, was objective in his assessment. In March, after the trauma of Big Week, he described the Fifteenth as "a pretty disorganized mob." But he knew talent when he saw it. He trusted Twining and generally approved of his subordinates. Unit commanders were "perfecting the reorganization and training of their groups pretty rapidly."[40]

Training was a perennial topic and a common problem. When the 484th Group arrived at Torretta in April, many of Colonel William B. Keese's men recognized the situation. Upon reflection, the unit diarist wrote long afterward:

> In training during the war due to the expediency of getting troops into battle quickly, grades often were not given at the end of classes. If one hoped to survive and return home after the war, the soldier had to pay close attention to what was being taught. A flier had to learn his aircraft and weapons like the back of his own hand. There was no cheating or use of crib sheets in combat. It was best to get the information stuffed between your ears for instant recall, or your butt and those of your aircrew buddies will be put in doubt.[41]

TARGET: MORALE

Following Big Week, the Allied air chiefs resumed "morale attacks" against Balkan population centers, hoping to sow enough discontent to cause cracks in the Axis dike.

The goal was based on theory rather than reality. Two decades earlier, the Italian airpower theorist general Giulio Douhet had posited that strategic bombing could avert another Great War by compelling enemy civilians to demand their government's capitulation. The strategy had not worked because Douhet missed an essential point: bombing civilians into submission could succeed only against an industrial democracy, if then. In the 1930s and 1940s, the only conceivable rivals within range of each other were France and Britain. The despotic regimes in Berlin, Rome, Tokyo, and elsewhere were immune to public opinion.

"Morale bombing" was the Allied euphemism for what the recipients termed "terror bombing." Some airmen, from bombardiers to generals, were uneasy with the practice, both for ethical and practical reasons. Nonetheless, the RAF returned to Sofia twice in March, setting more fires. Then at month's end a two-day Allied blitz created a firestorm that incinerated facilities as varied as the city arsenal, the national theater, and the Bulgarian Orthodox Church's Holy Synod.

Sofia was no stranger to war. It was razed by the Huns in the fifth century AD and captured by Czarist Russia in 1878. But as in the bombings of Coventry in 1940 and Hamburg in 1943, the superheated air caused the spontaneous combustion of materials and buildings. The remaining population ran short of food, and weeks passed before civic services fully resumed. Despite the civilians' misery, however, strategic results proved elusive.

The Allies faced a serious contradiction. They had condemned the German bombing of Warsaw, Rotterdam, Coventry, and other population centers, but they themselves found it necessary or advisable to target enemy civilians. In fairness to the airmen, often lost in the postwar argument was the technical limitation of 1940s bombardment, when the AAF expected at least half of its bombs to fall outside a thousand-foot radius of the target in daylight. The RAF, flying at night, expanded its target size from factory complexes to city centers.

Nevertheless, Hap Arnold and some of his subordinates tried to have it both ways. In his study of the ethics of bombing, the historian Ronald Schaffer writes, "American flyers were expected to terrorize Balkan civilians without appearing to use terror tactics."[42]

By March 1944 some senior American planners concluded that morale bombing was not going to succeed independently; it needed to be integrated into missions against hard targets. The doubters included the influential Major General Frederick L. Anderson, Arnold's strategic air operations officer. They argued that the Mediterranean air command lacked sufficient resources to force Bulgaria to capitulate while meeting other assignments, especially in Romania. Morale bombing therefore needed to be part of a broader Allied strategy including battlefield victories in Italy and Russia while razing more cities in Germany.

Politically, morale bombing pulled in two directions. It prompted civilian resentment of the pro-Axis regimes but also hatred of the Allies for killing civilians and reducing some historic cities to smoldering rubble. The raids also played into Soviet hands, as Balkan Communists disingenuously noted that the Russians seldom bombed cities, ignoring that the Red Air Force was a tactical organization possessing nothing like the Anglo-American strategic capability.

That capability was about to be turned in a new direction, thanks to a startling new airplane.

CHAPTER THREE

ITALIAN SPRING

MARCH–JUNE 1944

B ig Week had proved that the Fifteenth Air Force badly needed long-range fighters. Beginning in April, Twining got them.

The three P-38 groups could seldom provide more than penetration or withdrawal support to distant targets such as Vienna and Regensburg, and the 325th Group's P-47s had even shorter range. Luftwaffe interceptors, consequently, exacted a steady toll of "heavies." In its first seven months, the Fifteenth attributed 54 percent of its bomber losses to enemy fighters, a figure that peaked at 82 percent during February.[1]

Concentrating on targets closer to home after Big Week, the Fifteenth's bombers enjoyed better escort coverage. Bomber losses dropped from 131 in February to eighty-two in March, when most targets lay in Italy and Austria. A two-day mini-blitz against enemy airfields on March 18 and 19, however, cost twenty-five bombers and three fighters, while the 454th Group lost nine Liberators in one day over Graz.

With his bomber strength growing—eight more groups arrived from January through March—Twining made his case for more fighters. Three groups from the Twelfth Air Force were transferred between April and June: the Thirty-first and Fifty-second with Spitfires and the 332nd in P-47s. But before the new units could join the Fifteenth, they needed to change horses.

Their new mount was the Mustang.

North American's P-51, originally intended for Britain, began life with the same Allison engine as the Lightning. It performed well up to fifteen thousand feet, but thereafter speed fell off unless sufficiently supercharged. The problem was solved by installing the British Rolls-Royce Merlin engine, which thrived at high altitudes. The result was not only better performance, but greater range.

The Mustang was aerodynamically extremely "clean." Its laminar-flow wing was one of the most efficient airfoils of the era, and the air scoop mounted beneath the fuselage caused less drag than the nose-mounted radiators. Eventually its top speed was rated at 437 mph.

Colonel Charles M. McCorkle of the Thirty-first and Lieutenant Colonel Robert Levine of the Fifty-second oversaw the conversion from Spitfires to Mustangs. Though the airplanes were different breeds, they both used the Merlin, one of the finest aircraft engines of the war, simplifying maintenance.

Despite its devotion to the Spitfire—the most glamorous of all Allied fighters—the Thirty-first Group immediately recognized the P-51's advantages. In nearly a year and a half flying Spits, the Thirty-first had claimed 194 aerial victories. Pilots doubled that figure in less than five months with the hardy little North American pony. The Spitfire's monthly record had been thirty kills, set in January 1944, but the Thirty-first topped that figure in each of its first five months flying '51s.

For aggressive aviators, performance was only part of the equation. The other was range. The Mustang's long legs could take pilots where the action was. On April 16 the group flew a bomber escort almost to the Romanian border. The Mustangs were airborne for four hours and forty-five minutes, twice the endurance of a typical Spitfire mission.

The Fifty-second Group began transition on April 22 and logged its first Mustang mission on May 10, an escort to Nice, France.

Pilots immediately felt at home in a P-51. When American males averaged five foot eight, its cockpit layout was one of the best. The controls fell easily to hand, the result of North American's attention to detail. Visibility was decent in the B and C models, though the view rearward was restricted as in the Spitfire and the Messerschmitt 109.

As a weapon, the Mustang was tops. It originally packed four .50 caliber machine guns, but the D model featured the bubble canopy and six guns. With its speed, maneuverability, and range, it could take the fight to the enemy and engage him on better than even terms. At the same time, Mustangs protected American bombers from deadly Luftwaffe interceptors over any target. The P-51 was one of a handful of game-changers among military aircraft. It probably saved the daylight bombing offensive when relentless attrition threatened to force a change in AAF policy.

The 325th Group continued flying Thunderbolts until late May, leaving little time for transition. But in those carefree days of military aviation, the prevailing attitude was "They all have a stick and a throttle. Go fly 'em." So it was with the 325th, which parked its Thunderbolts on May 24 and launched the first Mustang mission three days later.

By then, Bob Baseler had rolled out of the group, reassigned to Brigadier General Strother's fighter wing staff. Baseler was succeeded by a Texan, Lieutenant Colonel Chester L. Sluder, on April 1. Baseler nevertheless continued flying occasional missions, maintaining the good-natured feud with his former crew chief. Because Baseler's P-47 had been *Big Stud*, Sergeant Eckert dubbed the smaller Mustang *Little Stud*. The colonel had learned his lesson previously and did not object.

Major Herschel "Herky" Green was top gun of the 325th, already an ace with nine victories in P-40s and P-47s. Recalling the Mustang, he said,

> Pilots reported getting into a turning duel with an enemy plane and suddenly finding they were having to push forward on the stick with all their strength to keep the aircraft from turning tighter and tighter and entering a high speed stall. Many reported they could not prevent the high speed stall. Several stated that the aircraft had stalled and snapped into a spin from which they felt fortunate to escape. It did not take us long to become fully aware of this critical problem and heed the placard warning.
>
> On long missions it was tempting to retain as much fuel in wing and fuselage tanks as possible, but we learned always to burn off at least 55 gallons from the fuselage tank before changing to the drop tanks.[2]

The last to convert to P-51s was the 332nd Group, the Tuskegee Airmen, which exchanged Thunderbolts for Mustangs in June. The Tuskegee Airmen were accustomed by then to changing mounts. The original Ninety-ninth Squadron had flown P-40s for nearly a year before converting to P-47s. The group commander was Colonel Benjamin O. Davis Jr., an army brat whose father had been America's first black general. Davis Jr. had graduated well up in the West Point class of 1936 and won his wings in 1942. He was a serious, no-nonsense officer driven to succeed.

Whatever their airplane, fighter pilots were practically kids. Of the Fifteenth Air Force's top fourteen aces (that is, those with ten or more aerial kills), eleven were under twenty-five. The top gun was John J. Voll, a twenty-two-year-old captain. Four of the leading scorers made ace as second lieutenants, and six others at twenty years old were still too young to drink or vote.

The old hands were twenty-six, and some group commanders, including full colonels, were under thirty.[3] In contrast, some bomber commanders were nearly forty. The average army pilot was twenty-four and earning more money than he could easily spend. In 1944 an unmarried first lieutenant received a monthly base pay of $166.66 plus $83.30 flight pay, $16.60 overseas pay, and $6.75 miscellaneous allowances: a princely $273.31. (The commensurate figure in 2014 would be about $3,628.) If he died in the line of duty, the beneficiary of his GI insurance policy received $10,000.[4]

A P-51 pilot flew a $51,500 aircraft that only a Howard Hughes could have afforded in civilian life. The Mustang jockey had 1,700 horses in his left hand and 2,100 rounds of machine gun ammunition under his right index finger. P-38 pilots reveled in even more deluxe machinery: in 1944 their twin-engine Lightning cost the taxpayers $97,100. It was so sleek that it cruised almost as fast on one engine as two.

The Lightning was the most distinctive aircraft in European skies. Its twin-boom configuration with a gondola housing the pilot and armament was unique. The design was radical for its era, more revolutionary than evolutionary. It featured a two-handed control yoke instead of a stick and a nose wheel. Powered by two supercharged 1,700-horsepower Allison engines, it made news from its debut in 1939. The P-38 was America's first production aircraft capable of 400 mph in level flight, and despite its large size (a fifty-two-foot wingspan), it was surprisingly agile. Counter-rotating props eliminated torque or the powerful "P-factor."

Fighter pilots often lorded it over lesser mortals, aloft and on the ground. Bomber crews at Amendola recalled a spectacular buzz job by the First Fighter Group. The P-38s from Salsola extended their flight pattern twelve miles southeast, screaming in so fast and low that their slipstreams collapsed some tents. The miscreants were never identified.

All the fighter pilot had to do was show up, fly, and shoot. He had few collateral duties. His exotic airplane, fuel, and ammunition were all provided, and there was no bag limit on the prey he hunted. Inevitably, his youthful, type-A personality combined with his bulletproof attitude to produce tragedy. Shortly after the Thirty-first Group converted to Mustangs, a twenty-six-year-old lieutenant with four kills stayed up late drinking with his buddies. At dawn Leonard H. Emery fired up his airplane, took off, buzzed the field, and disappeared. Much later the group learned that a lone P-51 had been shot down while strafing Bucharest. Some said the pilot had been grieving the loss of a friend, others that he had "the Messerschmitt twitch." As often happened in war, the full story was never known.[5]

FRIEND OR FOE?

A new aircraft in theater invited both curiosity and error; the Mustang was no exception.

From World War II onward, the incidence of friendly fire varied widely—between 2 and 15 percent of aircraft destroyed or damaged in combat—but whatever the number, "blue on blue" incidents were all too common. The most frequent cause was poor aircraft recognition. Innately aggressive twenty-something pilots in high-speed combat had to make decisions in a couple of heartbeats: mistakes were inevitable.[6] Although nothing else resembled a P-38, a Mustang—especially the B model—could be mistaken for a Messerschmitt 109. And from some angles, despite its elliptical wing, the radial-engine P-47 could resemble a Focke-Wulf 190.

On an April 1944 mission to Wiener Neustadt, a P-38 shot up Captain Harry Parker's Thunderbolt. The Checkertail pilot nursed his crippled "Jug" to friendly territory before ringing up the for-sale sign. He parachuted to safety, returning to down thirteen enemy aircraft.

On April 16, Liberator gunners who had not seen Mustangs before put a .50 caliber round through Lieutenant Howard Baetjer's engine. The Thirty-first Group pilot bailed out and was listed as missing in action. He turned up six weeks later courtesy of Yugoslavian Partisans. His friends plied him for details, but all returnees were prohibited from revealing information about their rescues. Baetjer returned to flying, though the Princeton graduate's luck ran out. He was shot down again and spent the rest of the war in POW camps.

The friendly fire losses were frustrating, but they eventually declined.

ESCORT POLICY

With far greater range than the Spitfire, the Mustang opened a new chapter in the history of the Fifteenth Air Force. But Strother's fighter pilots had their work cut out for them learning how to make the best use of their new mount, as George Loving of the Thirty-first Group relates:

> Lacking experience with the P-51, higher headquarters pretty much left it to our group commander, Sandy McCorkle, to come up with escort tactics we would use. Boiled down to the essence, Sandy's strategy was to have us maintain considerable height over the bombers, keep squadron integrity as long as possible, always leave part of the formation high over the bombers when going after enemy fighters, but not go to the deck or outside the battle area, and regroup as soon as possible.
>
> Typically, the lead squadron of Mustangs would be positioned three thousand or four thousand feet above the lead bomber group, a second squadron would be one thousand

feet higher over the middle of the bomber formation, and
the third squadron would be over the rearmost bomber
group, two thousand feet higher than the lead Mustang
squadron. Altitude could be converted quickly to airspeed,
which could be the vital factor in any air battle. For this
reason, we needed to stay high but still within easy reach
of any enemy fighters posing a threat to the bombers.[7]

The Checkertails' Barrie Davis writes, "I do not remember the
exact date orders changed, but until about April 1944, we had orders
to break off the chase at fifteen thousand feet and return to close escort
of the bombers." Subsequently headquarters in Bari issued a policy
change,

with instructions to chase the enemy until we got him—
even if the chase extended down to ground level.
    The orders to break off the chase at fifteen thousand feet
caused a false belief in the minds of enemy pilots. Several
years ago, during a Hungarian-sponsored Bucharest
reunion of airmen who fought in the air over Hungary, I
talked with former German and Hungarian fighter pilots
who believed the Me-109 could out-dive the Mustang. This
belief developed when they had dived to escape a pursuing
Mustang, went through fifteen thousand feet, looked
behind, and the Mustang was gone. It was a fatal belief.
Three of my six aerial victories came when the enemy fighters attempted to escape with a steep dive, which was not
successful.[8]

Arthur Fiedler, a twenty-year-old Mustang pilot, was an ace before
he could vote. His early experience demonstrated the difference between
the policies of staying with the bombers and "pursue and destroy."

On 24 June 1944 I bounced six Me-109s preparing to attack B-24s, I was returning to base alone with a rough engine. When I reached their altitude, only the last man was still there and I glommed onto him. Lost my gunsight bulb due to high Gs but finally managed to get hits on him as we passed through the B-24s who targeted both of us.

At fifteen thousand feet I had to leave him per orders and attempt to return to the bombers. At that time, he was trailing coolant and a tongue of flame was visible on his left fuselage. I was given credit for a probable.

Some time in the next four days, we were advised of Doolittle's [Eighth Air Force] policy, which was formulated after his evaluation of why the Germans failed against the English in the Battle of Britain. Essentially if an e/a attacked our escorted bombers, we were to pursue him until we eliminated him or the reverse occurred. On 28 June I received credit for two Me 109s although the new policy was not particularly germane as we were on a fighter sweep.[9]

The reference to Doolittle's escort policy for his British-based fighters was timely. When Ira Eaker moved to the Mediterranean in early 1944, he left in place his close-escort policy with the Eighth and apparently extended it to the Fifteenth. Doolittle and his Eighth Air Force fighter commander, Major General William E. Kepner, however, almost immediately reversed the policy. Both knew that the Luftwaffe had attempted close escort over Britain in 1940 and that the result had been heavy losses among German bombers. More than forty years later, Luftwaffe fighter chief Adolf Galland still chafed under the restriction, complaining that his Messerschmitt pilots, who were denied the initiative, had to react to RAF interceptors rather than attacking them on even terms.[10]

Fiedler continued,

> Initially the bomber folks complained bitterly about the
> new policy; however, since their losses decreased, the com-
> plaints eventually lessened considerably although there
> were exceptions. One could also question whether the loss
> of Ploesti contributed to decreased attacks on our bombers,
> or perhaps other considerations were in play?
>
> Now assume you are a German fighter pilot. You know
> that if you attack a group of bombers escorted by one
> specific group of P-51s, you probably can make a high
> speed attack from altitude, hit the bombers, dive away,
> and the fighters will not follow you. You are also aware
> that if you attack bombers escorted by the other three P-51
> groups, they may follow you wherever you go until they
> either eliminate you or you are fortunate and able to down
> the pursuing P-51[s]. You also know from past encounters,
> that in a knock down, drag out contest, neither the Me-109
> nor the FW-190 have been particularly successful in sur-
> viving when confronted by a Mustang flown by a good
> pilot![11]

Apparently both strategic air forces allowed fighter group commanders to choose their own escort policy. Most chose the flexible,
roving tactics described by the Thirty-first and 325th rather than
sticking with the "heavies" most of the time. While reducing bomber
losses was important, it was secondary to achieving air superiority,
and destroying the enemy air force was not accomplished by flying
formation on the bombers. Besides, once the Axis fighters were beaten,
U.S. bomber losses would plummet. So from June 1944 the Mustang
dominated Fifteenth Air Force escort missions. At war's end, the three
top-scoring groups flew P-51s, and among the fourteen double aces or
better, only one flew a Lightning.

BOMBERS

The Fifteenth had added one new B-24 group in December, four in January, and three in February. Twining continued building his air force that spring, adding another group of Liberators in March and three in April. The AAF was turning out heavy bomb groups with the same efficiency as the Willow Run production line was turning out Liberators. The typical unit went from authorization to activation in about two months. The groups formed up at remote bases in Idaho, Utah, New Mexico, and Nebraska, and their names tell the story: the 450th from Boise to Manduria, the 455th from Alamogordo to San Giovanni, the 464th from Wendover to Panatella. A bomb group's four squadrons spent seven or eight months training before deploying overseas, though two groups—the 464th and 465th—were nearly a year reaching Panatella.

There was a building-block approach to unit training, which was conducted in three phases. The first phase, focused on individual crewmembers, introduced pilots to their planes and molded ten individuals into a combat team. In the second phase, crews concentrated on formation flying and aerial gunnery, usually progressing from three-plane flights to six- and nine-plane squadrons. In the final phase, crews conducted long-range navigation flights, often over water. Training focused on essential combat tasks with more gunnery and often daily bombing.

The Fifteenth took six months to grow to maturity. In December 1943, it comprised 4,873 officers and 32,867 men. Its 1,115 bomber crews (about 11,150 men, nearly 30 percent of the Fifteenth's total personnel) operated 739 B-24s and 200 B-17s. With arrival of the Fifty-fifth Bomb Wing's last two groups (465th and 485th) in April 1944, Twining owned twenty-one bomb groups and seven fighter groups. It was half of the Eighth Air Force's final strength, but by the spring of 1944 he had what he needed to accomplish his primary mission: to shut off Germany's Balkan oil. In the meantime, however, there were other items on the Fifteenth's growing agenda.

MORALE TARGETS:
SOFIA AND BUCHAREST

Operating over the Balkans in the spring and summer of 1944, the Fifteenth began to encounter aircraft from two other Axis nations— Romania and its southern neighbor, Bulgaria.

Romania's oil and transport systems were obvious targets for the Allies, and the Fifteenth repeatedly struck Bucharest and Ploesti. From early April through June, Twining launched six bombing missions against the capital with as many as three hundred Forts and Liberators at a time hitting marshalling yards and refineries. In June, Fifteenth fighters swept over the city on two occasions, dropping down to strafe airfields, locomotives, and most anything that moved.[12]

Romanian fighters had intercepted B-24s during Operation Tidal Wave, the low-level Ploesti raid in August 1943, and they intercepted Fifteenth Air Force bombers from April 1944 onward. The yellow-crossed Messerschmitts clashed with Mustangs for the first time during a shuttle mission to Russia on June 6. Captain Constantin Cantacuzino, an international sportsman before the war, had a string of victories over the Soviets but relished the chance to fight P-51s. He made the most of the opportunity when the Seventh Fighter Group tied into a formation of 325th Checkertails, brand new to the Mustang. Escorting bombers to Galati, Romania, the Checkertails encountered stiff opposition, losing two planes while claiming six kills. Cantacuzino shot down Lieutenant John D. Mumford, who eluded capture and reached the Soviet lines.[13]

As a rule, the Balkan aviators were older than their opponents, often by as much as a decade, and experienced both in flying and in combat. The top Romanian aces, Cantacuzino and Alexandru Serbanescu, were thirty-eight and thirty-two, respectively. Stoyan Stoyanov, the leading Bulgarian pilot, was thirty-one, and Major Aladar Heppes, the senior Hungarian in combat, was forty.

A minor Luftwaffe partner, the Bulgarian Air Force—the *Vozdu-shni Voiski*—flew aircraft sporting a black X on a white field. Though deploying only 250 front-line aircraft in May, the *Vozdushni Voiski* nonetheless made a good showing. In 1943 and 1944, the Bulgars claimed sixty American aircraft downed (forty-six bombers), with 108 AAF fliers killed and 329 captured. Sixteen Bulgarian pilots died in the effort.[14]

After a hard-fought engagement over the Romanian-Bulgarian border on June 11, the Fifty-second Group reported, "There was no disposition on the part of the enemy to avoid combat. In view of the evident ability of the enemy pilots, there was some surprise at the ... poor marksmanship on their part." The yellow-tailed Mustangs claimed thirteen kills against one loss, with known Axis losses of four JG 301 pilots and a Bulgarian 109 pilot.[15]

Bulgaria's role in World War II is little known in the West, but it figured prominently in Fifteenth Air Force operations. The Allies flew eleven missions against its capital, Sofia, from November 1943 to April 1944, striking some 12,000 buildings and killing 1,374 persons. A local writer describes the destruction: "Industrial, governmental and cultural buildings were badly damaged and whole residential areas were charred. Streets and sidewalks were ploughed and tram lines ripped apart. The water, electrical, and telephone systems were also severely disrupted. There seemed to be no citizen of Sofia left untouched by the bombings."[16]

On April 4, 1944, three hundred of Twining's heavies attacked Sofia's marshalling yards, destroying 1,400 railroad cars and numerous buildings, leaving fires that burned for two days. The Americans attempted precision but failed to achieve it; the heaviest concentration of bombs landed beyond the rail yards, striking the city.[17]

Thirteen days later, on what Sofians would remember as "Black Easter," 470 bombers escorted by two hundred fighters attacked

Belgrade and Sofia. Twenty-five hundred bombs fell on rail and transport targets. Perhaps 750 buildings were destroyed, with three times that number left irreparable, and 128 persons were killed.[18]

Black Easter ended a vain five-month effort to force Bulgaria out of the Axis camp. As early as January, neutral press reports stated that three hundred thousand people had abandoned Sofia, which had a population of roughly four hundred thousand. Nationwide, 187 cities and towns had been bombed, and 4,100 people had been killed or injured. The doubts of some Allied strategists early that year were confirmed: bombing failed to force Bulgaria to capitulate, just as it had failed in Britain and Germany.[19]

The Americans bombed Bucharest on April 4. Relying upon questionable data, Ira Eaker shared his dismay at the civilian casualties with Hap Arnold: "Our attack on the marshaling yards at Bucharest was a bloody affair. We killed about 12,000 people, six thousand of them were refugees on trains in the yards; six thousand of them were Rumanians living around the yards."[20] The toll was actually far less. Romanian sources report about 2,600 killed and nearly as many wounded, victims, apparently, of strong winds aloft that blew ordnance off the intended target, the city's main marshalling yard. The lone bomb group to reach the target, the 449th, sustained heavy losses, with seven of twenty-eight Liberators destroyed and many damaged.[21]

BLOODY VIENNA

Vienna became the Fifteenth's toughest target—even tougher than the fiercely defended refineries around Ploesti. Intelligence officers briefed aircrews that the Austrian capital's defenses were exceeded in strength only by Berlin's, though Hamburg—out of range of Foggia—probably boasted more flak than Vienna. Berlin and Vienna each had three of the Reich's eight major flak tower complexes; Hamburg had two. Arranged in pairs (one gun tower and a fire-control platform), they were tall, brooding gray monoliths bristling with light and medium antiaircraft guns, 20mm to five-inch, many radar controlled.[22] Hundreds of heavy and medium guns were arrayed in cordons circling the city. And the flak crews got plenty of practice: from late 1943 Vienna was bombed nearly fifty times.

On June 26, 677 bombers set off from Foggia against multiple targets in the Vienna area: an aircraft factory, a rail marshalling yard, and six petroleum plants. Moosbierbaum was a priority, receiving the first of a dozen strikes over the next nine months. Its chemical plant delivered large quantities of naphtha for liquid oil dehydrogenation, and a refinery was nearby.

XV Fighter Command put up 260 or more Mustangs and Lightnings, but the defenders nearly matched that total. The result was one of the greatest air battles in the Fifteenth's history.

From his headquarters in Vienna, Colonel Gotthard Handrick—the Olympic gold medalist—astutely deployed 240 interceptors. His Eighth Division controllers pulled in twin-engine fighters from as far off as Prague (150 miles) and Slovakian 109s from Bratislava just across the Danube. The Germans deployed them well.

The 304th Wing's 161 Liberators were led by the 455th Group's thirty-eight planes ahead of the 454th, 456th, and 459th. During the turn at the initial point, the 455th's second section of eighteen B-24s swung to the right, extending into a vulnerable position. Flying formation could be difficult when straight and level, but maintaining position in a banked turn with eighteen bombers required careful handling and timing. Inevitably some formations drifted wide, and the Germans took note.

A Messerschmitt 110 unit was positioned to cut off the box as the wing arrived at the turning point for the final run to Moosbierbaum.

Nearly thirty *Zerstörer* (destroyers) tackled the Liberators head-on then kept going to deny the escorts a shot at them. Meanwhile, sixty 109s and 190s rolled in from a forward perch with remarkable aggressiveness. They pressed their attacks to collision range, unconcerned with Yankee fighters or German flak.

According to the 455th's history, the vulnerable formation "was attacked from every angle by approximately sixty twin-engine and sixty single-engine fighters, a relentless attack on the bombers. One of the bombers collided head-on with one of the fighters. Despite its mortal wounds it persisted through the bomb run, dropped its bombs and plummeted to the ground. Two other aircraft set afire in the attack struggled over the target, released their bombs and then the crews abandoned their airplanes."[23]

The cost of the combined assault was devastating. The 455th Group wrote off ten planes and crews, a unit record, with eight more downed from the 304th Wing. The follow-up assault by the single-engine fighters claimed twenty-eight kills or "culls," cutting out individual bombers from the formation. Nine 109s or 190s and four 110s went down in the melee.

The wing lost eighteen bombers, all to enemy aircraft, while claiming fifty-three defenders downed. Only twenty-six of the Vulgar Vultures returned to San Giovanni, three with severe damage. Several of the 742nd Squadron's fifty-nine missing men had been flying their last mission. They were old hands, the group's original cadre when it arrived at San Giovanni in January; many had flown the first mission in mid-February.

But there were losses on both sides. One *Zerstörer* group (I/ZG76) met a wall of .50 caliber fire, losing eight Bf 110s to bomber guns. It was testimony to the Germans' aggressiveness, as twin-engine fighters usually kept their distance to employ their heavier weapons.[24]

The defenders included thirty Hungarians and eight Slovaks, their 109s presenting a kaleidoscope of insignia: the Luftwaffe's black cross and swastika, Hungary's white cross on a black field, and Slovakia's blue cross with red center.

Some of the Slovak pilots had experience against the Soviets but none had seen anything resembling the Fifteenth's armada. Preparing to attack the Americans, the 109s dropped their belly tanks and turned in at thirty thousand feet. They downed a 459th Group Liberator, and then the roof fell in.

In minutes U.S. fighters shredded the Slovak unit. Master Sergeant Pavel Zalenak, a twelve-victory ace, was selected for destruction by three P-38s, which drove him to ground level, forcing him into a high-speed crash landing. Though wounded, he survived. Others were not as fortunate. The Americans downed or damaged seven of the eight Slovak Messerschmitts, killing three pilots and seriously wounding one. One of the slain was reported either to have been killed in his chute or to have fallen from his harness.[25]

The escorts chalked up forty-four kills in all, one less than the record on January 30. As usual, Mustangs got the best of the shooting; the Thirty-first and Fifty-second Groups claimed thirty kills between them. But the Eighty-second Lightnings did well, returning to Vincenzo with fourteen victories against four losses. Four Mustangs also failed to return, but it was an overwhelming American victory. The Luftwaffe could not endure many more of them.

Bomber crews reported the sluggish Me 210s showed more than their usual willingness to fight. "They made every effort to draw off the escorting fighters so as to leave the bombers unprotected."[26]

Top gun was Major Samuel J. Brown, a burly Mustang squadron commander who ran his score to thirteen in a vertical combat. Spotting two large gaggles approaching the bombers, he positioned himself and wingman Flight Officer Edward Jay to intercept the Me 410s. After directing the rest of the 307th Squadron against the 109s, Brown and Jay displayed some exceptional teamwork. The CO dropped two and Jay another almost before the *Zerstörer* could react.

Slamming forward on his throttle, Brown grabbed for altitude, stalking some 109s from below. He hammered one that stalled then spun
earthward while the others dived away. The two Mustangs executed
a simultaneous hammerhead turn—nose high, running airspeed to
nearly zero before booting rudder to slice downward. On the descent
they picked out more 410s and each destroyed one before heading
home low on ammunition. They had six kills and two damaged
between them.

A fellow Thirty-firster, Second Lieutenant John Voll, downed
two, having opened his victory log three days before. Another "second balloon" was James D. Holloway of the Eighty-second, who
became an ace by adding three twin-engine fighters to his previous
score.

Despite bomber and fighter claims of sixty or more Axis planes
downed, the large Luftwaffe response achieved results. Forty-three
American aircraft were lost, matching the Big Week mission against
Regensburg. Hardest hit was the 455th Group, which lost ten Liberators. Nevertheless, the Luftwaffe paid heavily. Forty-one fighters
were destroyed, including sixteen *Zerstörer*, with more than forty
aircrews lost. Both sides were engaged in attrition warfare, and neither
was going to back off.[27]

LIVING THERE

Far, far below the geostrategists in Washington, London, and Foggia, and even below the wing commanders, were the individuals supporting every military campaign: the unheralded thousands in khaki
who made each mission possible.

By definition an air force is a technical organization. There is often
as much enthusiasm about the hardware among the non-fliers as there
is among pilots. In early May the Fourteenth Fighter Group reported,
"Nine of our old [P-38Gs] have been prepared to leave tomorrow

morning. They are being replaced with new J's. Number Four has 716 hours on it and Number Seven has 707, each with over 100 missions. The nine planes average over 500 hours apiece and are still in good condition. Bouquets to our mechanics. Typhus shots were given by the needle jabbers."

The next day: "Ten new Js were received this morning and beautiful birds of the air they are."[28]

Despite a rigid rank structure, most units learned the value of certain noncommissioned officers and enlisted men. Intelligent commanders gave ample latitude to subordinates with a knack for getting things done, sometimes looking the other way when pragmatism clashed with regulations. The Thirty-first Fighter Group recorded, "Corporal Valorose, 308th Squadron, took a trip to Rome and nothing would get done properly until he returned."[29]

The army tried to provide diversion for GIs, ranging from athletics to bingo to talent shows and movies. At Triolo, the cinema fare in May 1944 was usually five or six months old. Some films had been released as recently as Christmas. The airmen could be tough critics, as the diary of a P-38 unit shows:

[May 5:] Deanna Durbin and Franchot Tone played in "The Butler's Sister" and Deanna displayed no end of S.A., which of course was gratifying to all. Deanna Durbin, the twenty-two-year-old brunette and occasional blonde crooner, rated high in sex appeal.

[May 8:] No mission today. A propaganda picture "Behind the Rising Sun" credited some Japanese as being human but succeeded in leaving its audience filled with hate for the Nipponese.

[May 10:] The movie provided the only interest of the day, "Moonlight in Vermont" with Gloria Jean, a very poor picture.

[May 13:] The Ritz Brothers and Frances Langford played in a class C musical, "Never a Dull Moment."

[May 20:] "Jack London" proved a very inferior movie this evening.

[May 27:] It was a spring rain in earnest today. No mission. Lousy show this evening. Ted Lewis in "Is Everybody Happy?" An emphatic *No* was on everybody's lips as they left after seeing it.[30]

At Salsola ("Foggia Number Three"), the First Group's theater was dubbed "the Barn," seating five hundred and often with standing room only. A show consisting of newsreels and a movie was run three times daily, three days a week, "and usually plays to a full house."

In June the Eighty-second Fighter Group's softball team hosted a visiting team that drew a record audience at Vincenzo. The Women's Army Corps team from Foggia took the field, and even the men who were not sports fans considered it "a thrilling sight, everyone's eyes on the WACs instead of the ball. Even the umpire, Staff Sergeant Bill Jones, didn't know the score at the end of the game."[31]

Meanwhile, San Severo became "progressively more civilized." In addition to decent living quarters, an acceptable mess facility, an officers' club, and a movie twice a week, it now offered a laundry operated by Italian women (fifty cents a bundle). But civilization came at a cost. "Regulations that heretofore had gone unenforced were now being resurrected," recalled one pilot, especially in connection with transportation. Previously, five or six men might cram into a jeep, but under the new regime, only four were permitted, and a "trip ticket" had to be obtained from the motor pool. Pilots noticed that MPs at the front gate were not as friendly as before. They were obviously feeling the heat too.[32]

Creeping civilization (especially better quarters, varied food, ample toilet paper, and more frequent entertainment) had some onerous consequences: dress standards and military courtesy. The Fifty-second Group lamented:

> The price of these luxuries was that a certain decorum was expected of us. No longer was a pair of underwear shorts considered adequate for the necessary early morning trip out back. Bathing from a helmet standing in front of a tent before God and everybody was discouraged. Some degree of neatness in uniforming was now expected, now that laundry and dry cleaning service was available.
>
> The military custom of saluting was encouraged, particularly when there were high-ranking strangers in camp. After an embarrassing experience involving the group CO and a visiting general, formations were called in each squadron and everybody was warned to salute anything above a captain. So for the next 24 hours military tradition was strictly observed. Then matters once more settled back to normal.[33]

However onerous military protocol may have been, the Fifteenth tried to give combat crews a break midway through their tours. Officially, "R and R" stood for rest and recreation (or recuperation), but GIs sometimes referred to "rape and rampage." The most popular R and R destination was the fabled Isle of Capri, south of Naples in the Tyrrhenian Sea.

Capri lived up to expectations. A 456th Group Liberator pilot, Robert S. Capps, described his visit as "a wonderful, restful, luxurious experience. We had very good accommodations and there were excellent, first-class restaurants in the hotels run by highly skilled Italians.... It was a great change from our rough tent life and eating off metal mess kits at our air base." A future Ph.D., Capps wrote, "I can readily understand why the Roman emperor, Tiberius, decided to make his castle here and live the last years of his life from 26 to 37 A.D." The delights of Capri ended too soon for Capps and his comrades. "We had to return to reality, the constant threat to our lives, and the rustic style of living we were accustomed to at our base. We had to start sweating out combat missions again."[34]

Besides strategic targets such as Ploesti and Vienna, those combat missions included smaller strikes, often in northern Italy. Usually losses were few, but drama still occurred, as on the 451st Group's Mission 44 to the Padua marshalling yard in mid-May. The briefers described a "milk run," and the prediction held up until the Liberators began their bomb run at only eighteen thousand feet. At that point heavy flak opened up.

Lieutenant William Booker's plane took a solid hit. The pilot was wounded in the legs and the cockpit filled with smoke. Copilot Charles Brown took over, completing the bomb run, then crewmen began treating Booker and the nose gunner, who was seriously wounded.

Headed for Gioia del Colle, Brown called for a damage check. The flight engineer began a dolorous litany: hydraulics failing, radio out, and landing gear damaged. Then, while descending toward base, Brown learned that the nose wheel was flat, as was the left main landing gear tire. Without hydraulics the crew had to crank the wheels down manually.

While wondering how he would land the crippled Liberator, Brown received unexpected help. Above all, a bomber crew was a team, and everyone could make a contribution. Brown explained, "One of the crew read somewhere in a similar situation, parachutes were opened via the waist windows just before touchdown. We decided to try it. They attached the chutes to the waist gun mounts."

Brown made a low initial approach, firing red flares to indicate casualties onboard, then powered into a circuit for the landing attempt on the "crash strip" to free up the main runway. His flight engineer, Sergeant Arthur Brewer, sat in the left seat to call out airspeeds.

"I dragged the airplane in on the landing approach," Brown said. "We made what I thought was a pretty good power-on, nose-high landing on the right wheel. When the plane touched and slowed, the left wheel came down and we veered to the left on the strip ... Upon impact the nose wheel collapsed and we skidded to a stop with the nose telescoping up towards the flight deck. I can remember watching the nose section coming up and hoping that the plane would stop before our legs were crushed by the instrument panel. After an eternity, we stopped."

The group commander, Colonel Robert Eaton, expressed concern over the nonstandard parachute braking procedure, but Brown noted, "We completed the landing with no further injuries to the crew."[35]

THE LUFTWAFFE IN CRISIS

While American airmen enjoyed more amenities on the Foggia fields, their Luftwaffe counterparts faced a grim present and an uncertain future.

When German fighters rose to defend petroleum targets, the Jagdwaffe's mission was twofold: to protect the Reich's vital lifeblood and to permit air operations to continue. Both proved a losing battle.

Faced with reduced oil in 1944, the Luftwaffe had no choice but to cut training—the bedrock of every air force. Hundreds of bomber pilots converted to fighters, but they could not make up the deficit among growing monthly losses. Something had to give, and that meant training hours.

The 1944 Luftwaffe curriculum was cut to 111 hours over eight months—half the figure of two years before. Many new *Jagdflieger* reported to their units with merely twenty hours in Messerschmitts or Focke-Wulfs. In contrast, their newly arrived opponents averaged about five hundred hours, often with more than two hundred in fighters with far better gunnery training.[36]

The Yanks also were better trained in instrument flying—a crucial skill in cloudy European skies. Thus, by summer 1944 the typical German fighter pilot was triple damned: outnumbered by better-trained opponents flying generally superior aircraft.[37]

KILLING BOMBERS

With fewer well-trained fighter pilots, the German Air Force needed a simple yet effective way to shoot down four-engine bombers. The answer had been found in Northern Europe in late 1942 when Focke-Wulf 190 pilots began attacking *Viermots* head-on rather than from behind. The originator of the procedure, Lieutenant Colonel Egon Mayer, was credited with twenty-six bombers before his death in 1944.[38]

Frontal attacks on bomber formations had the advantage of concentrating the firepower of multiple fighters on the few targets at the head of the stream. Sweeping in three, four, or more abreast, the *Jagdflieger* accepted the limited firing time in a combined 400 mph closing speed or more. If they pressed close enough, their concentrated machinegun and cannon ammunition could cripple or kill a four-engine plane in seconds.

However, the Americans took corrective measures. In B-17G models, a remotely operated "chin" turret was mounted with two .50 calibers able to sweep the forward quarter of airspace. Aimed by the bombardier, the new turret augmented the top and belly turrets that also could shoot straight ahead.

One of the senior Luftwaffe leaders was Colonel Johannes Steinhoff, who commanded Jagdgeschwader 77 in the Mediterranean. A thirty-one-year-old sophisticate considered one of the handsomest men in the Luftwaffe, he spoke impeccable English and enjoyed hosting downed opponents. His combat philosophy was based upon centration—maintaining one's own force while dispersing the enemy. Collisions occurred, but determined fighters pressing their attacks through the formation often caused individual bombers to break away, trying to avoid collisions. A lone bomber was easy meat.

In describing the challenge of destroying four-engine bombers, Steinhoff said, "The best way to attack a bomber is from directly overhead because the gunners cannot get a good shot at you, and it gives the fighter a bigger target and more firing time. But that required more training than we could afford, especially with fuel shortages. So we used the company front technique."[39]

A junior pilot in JG 3 was Lieutenant Oskar Boesch, who volunteered for the wing's *Sturmstaffel*, the squadron sworn to ram bombers if pilots ran out of ammunition. Describing the ramming mindset, he recalled, "You are twenty years old and you think you are rough and tough. You can drink all night and please the girls, then in the morning you climb into your 190 with a huge hangover. You turn the oxygen regulator to 100 percent, and when you take off to engage 500 *Viermots*, you are immediately sober!"[40]

British and American airmen flew a specified number of combat hours or missions before rotating out, perhaps to return, perhaps not. The Germans had no such luxury. Perennially short of experienced men, the Luftwaffe left many pilots in combat indefinitely. The Darwinian nature of the air war produced enormous casualties, but it also yielded a few hundred *Experten*, unexcelled masters of aerial combat.

Yet even the heroes with Knight's Crosses at their throats sustained losses. Lieutenant Franz Stigler, who finished the war in jets, said that he was shot down so often that he should have received paratrooper pay. The top bomber slayer, Major Georg-Peter Eder, was downed seventeen times, sustaining wounds on all but three occasions. Yet he thrived against the *Viermots*, credited with thirty-six among his total seventy-eight.[41]

Sergeant Konrad Bauer was shot down seven times, losing two fingers on his right hand while downing fourteen bombers.

Not even vision problems grounded some determined aces. Lieutenant Ekkehard Tichy continued flying after being wounded in one eye and collided with his ninth bomber, possibly owing to impaired depth perception.

Lieutenant Hans-Heinrich Koenig was half-blinded as a night fighter but converted to day flying and ran his tally to twenty *Viermots*, when he was killed attacking a B-17 at close range.

Likewise, Lieutenant Rudolf Klemm lost an eye to "friendly" flak but continued flying to lead a squadron.

Major Gunther Specht, barely five feet tall, led a wing despite the loss of an eye and died fighting over Belgium in 1945.

In all, nine of the top twenty-five bomber killers died in action—a 40-percent casualty rate.[42]

In the second half of 1943, with an average 4-percent loss rate, it had been statistically impossible for many U.S. bomber crews to complete a twenty-five-mission tour. But in the first half of 1944, the attrition lines had crossed on the air war chart. In May, with Mustangs fully operational, Luftwaffe losses reached 25 percent pilots and 50 percent aircraft *per month*. The *Jagdflieger* had become an endangered species: the strategic air campaign could only go one way, and the tide ran increasingly against Germany.[43]

CHAPTER FOUR

EAST TO PLOESTI

APRIL–JUNE 1944

The Fifteenth Air Force had a priority target: oil. In fact, the Second World War was about oil. The war would not have been possible without it.

The importance of oil had been recognized decades earlier. Shortly after the Great War, the French diplomat Victor Henri Berenger wrote, "He who owns the oil will own the world, for he will rule the sea by means of the heavy oils, the air by means of the ultra-refined oils, and the land by means of petrol and the illuminating oils. And, in addition to these, he will rule his fellow men in an economic sense, by reason of the fantastic wealth he will derive from oil."[1]

Oil was first refined in Scotland nearly ninety years before World War II erupted in Europe, but the first commercially successful refinery opened at Campina, Romania, in 1857, ironically (in view of later events) with heavy American financing. Campina was a few miles north of a city called Ploesti.

The world's dependence upon petroleum grew enormously over the next six decades, and oil and gasoline fueled the twentieth-century engines of war. Navies began converting from coal- to oil-fired ships before World War I, and fuel oil was essential to submarines. The importance of fossil fuels grew with the number of military vehicles and aircraft. By 1914, no major nation could conduct conventional warfare without a petroleum industry. The only major mode of transportation not reliant on oil was the railroads, which in Europe remained largely steam powered until mid-century.

Anticipating a shortage of oil, Germany developed synthetic petroleum before the war and in 1940 established ties with Romania. Hitler's eastward drive in 1942 was aimed at the oil fields of the Caucasus rather than Moscow.

In 1941 the Roosevelt administration embargoed oil and gasoline shipments to Japan in response to Tokyo's depredations in China. Because America provided 80 percent of Japan's fuel, the geopolitical clock was running: the Imperial Navy had perhaps two years' worth of oil stockpiled. The attack on Pearl Harbor, accordingly, was intended to neutralize the U.S. Pacific Fleet while the emperor's forces seized the petroleum wealth of the East Indies. In Asia as in Europe, oil determined the fate of nations.

FROM CRUDE TO GASOLINE

Refining oil was, and is, a complex process. The crude product undergoes atmospheric distillation to separate water and chemicals, and under intense heat it produces a variety of fuels.

Petroleum distillation produces three main products, depending on how they are separated into fractions, or distillates. Light distillates are most valued, as they include gasoline, especially the high-octane variety used in aviation. Middle distillates include diesel and kerosene, while heavier distillates provide fuel oil and lubricating oils. Heavy products, requiring less refining, are cheaper to produce than the lighter fractions.

The refineries of Europe produced different types of petroleum, but they all shared a basic design. Crude oil was super-heated, to as much as six hundred degrees centigrade (1,100° Fahrenheit) and pumped into a distillation tower, where the heavier fractions sank to the bottom and gases rose to the top. A cracking unit broke large hydrocarbons into smaller ones, yielding gas oil and lubricating oil. A refinery required one or more boiler houses, generators, and pumping stations, plus many pipes and holding tanks.

Through much of the war, bombers targeted specific portions of a refinery, but inevitably the effort was wasted. With decent visibility, a crew could land some of its bombs inside the refinery's bounds, but striking a boiler house, for instance, was difficult. Eventually airmen learned to "hold in the middle" and trust in the unavoidable dispersion of bombing.

The heart of Axis oil production was Ploesti, a city of eighty thousand located thirty-five miles north of Bucharest. Around 1900, Romania had become the first exporter of gasoline, and by 1941 ten major refineries surrounded Ploesti. Those refineries, in order of importance, were Astra Romana, Concordia Vega, Romana Americana, Phoenix, Colombia Aquila and Creditul Minier (at Brazi), Standard Petrol, Unirea Sperantza, Xenia, and Dacia Romana.

Prewar British assessments had identified the Ploesti complex as a vital target, but it lay far beyond the range of bombers based in Britain, and Greece fell to the Nazis before any missions could be mounted. The RAF's first bombing campaign against oil sites, in 1940–41, accomplished nothing. The effort lacked aircraft, bombs, and especially persistence.

The Soviets had flown some small-scale missions against Ploesti after Germany invaded Russia in June 1941, and ten American bombers had struck the Astra Romana plant in June 1942. None of those raids accomplished much. It was clear that a far stronger effort was required.

TIDAL WAVE

Thus began the notorious mission of August 1, 1943. Operation Tidal Wave was a spectacular low-level attack against the greater Ploesti complex, flown by nearly 170 Liberators. Launching from Benghazi, Libya, the bombers targeted seven of ten refineries. Two were knocked out. Creditul Minier never returned to service and Colombia Aquila was inoperable until July 1944, shortly before Romania capitulated. Steaua Romano, badly damaged, never regained full production.

Tidal Wave reduced Ploesti's potential production by more than 40 percent, but the Romanians and Germans were persistent and competent. The other refineries took up the slack, and by the following April, Ploesti's production was back at pre-attack levels.[2]

Some fifty-five Tidal Wave Liberators were shot down, crashed, or were interned upon landing in Turkey. Of 1,765 crewmembers, 310 were killed and 186 captured or interned—an appalling 28-percent loss rate.[3]

It was clear that Ploesti's refineries were not going to be destroyed in one or even ten missions. Like other industrial targets, the oil beast had to be hacked to pieces or crushed to death; the Allies couldn't shoot it through the heart. But before bombs could fall on Ploesti again, another battle had to be fought and won.

APRIL ONSLAUGHT

There was a political battle to be fought in the spring of 1944 before Ira Eaker and Nate Twining could loose their bombers. Supreme Headquarters, Allied Expeditionary Force, in London was concerned with how to support the impending Normandy landings.

Should they reduce Axis oil production or interdict German transport in northern France? The players in the drama, below Eisenhower, were two Britons and an American: Eisenhower's deputy commander, Air Marshal Sir Arthur Tedder; Air Marshal Sir Charles Portal, chief of the Royal Air Force; and Lieutenant General Carl A. Spaatz, overseeing all American strategic air operations in Europe.

Spaatz favored the "oil plan," attacking refineries in Germany and the Balkans. In early March, Air Marshal Sir Douglas Evill, Portal's main staffer for the combined bombing offensive, urged "immediate clearance be given for the early attack of Ploesti by the Fifteenth Air Force."[4]

Tedder, at Eisenhower's right hand, understood the vulnerability of Axis oil to prolonged air attack. But he reckoned, correctly, that enemy petroleum production could not be crippled sufficiently before D-Day, and he clashed with "Tooey" Spaatz. Once Eisenhower approved the "transport plan," Spaatz complied—with a subtle wink southward in Eaker's direction. Between them, the two air commanders agreed, "We mean to finish off this job in the Ploesti area with the first favorable weather."[5]

The oil component of the transport plan focused on railroads transporting fuel from Axis refineries. Spaatz, Eaker, and, by implication, Twining seized the opportunity to get their way. They sent bombers to pound the marshalling yards at Ploesti, Bucharest, and elsewhere, knowing that America's vaunted precision bombing was seldom precise and that "spillage" would inflict damage on nearby refineries.

Aircrews quickly discerned their superiors' intent. Navigators and bombardiers studying their target folders in April noted several aim points perilously close to refineries. "It was obvious," recalled one flier based at Manduria, "that no one would be upset if the whole damned place went up!"[6]

The officers' guile amounted to insubordination, which was especially rare at the two- and three-star level, the preserve of company men jealous of their careers. But Spaatz and Eaker were willing to press the limits of their orders.

Their scheme would not be easy. By April, Ploesti was defended by 150 Axis fighters and 220 or more antiaircraft guns, including 140 of the heavy-caliber variety (88, 105, and 128 mm). An AAF evaluation board conceded, "Damaging oil refineries successfully by aerial bombardment is one of the most difficult missions assigned a strategic air force. Where a target such as Ploesti is so heavily defended that it requires a large proportion of blind or obscured bombing from high altitude, this difficulty is accentuated."

Another problem was the weather. The route from Foggia to Ploesti passed through western Yugoslavia, the rainiest spot in Europe. Clouds often built up twenty thousand feet, and from April to August (the window available to Twining) there were only twelve to fifteen days a month that were not completely overcast. Visual bombing was going to be a problem.

The attackers recognized the difficulties. Some refineries were porous targets with considerable open space, and their vulnerable points could be widely separated. In one study of nearly twelve thousand bombs dropped on synthetic oil plants, only 155 (12.9 percent) struck within the refinery perimeters, and only forty (3.6 percent) hit something vital.[7]

TARGET PLOESTI

On April 5, Twining sent three bomb wings with nine B-24 groups and four B-17 groups to Ploesti, inaugurating a four-month campaign. During the nearly six-hundred-mile outbound leg, weather diverted four Liberator groups, but the other nine pressed ahead.

The bombers met serious opposition. Romanian fighters attacked head-on while twin-engine Luftwaffe interceptors lobbed rockets from both sides. Anti-aircraft fire over the target was predictably heavy though largely ineffective, as was the smoke screen the defenders spread.

The 230 Allied bombers unloaded 588 tons of ordnance, ostensibly on the rail yard, but photo interpreters later plotted sixteen hits in the Standard refinery and a few random hits at Concordia Vega, northeast of town.

The 450th Group put up an unusually large formation: forty Liberators took off "to bomb Ploesti Marshalling Yard and adjacent industrial area."[8] The Cottontails (named for their white rudders) lost six aircraft, the heaviest losses of the raid. The Liberators were largely unescorted, though P-38s joined on the way home. Luftwaffe squadrons jumped the group twenty-five minutes out, executing a surprise attack from twelve o'clock high, shooting three Liberators out of formation. The mission report concluded, "The attack was coordinated and the fighters came through in twos, threes, and fours. They would rally to the rear of our formation, make a side pass, gain altitude and use the same tactics again."

Closer to the drop point, fifty or more single- and twin-engine interceptors rolled in, some pressing fifty feet from the bombers. The Americans respected the enemy's skill and motivation, noting, "No break-off in intensity was noted over target, and enemy fighters flew through flak to harass our formation.... The fighter pilots were either very experienced or were driven by desperation."[9]

Despite the smoke screen, many bombardiers dropped visually. Observers reported good coverage with hits on distillation units and storage tanks and damage to rail facilities. But the group paid a price: only seven parachutes were seen dropping from the six downed bombers, and nineteen planes took flak damage.

Amid the bedlam of multiple fighter attacks, aircrews found time to make some surprisingly detailed observations. "One Me-109 had British markings on the underneath side of each wing while one FW-190 painted yellow and green fuselage and wings with yellow nose had American insignia on the top of left wing."[10] Some fliers probably confused Romania's yellow markings on IAR 180s for FW 190s.

The Americans lost thirteen bombers, 5.6 percent of the attackers—not nearly as bad as Tidal Wave's 30-percent loss. But the April 5 raid inflicted less damage and demonstrated that Ploesti remained a tough target.

PATHFINDERS

On April 15, Twining split his force—ordinarily a tactical sin—but he had a reason. The bombers conducted simultaneous attacks on Bucharest and Ploesti, the Fortresses of the Fifth Wing dropping visually because of the sparse smoke screen. With a P-38 escort, the B-17s got off lightly, losing only three planes when the defenders' 169 fighters had to cover two targets. Protecting the B-24 task force, First and Fourteenth Group Lightnings claimed eight kills near Bucharest.

On this mission, the 450th Group Cottontails introduced pathfinders to the Fifteenth Air Force. Pathfinders were radar-equipped lead bombers that put a group formation on target when visibility was reduced. The Eighth had used pathfinders in the summer of 1943.

British "boffins" had produced the H2S radar that presented a crude terrain map on a scope, actually a cathode ray tube much like a television screen. Reportedly the alpha-numeric designation was based on a pun by Churchill's science advisor, Professor Frederick Lindemann, product of a German father and American mother, who insisted "it was stinking that it had not been invented sooner." H2S is said to refer to hydrogen sulfide (H_2S), which smelled like rotten eggs.[11]

As they often did in wartime, the Americans took a British invention and ran with it. MIT's radiation laboratory began hand-building early sets while Philco was contracted to produce thousands more, operating on a shorter wavelength that yielded superior resolution of surface features. Designated H2X, the American product went operational in late 1943 but did not reach the Fifteenth until the following spring.

The basic technology of airborne radar was four years old and shrouded in secrecy. Twining's electronics warriors dubbed the set "Mickey," after Mickey Mouse, but it was neither small nor cute like the Disney rodent. An H2X weighed three hundred pounds and contained eighty vacuum tubes. It was mounted in a fuselage receptacle that replaced a B-24's belly turret and was operated by one highly trained technician who displaced the turret gunner and the usual bombardier. The image projected to the radar bombardier afforded exceptional accuracy through weather or darkness.

A Cottontail flier who participated in the pathfinder debut on April 15 recalled,

> On this mission to Bucharest the 720th Squadron led the 450th Group, which in turn led the 47th Wing.... Cloud over Yugoslavia was fairly dense and worsened as the formation neared the IP.
>
> By the time they reached the target, the cloud cover had increased to between 8/10 and 10/10. At 1210 the 450th dropped its deadly cargo through the solid cloud cover. Two minutes later the 449th Bomb Group, also guided by pathfinders, dropped its bombs. Flak over the target was heavy [caliber], light [intensity], and inaccurate, and was not encountered until after the bomb run. Clouds prevented any assessment, but as [Sergeant Maurice] Gilliam recorded in his diary, "The Pathfinder found the way to the target." Later reconnaissance showed that the mission was a success with heavy hits in the southwest corner of the city.[12]

Mickey had proved itself, but it was no panacea. If the radar bombardier made a routine error or misread the image, or if the set malfunctioned, the entire formation missed the target.

Weather prompted a recall on April 21, but few formation leaders heard the message, so most groups proceeded independently. Though the bombers were late, Major James G. Thorsen's Mustangs galloped into "a hell of a fight that erupted over the target and all around it." The Thirty-firsters described their foes as "full of hate and destruction" while fighting "ferociously and heroically." Though outnumbered, the P-51s trampled elements of three Romanian fighter groups, killing ten pilots and destroying fourteen aircraft while losing three Mustangs. It was a serious setback to the *vân tori* (aerial hunters) from a force of thirty 109s and seventy homegrown IARs.[13]

Across the border, the Royal Hungarian Air Force suddenly faced the necessity of home defense. Though well blooded in Russia, the Magyar aviators first clashed with the Fifteenth in April, adjusting to the vast difference between the Soviet and the American air forces. After a few initial combats, Budapest recognized the need for a dedicated air defense unit and in May established 101 "Puma" Fighter Group as the basis of a wing. The group commander was a veteran, forty-year-old major Aladar Heppes, commanding three squadrons of Bf 109Gs. "The Old Puma" began leading interceptions in late May, adding to his tally of Russian kills. Group headquarters was established at Veszprem-Jutas near Lake Balaton, southwest of Budapest. The white-crossed Messerschmitts would be drawn into more and more missions against the Fifteenth Air Force.

✪ ✪ ✪

On the third Ploesti mission, April 24, the Fifth and Forty-seventh Wings dispatched 290 bombers, which inflicted worthwhile damage on Astra Romana and Concordia Vega, despite the official emphasis on transport. Astra was especially hard hit, with 134 bombs (six duds) inflicting "very severe damage" to coolers, furnace, and pumps.[14]

Postwar evaluation showed that some portions of Concordia were permanently disabled at a cost of eight planes. Flak was "intense and accurate," with the defenders employing both tracking and barrage fire. The gunners had their solutions dialed in: twenty-eight of the Second Group's B-17s returned with flak damage.[15]

April's losses over all targets totaled 205 aircraft, including thirty-four fighters and recon planes, a 56-percent increase over February's record of 131 with Big Week attrition. The defenses were getting tougher throughout the Fifteenth's operating area.

MAXIMUM EFFORT

On May 5, Nathan Twining launched his first maximum effort against Ploesti: all five wings, totaling 485 bombers. They delivered 1,220 tons on the rail yards, sustaining the heaviest losses yet. The antiaircraft defenses had nearly doubled in a month, and eighteen American planes failed to return—a loss rate under 4 percent and therefore sustainable as the Fifteenth was nearing its peak strength.

The 456th Group Liberators escaped interception until five minutes before bombs away. Messerschmitts and Focke-Wulfs attacked from "around the clock" but inflicted no serious damage. One flier recalled, "As usual for Ploesti, flak was heavy, intense, and accurate, and three planes were lost."[16]

The enemy met the May 5 mission with a new trick. The Luftwaffe flew "Thistle" aircraft—captured U.S. planes—near the bomber stream to report the raiders' course, speed, and altitude. They usually vanished before anyone detected the deception.

On the other hand, springtime brought some relief for the frozen fliers. At 20,300 feet the temperature was now a tolerable eighteen degrees below zero centigrade, or zero Fahrenheit. "It was getting warmer. Aircrews could feel the difference and welcomed it."[17]

LAST RAIL TARGETS

The 304th Wing logged the last Ploesti mission against marshalling yards on May 6. Though still officially targeting transportation, the intelligence annex to the field order said the mission *"continues* systematic destruction of oil refinery capacity and rail transport facilities in Romania." Again the smoke screen was ineffective, while the wing lost six of 135 aircraft.[18]

The six missions officially flown under the transport plan were rated a partial success. Ploesti dispatched half a million tons less oil than when the bombing began, but it remained a valuable resource for the Axis. With reduced rail capability, more of its oil was pumped to stations on the Danube, where barges assumed a greater share of the load. The British countered with a mining campaign whose success demonstrated the effectiveness of aerial mines a year before B-29s launched Operation Strangle against Japanese coastal waters.[19]

Losses had remained well within limits: forty-eight of 1,320 effective bomber sorties on the Ploesti "rail yard" targets.

✪ ✪ ✪

While continuing the Ploesti campaign, the Fifteenth struck other targets as well. On May 10 Wiener Neustadt, always a tough target, cost the AAF twenty-seven bombers. The 463rd Group was hardest hit, losing eight Fortresses. The group commander, Colonel Frank Kurtz, was a two-time Olympic diver who had taken a bronze at Los Angeles in 1932. In 1941–42 he became known as pilot of the B-17D, *The Swoose*, that evacuated personnel from the Philippines.[20]

TARGET: REFINERIES

On May 17, Eisenhower in London made destruction of the Luftwaffe the AAF's priority. Knowing that the Germans could not defend every target, Spaatz and Eaker counted on the enemy's protecting its fuel sources. On May 18, with permission to strike oil production,

Twining sent 206 bombers from three wings, each targeting a specific refinery. More than half the force—111 Liberators of the 304th Wing—struck the Redeventa refinery with 270 tons of ordnance. But even with pathfinders and offset bombing techniques, the results were pitiful. The large Romana Americana facility east of town took only eight hits.[21]

Experience gained in the first six attacks permitted the defenders to optimize their passive—and most effective—weapon. May 18 was the first time that Ploesti produced a fully effective smoke screen.

MAKING SMOKE

Romania had established a commander of Passive Defenses for Bucharest and Ploesti, armed with chlorosulfite acid generators to produce large smoke screens. Steel barrels each containing four hundred pounds of acid were connected to large canisters of high-pressure compressed air that expelled the acid into the atmosphere. When there was a verified report of inbound bombers, the Romanians started the generators forty to sixty minutes before expected target time. The smoke could linger for three hours or more, depending on local winds.

At the end of the campaign, Ploesti deployed some 1,900 generators—twice as many as during Operation Tidal Wave a year before.

The three wings attacking on May 18 (the Fifth, Fifty-fifth, and 304th) lost fourteen aircraft. A Fortress group, the 463rd, returned to Celone short five planes after a prolonged shootout with German and Romanian fighters. Among the Axis losses was a Romanian squadron commander, Captain Gheorghe Cristea, who had just scored his fourth shootdown. American fighters claimed fourteen Germans and Romanians, though four of the victims were misidentified as Italians.

The Fifteenth recognized the growing effectiveness of Ploesti's passive defenses and began considering countermeasures. Twining's operations staff began evaluating blind bombing techniques, including radar-assisted bombing from pathfinder aircraft and "offset bombing," in which targets were determined by their known bearing and distance from some identifiable point.

✪ ✪ ✪

In the run-up to D-Day, Spaatz had two hands to play. He sent the Eighth against refineries on May 28 and 29 while the Fifteenth returned to Ploesti on the thirty-first. Again Twining launched all five bomb wings, each to a particular refinery, with good results. Despite a thick smoke screen, some formations drew a deadly bead on their targets. Thanks in part to the sharp-eyed 451st Group bombardiers, the Forty-ninth Wing smothered Concordia Vega, northeast of the city, with 156 bombs, trashing the boiler house and halting production for two weeks.

The Forty-seventh Wing crippled Romana Americana for a month while fires erupted in the little-struck Standard refinery.

The 122 German and Romanian interceptors downed a dozen B-24s out of 481 bombers, and they took out four fighters, the heaviest loss since May 8. The yellow-tailed Mustangs of the Fifty-second Group accounted for fourteen of twenty-two fighter claims that day. Lieutenant Fred Ohr chased a Messerschmitt into the ground, his second notch en route to becoming the only American ace of Korean descent. The group lost two pilots, including one who apparently collided with a Focke-Wulf.

✪ ✪ ✪

The best bombing in May came from the Forty-seventh Wing, composed of the Ninety-eighth, 449th, and 450th Groups. The new wing commander, Colonel Hugo P. Rush, formerly the leader of the Ninety-eighth Group in North Africa, had the experience and organizational ability to produce results within three months of taking over at Manduria. His headquarters was perhaps the most picturesque in the Fifteenth—whitewashed buildings set among olive groves, with recreational outlets for basketball, volleyball, and horseshoes. But Rush paid close attention to business. In May his groups put as much as 52 percent of their ordnance within the desired thousand-foot circle of the aim point.

Rush's success was part technical, part psychological. Under the 376th Group's former commander, Lieutenant Colonel Robert H. Warren, the wing staff streamlined procedures for takeoff and rendezvous, producing tighter formations early in a mission profile. Smoky "sky markers" were loosed at the initial point prior to the final bomb run, giving trailing groups a better idea of their position.

Rush also appealed to his airmen's egos, as the group with the best recent bombing record was given the leading place in the wing. The unit with the poorest record, naturally, flew "tail end Charlie" until it worked its way out of the cellar.[22]

✪ ✪ ✪

When the Fifteenth reached full strength that May (minus the allotted photo-recon group), it amounted to about half of Doolittle's command in Britain. The Mighty Eighth numbered thirty-nine bomb groups and had just received its fifteenth and final fighter group. The last two B-24 groups went operational the next month. On D-Day the heavies favored B-17s with twenty-two groups, and four Liberator outfits converted to Fortresses that summer.

When Carl Spaatz's two segments of the United States Strategic Air Forces in Europe were thus complete, mature, and ready to proceed with their assigned missions, an unlikely partner arrived.

FRANTIC IN JUNE

In a rare example of Soviet cooperation, Stalin consented in early 1944 to make Russian bases available to U.S. Army Air Force units to attack otherwise inaccessible industrial targets in eastern Europe.

This "shuttle bombing" would permit eastbound missions to strike targets en route to Russia, land there, and hit other targets on the return flight. Stalin approved the plan in early February, setting off four months of preparations.

The campaign was originally dubbed Operation Frantic Joe—and the preparations were indeed frantic. Perhaps to alleviate diplomatic concern about offending the Soviet ruler, the name was shortened to Operation Frantic. The primary aim was geopolitical, as President Roosevelt wanted to build a stronger relationship with Stalin and possibly pave the way to Siberian bases for missions against Japan. The European airmen's agenda was necessarily narrower, but Spaatz and Eaker hoped to bomb industrial plants in Latvia and Poland beyond range of the Eighth and Fifteenth.

The geopolitical maneuvering behind the shuttle missions tested the entente at every level. The Soviets wanted the operational benefits of heavy air attacks on targets beyond the Red Air Force's range or capability, and AAF planners quickly recognized that Frantic would benefit the hosts far more than the visitors. The Soviets allowed only 1,200 American support personnel under Major General Robert L. Walsh of the U.S. Eastern Command.

Considerable logistic effort was required to pre-position supplies and provide facilities for sustained operations. The Russian allies were unaccustomed to contact with the West, so the U.S. Air Transport Command had to fly in aircraft parts, ordnance, and accommodations from Iran. The Americans also had to deliver their own fuel, since the Red Air Force's gasoline was a lower octane.

The Soviets provided three Ukrainian airfields for the visitors: Poltava and Mirgorod for bombers and the shorter Pyriatin for fighters. Poltava lay nearly seven hundred miles northeast of Budapest and 1,185 miles from Foggia. All the Frantic bases lay along a northwest-southeast bearing within about a hundred miles of Poltava. The Americans had to rely on basic navigation, however. Their only homing beacon had a range of about fifteen miles—nearly useless in the vast Eurasian steppe.

Unknown to aircrews, four of the Fifth Bomb Wing's six B-17 groups were selected for Frantic One: the Second, Ninety-seventh, Ninety-ninth, and 483rd. The 301st and 463rd would continue operations from Foggia. The 325th Fighter Group's P-51s provided long-range escort.

The first shuttle operation was a closely held secret, even from the airmen who would fly the missions. The briefing was sprung on aircrews between three days and two hours before takeoff. At the Ninety-ninth Group's headquarters at Tortorella, Colonel Ford J. Lauer explained the grand strategy—to bomb distant synthetic oil plants in Poland—which failed to develop as planned, but Lauer shared another objective. He told his crews, "One hundred thirty million Americans will look upon you today, and you are their representatives in a land where you will be the first American combat men."[23]

The bombers took extra men to Russia: 325th Group crew chiefs and mechanics to tend the Checkertail Mustangs. Given the ten-day duration of the shuttle mission with three combat missions, maintenance would be necessary on many of the fighters.

Frantic One launched the morning of June 2 with 130 B-17s shepherded by sixty-nine Mustangs bound for the rail yard at Debrecen, 120 miles east of Budapest. Eaker flew the outbound leg from Foggia, occupying the copilot's seat in a Ninety-seventh Group B-17 named *Yankee Doodle II*. He had led the first Eighth Air Force heavy bombing mission in the group's original *Yankee Doodle* in August 1942, before the unit went to the Mediterranean.

With little opposition, the raiders could take their time over Debrecen. The Ninety-ninth preceded the Ninety-seventh, raising so much smoke and dust that the latter had to go around for a second pass before its bombardiers could drop. The results were excellent.

The Ninety-seventh lost a B-17, *Shirley Our Girlie*, with three men killed. One of the passengers was a Mustang crew chief.

Coming off target, the task force set course east-northeast, droning above the vast Ukrainian flatness to the last major navigation checkpoint, the Dnieper River. Once there, navigators began to relax; Mirgorod and Poltava lay sixty and eighty miles beyond.

That left Chet Sluder, a thirty-year-old Texan and former Doolittle staffer from North African days, leading the fighters. When the B-17s motored on to Poltava and Mirgorod, he herded his Mustangs for Piriatyn.

Easier briefed than done. The Checkertail group commander had his hands full as lead navigator. Sluder relied on three maps, each with a different scale and topographical scheme, and a low cloud deck forced him to rely on dead reckoning. When he could see the ground, it was of little help. "That part of Russia is flat and featureless so I had to fly strictly by compass," he recalled.[24]

Sluder shouldered a large responsibility: a major mission, sixty-eight other pilots, and 3.5 million dollars' worth of airplanes (the equivalent of 41.5 million dollars in 2012). Realizing that he had probably overflown his destination, he reversed course and felt much relieved when he recognized the Dnieper, then headed for Pyriatyn fifty miles northeast.

At Poltava, Eaker inspected the camps, hospital, and mess halls with a group of Allied reporters in tow. But he was needed elsewhere. Eaker's reputation and rank lent weight and prestige to AAF dealings with the Soviets, allowing him to address the senior officers on equal terms. He spent ten days in Russia, but much of his time in Moscow was largely wasted in diplomatic receptions and fruitless conferences.[25]

Fraternization between the Americans and the locals began almost immediately, including pickup volleyball games, often with mixed-nationality teams. On at least one occasion, airmen gawked at the balding middle-aged player with three stars on his collar: Ira Eaker.

The general described a warm welcome from citizens of Poltava and Mirgorod. "The local people were very friendly, particularly at first. They were kindly and cordial and the young girls especially, who worked on the base, were friends toward our crews." By the third day, however, more officials from Moscow made themselves felt, to the point that some Yanks heard of irate females taking clubs to the commissars. But socialist doctrine was reinforced: accepting a magazine from an American was cause for discipline.[26]

Local tours were arranged for those visiting airmen interested in seeing the sights—such as they were. Though the Fifteenth was accustomed to seeing destruction, Poltava impressed the Ninety-ninth Group: "The town had taken the full brunt of the war. There was hardly a building left intact. When the Germans overran this part of the country, the Russians retreated and left behind only 'scorched earth.' Every building, every bridge, power line and water main was totally destroyed. Only shells of buildings remained."[27]

Some of the Americans got over their initial reluctance to dance with Ukrainian women, but the cordiality of their hosts was limited. The Soviets, xenophobic to their marrow, were suspicious of so many Americans on the *Rodina*'s soil, and ample vodka ensured fights and arguments. Meanwhile, the Yanks brought all manner of desirable items from candy bars to nylons, contributing to a ready-made black market.

There were not enough American maintenance men at the Ukrainian bases, so the AAF had to use Soviet personnel. One bomber crew, which received five Russian technicians, was fortunate to have a B-17 crew chief who spoke fluent Polish and some Russian. Captain Harry Miller of the Second Group wrote, "Those Russkies worked like hell! They laughed and joked constantly. They were extremely careful about everything. I think all the careless ones had already been shot.... They did not strip any threads or lose a single nut or bolt. They changed the engine in almost as little time as my prize engine change crew in Italy. They left us with a good feeling about the Russian GIs."[28]

It wasn't all boredom. Four days after arriving, the task force attacked the airfield at Galati, Romania, a seven-hundred-mile mission just across the Ukrainian border. Bombing results were judged good to excellent, though a one-time attack could inflict little permanent damage. The Checkertails claimed six kills, losing two Mustangs with one pilot captured. Group commander Chet Sluder said, "I clobbered an FW 190, and Captain Roy Hogg nearly got himself killed shoving six more off my back." The Clan crowned three new aces that day: Hogg, CO of the 318th Squadron, along with Lieutenants Cullen Hoffman and Bob Barkey.

The fighters did their job: a 463rd Group Fortress went down over Yugoslavia but the other bombers got off lightly.

Twenty-five-year-old Lieutenant Ion Dobran flew one of the yellow-crossed Bf 109s that scrambled from Tecuci, near the wooded hills of Moldavia fifty miles northwest of Galati. Vectored onto the intruders by radar controller Albatross, he engaged at nearly twenty thousand feet. Dobran latched on to a Mustang and opened fire, scoring hits. But almost immediately the American's three partners were after him. He stuffed the nose down, trying to escape in a screaming dive—generally useless against the sleek Mustang. Despite his maneuvers, one persistent Checkertail pilot stuck with him, forcing the Romanian into an emergency landing in a barley field. He opened the "coffin lid" canopy and scrambled out, expecting to be strafed. He heard only the receding sound of a high-performance engine. Then silence. Dobran recalled, "Then from inside, like a huge river, an unspeakable joy—the joy of a man who can see again the sky, the sun, and the grass. The wind is caressing me. Oh God, how beautiful is life when you start from broken pieces. We are modern gladiators—one of the two fighters should die. Who pointed the thumb up for forgiveness?"[29]

Upon return to Poltava the men in the Mediterranean Theater learned of events sixteen hundred miles northwest. Recalled one officer, "Everyone was excited by the news of the Allied invasion on the beaches at Normandy. It was reported that this operation was to hold

German fighters from the invasion landings." Closer to home, the Fifth Army entered Rome two days before D-Day, signaling a further decline in Axis fortunes.[30]

RETURN TO PLOESTI

While Frantic bombers hit Galati, half a dozen groups based in Italy went after transportation targets across Romania. The heavy losses suffered in May prompted the Fifteenth's operations staff to come up with a new strategy for June 6. The goal was to spread enemy fighters across as broad a front as possible, preventing them from concentrating on one or two formations. Both phases of the plan were intended to reduce the opposition faced by three wings attacking both Ploesti and petroleum storage and transport facilities at Giurgiu, a Danube shipment port.

Liberators from the Forty-seventh, Forty-ninth, and Fifty-fifth Wings flew against Romana Americana, Xenia, and Dacia. Thirteen bombers of the 310 dispatched were lost, five from the 464th Group alone. They encountered 120 enemy fighters and another effective smoke screen, and their seven hundred tons of bombs produced disappointing results. The loss rate of 4.6 percent would have been acceptable if the results had been better, but in this case the results were not worth the cost.

RETURN FROM THE UKRAINE

During the June 11 return leg from Soviet territory, more than a hundred B-17s bombed Focsani, Romania, receiving an enthusiastic response from flak gunners on both sides of the front lines. German fighters attempted to intercept, but the 325th intervened, claiming three Bf 109s downed. A Ninety-seventh Group Fortress was lost on the return to Italy, as the Fifteenth completed its only shuttle-bombing mission to the Soviet Union.

The Americans continued pressing for approval to attack strategic targets, but the Russians refused, limiting targets to airfields and rail yards. Eventually the Soviets relented for an Eighth Air Force mission, but weather canceled the operation.

FIGHTERS OVER PLOESTI

The heavies weren't wrecking Ploesti.

Although the oil campaign had been in full swing since April, its seven high-altitude bombing missions had left much of the refinery complex intact or reparable. With ample warning of approaching B-17s and B-24s, the defenders invariably obscured the targets with heavy smokescreens.

Frustrated with the meager results of the original plan, Twining decided to try something unorthodox. He would send P-38s to dive-bomb Ploesti. The Lightnings could fly low, avoiding enemy radar, then pop up to altitude and deliver their bombs with precision.

It seemed worth a try.

The first target was the Romana Americana refinery, which had escaped serious damage and reportedly was producing nearly 15 percent of all Axis oil. Two P-38 groups were assigned the mission: the Eighty-second to do the bombing, with the First providing escort. Both units would provide forty-eight aircraft, launching at sunup on June 10.

The fighter-bombers carried extra-large drop tanks on one pylon and a thousand-pounder on the other. Flying low under radio silence, navigating by map and dead reckoning, the Lightnings crossed the Adriatic into Yugoslavia. At this point nearly twenty planes aborted—an unusually high number—including a dozen from the Eighty-second. The strike force was reduced to thirty-six bombers and thirty-nine escorts. Still, the lead squadron, the Twenty-seventh from the First Group, hit its final landmark within five minutes of ETA—excellent work nearly six hundred miles from home.

Then things turned to hash.

Flying low over rugged, unfamiliar terrain, some flights got separated. Approaching the target area, some First Group pilots sighted several German bombers and pounced on them. Six of the enemy went down in the melee, but the action stirred up the locals. About twenty Romanian IAR-80 fighters scrambled to intercept, and they tore into the dozen Lightnings. Given the defenders' advantages of altitude, position, and numbers, the fight could only go one way. The big IARs, potently armed, mauled the P-38s, destroying nine. Apparently the only American to retaliate was Lieutenant Carl Hoenshell, who probably downed three but never returned.

Meanwhile, the Ninety-fourth Squadron also encountered airborne Germans, shooting down seven bombers or trainers. All hope of surprise was now lost.

The Romanians had time to spool up their smoke generators, and the antiaircraft gunners were loaded and ready. When the Eighty-second Group rolled in on Romana Americana east of Ploesti, the sky lit up with bursting shells and tracers. Seven Lightnings went down in the flak. The retreating P-38s had made direct hits on a cracking plant, storage tanks, and other facilities.

The Lightnings had to shoot their way out. West of the target, the Twenty-seventh Squadron clashed with thirty or more Bf 109s, breaking even at four kills and four losses. Other P-38s strafed anything that looked worthwhile, exiting southwesterly.

Flying in the Seventy-first Squadron was Second Lieutenant Herbert Hatch. He led his wingman Joe Morrison into a pack of radial-engined fighters that he identified as Focke-Wulfs but actually were IAR-80s. It was a churning, broiling, low-level dogfight, fought on the deck in a depression between the hills: "I cannot overemphasize what a melee that was," Hatch reported. "There were at least twelve P-38s in that little area, all of them at very low altitude. Somewhere between twenty-five and thirty 109s were also there. None of us was at more than two hundred or three hundred feet, and some were quite a bit lower."[31]

In that churning aerial fur ball, "Stub" Hatch gunned eight planes, claiming five kills. He was lucky to survive—one of his victims clipped his airplane, knocking three inches off his left rudder.

When noses were counted, the First Group had lost fourteen planes and the Eighty-second eight more: twenty-two of the seventy-five that reached the target area. Most of the damage to the refinery was repaired in eight days. A 30-percent loss rate to deliver 18.5 tons of bombs was unsupportable. Fighters never attacked Ploesti again.

Nevertheless, newspapers back home hailed the fighter-bombing operation as a success. "Last Ploesti Refinery Smashed," ran a typical headline.[32]

The antiaircraft gunners had a different view. An AAF summary noted, "Low level attacks were considered a good opportunity for flak areas to bolster their scores."[33]

THE FIRST PRIORITY

Two days after D-Day in Normandy, Ira Eaker got the order he craved. Spaatz wired that the Fifteenth would "have as its first priority the complete destruction of the Rumanian oil refineries."[34]

By then, Twining's bombers had partly damaged nearly half of the sixty-plus refineries within range of Foggia. But the Germans, experts at repair and reorganization, spared no effort or cost to restore the petroleum plants. Continuing photo reconnaissance allowed Allied intelligence officers to estimate the amount of time required to return a refinery to previous production, usually with some precision.

The British had discovered that five-hundred-pound bombs were nearly as effective against refineries as thousand-pounders, and twice as many could be dropped per sortie. The concept had been reinforced by examining Luftwaffe results against English targets in 1940–1941. Because few Romanian facilities had protective walls around storage tanks, the thin-skinned receptacles were even more vulnerable to blast damage.[35]

With the shuttle concept proved, the Eighth Air Force launched its first Frantic mission on June 21. The Germans tracked the Fortresses to Poltava, however, and that night Luftwaffe bombers dropped in. Forty-seven of the seventy-three B-17s were destroyed on the ground, and most of the others were badly damaged. The Russian defenses proved wholly inadequate, leaving the surviving Mighty Eighth bombers to return home by way of Italy on July 5.

The official AAF study of Operation Frantic concluded, "Altogether the experiment was of little importance tactically and early estimates that it had fostered better relations between the two allies were overly optimistic. Americans did learn something of the Russians' genius for obstruction...."[36]

ON THE DECK

Fifteenth fighters were unusually active on June 15, with five groups attacking airfields in southern France. The First and Fourteenth Groups lost five Lightnings, while the 325th got hammered. One squadron arrived over an airdrome near Avignon that had already been attacked but destroyed or damaged only four planes on the ground. First Lieutenant Hiawatha Mohawk, flying a Mustang named *Blond Squaw*, got the only aerial victory.

Seven pilots from the 319th Squadron were killed or captured; three were flying so low to avoid flak that they struck the ground, water, or power lines. Another lost a dogfight with a Messerschmitt. Strafing was always more dangerous than air combat, and pilots groused that the mission results in no way compensated for the cost.

BRATISLAVA

The oil campaign was not limited to Ploesti, and on June 16 the Fifteenth attacked petroleum facilities in Austria and Czechoslovakia. As usual, oil targets drew a strong response, and more than two hundred enemy fighters opposed the six task forces. U.S. fighters claimed to have downed forty planes in the combat, the highest toll since the January 30 mission to northern Italy.

The Forty-seventh Wing targeted the Apollo oil refinery at Bratislava, Czechoslovakia, one of the ten largest outside Romania. Led by the 376th's Lieutenant Colonel R. C. McIlheran, the task force encountered forty single- and twin-engine fighters that rolled in from twelve o'clock high, striking "like Thor's hammer."[37]

Subsequent passes were increasingly aggressive, "hitting from all angles at distances from 50 to 200 yards, and in some cases flying right through our formation." One Messerschmitt struck a Liberator, destroying both planes. Meanwhile, Ju 88s lobbed rockets into the bombers from the flanks a thousand yards out, then continued with gunnery passes to three hundred yards. All the while the Liberators motored through "a terrific barrage of heavy caliber anti-aircraft fire before, during, and after the bombing run."[38]

The bombardiers put their ordnance on target, inflicting "grave damage to vital installations," including storage tanks, the distillation and cracking plant, and a rail yard. On the egress, aircrews reported fires visible seventy miles away. The mission cost the 376th two B-24s among the thirteen bombers lost but resulted in the Liberandos' second Distinguished Unit Citation with the Fifteenth, their third of the war.[39]

The interceptors were persistent, and in a 376th Liberator, bombardier Lieutenant George Crawford could stand it no longer. He belonged to a flying family from Breckenridge, Texas. His older brother Raymond flew B-24s in China, and Fred was a Fifteenth fighter pilot. After bombs away, George made his way aft to the left waist position, as the crew was one gunner short. In the narrow fuselage he was back to back with Technical Sergeant C. O. Schambacker.

Crawford saw two Liberators explode and spiral to destruction under fire from Me 110s. He had passed gunnery school in New Mexico but had little opportunity to use his skills until now. Throughout the mission he fired more than two thousand rounds without much effect—mostly snap shots at fleeting targets. But at length a single 110 eased into range on the same heading, six hundred yards out, and Crawford drew a bead. "Using my tracers to judge where the bullets were hitting, I fired burst after burst and saw the tracers strike home.... I could see tracers hitting the cockpit and then walking their way down the fuselage...." Encouraged by enthusiastic thumps on the back from Sergeant Schambacker, Crawford kept firing until the fighter dropped into the undercast.[40]

One of the escorting Mustangs that day was flown by George's brother Fred, of the Fifty-second Fighter Group. His squadron overflew the 376th formation, and Fred considered prospects for a personal escort on the way home.

Following a "bounce" on some 109s, Fred noticed some P-38s bearing First Fighter Group markings. One of them pointed its nose at the Mustang—and opened fire. A 20mm shell tore a hole in the right wing "as big as Bulldog Field's home plate." With smoke in the cockpit, Fred pulled the canopy release, unfastened his belt, and stood up. Diving over the right side, he bounced off the fuselage as his radio and oxygen leads tore loose. His right ankle struck the horizontal tail, then he found himself in midair ten thousand feet over Hungary. Briefly he wondered if the Lightning pilot would come back to finish him off. Then he pulled the ripcord. His canopy blossomed and he alit with a painful thump.

Almost immediately Fred was surrounded by a mob of angry civilians, unaccountably screaming "Jewd, Jewd!" He sank beneath a barrage of blows from fists and tools, but as a good Presbyterian he displayed a small cross. An elderly man saw the symbol and stopped the pelting. Eventually delivered to police, he was visited by a priest and entered the world of a prisoner of war. He was one of nine fighters who failed to return. In Texas his parents received the second telegram from the War Department—Raymond was already missing in China.

LIVING THERE

In June 1944 the Fifteenth glimpsed the shape of the future. High in the cerulean vault, P-38 pilots saw the shark-nosed jet-propelled Messerschmitt 262 entering operational evaluation at Augsburg in Bavaria. "The first sight of that plane always provoked disbelief—nothing could go that fast at that height, but there it was. It could and it did!"[41]

Meanwhile, more mundane developments continued around Foggia. The First Fighter Group concluded that Italy in the summer was "(A) very hot and (B) very dusty," with four-man tents leaving something to be desired. The area was rife with malaria, requiring a daily Atabrine (quinacrine) tablet that gave the skin a yellow cast.

After seven months in operation, the Fifteenth got to know more Italians as individuals, concluding, "They were friendly, desperately poor, and invariably seemed to have relatives living in Boston or San Francisco or Chicago." The Ninety-fourth Fighter Squadron at Salsola, ten miles north of Foggia, employed a paroled POW known as Gino. He made himself useful in the mess hall, where any complaints about the fare brought a referral to "Spic son of a bitch sergeant!"[42]

At the same base, the Twenty-seventh Squadron adopted one of many urchins and orphans, an outgoing youngster of twelve or so. Young Antonio Castriota was fitted with a cut-down non-com's uniform, complete with suitable patches, evolving into "Sergeant Tony."

BACK TO PLOESTI

The Fifteenth resumed its strikes on Ploesti on June 23, sending two wings against Dacia. The Forty-seventh's Liberators were turned back by weather, sparing Romana Americana another pasting. But nearly 140 Fortresses attacked Dacia, losing six bombers. The smoke screen was typically effective, limiting the damage.

Continuing the policy of spreading out the defenders, Twining sent the Fifty-fifth Wing against Giurgia, a target of the recent shuttle mission, and the 304th returned to working on the railroad, striking a Bucharest marshalling yard.

The Axis launched almost two hundred fighters, affording plenty of shooting for three Mustang groups, which claimed twenty-five victories. It was a costly mission for the Romanian Air Force, as two of its four fighter group commanders were killed. Captain Virgil Trandafirescu of the Seventh Group had been flying against the Russians since June 1941. He took eleven Messerschmitts against the Americans, claimed a P-51 (four were downed), then succumbed to the odds. Captain Commander Ioan Sandu of the First Group also functioned as the fighter wing commander. He led his nine IAR-180s into the bombers, possibly downed one of six B-17s destroyed, then was swarmed by the escorts. The forty-four-year-old Sandu was the senior Romanian pilot killed during World War II, allegedly strafed in his chute.

The attrition was unsustainable: two weeks later Bucharest's air ministry reported that operational fighters had spiraled down from 115 in early April, when U.S. operations began, to only fifty in early July, with thirty-three pilots killed. The homegrown IAR 80, clearly inferior to the P-51, was withdrawn from front-line service, replaced by Messerschmitts in the time remaining.

The Fifty-second Group accounted for nearly half the U.S. fighter claims but reported three Italian aircraft among the dozen destroyed. There were no Macchis or Fiats, of course—just IAR 80s and Bf 109s. The next day the Checkertails tangled with Romanians and correctly identified three IARs among six confirmed kills.

ABOVE AND BEYOND

The Fifth Wing's target on the twenty-third was oil storage at Giurgiu and two refineries near Ploesti. During the run to the Danube, a Ninety-seventh Group B-17 irreverently named *Opissonya* was rocked by flak and dropped out of formation, losing altitude. The pilot, First Lieutenant Edwin Anderson, was determined, however, to put his bombardier over the target.

Crouched over his Norden sight was Second Lieutenant David R. Kingsley, an Oregonian three days shy of his twenty-sixth birthday. He had reported to the Ninety-seventh Group at Amendola in April. Since then he had become a veteran, logging nineteen missions in barely two months.

Kingsley tried to ignore the German fighters that attacked before the group reached Giurgiu and concentrated on the image in his sight. The smoke obscuring the target and the flak were so thick, said one crewman, "You could almost walk on it."[43]

Opissonya took a beating over the target. With damaged controls, Anderson and copilot William Symons eased their battered Boeing away on three engines with one fuel tank ripped loose. Quick to finish a straggler, enemy fighters pounced on the lone Fortress. The tail gunner, Sergeant Michael Sullivan, was struck by 20mm shell fragments, which also destroyed his intercom; he could not call for help.

Barely able to crawl, Sullivan pulled himself forward to the waist position. The two gunners tried to administer first aid but his right shoulder was bleeding badly. They carried him to the radio compartment and called for Kingsley. After bombs away, the bombardier was the logical crewman to help. It was certain that the gunners would remain busy.

Working in the confined space, Kingsley pulled off Sullivan's damaged parachute harness and jacket, exposing the bleeding shoulder. Despite the awkward angle, the bombardier applied a tourniquet and stanched the hemorrhage, but Sullivan was approaching shock. Nearly five hundred miles from base, with one propeller feathered and eight-thousand-foot mountains ahead, it looked like a long flight to safety. Sullivan needed help—soon. For a time, two Mustangs had tagged along, guarding the vulnerable bomber, but all too soon they broke off, low on fuel.

At that point eight Messerschmitt 109s dived out of the sun. For perhaps fifteen minutes they made repeated firing passes, holing the wings and fuselage of the undefended Boeing and wounding the ball turret gunner. There was no option but to abandon ship. Edwin Anderson rang the bailout bell.

Kingsley helped the wounded men prepare to jump. When Sullivan's damaged parachute harness could not be found, the bombardier, in a stunning act of sacrifice, removed his own parachute and wrestled Sullivan into it. Kingsley took Sullivan in his arms and struggled to the bomb bay, where he told Sullivan to keep his hand on the ripcord. The gunner would pull the handle when he was clear of the ship. "Then he told me to bail out," Sullivan recalled. "Before I jumped, I looked up at him and the look he had on his face was firm and solemn. He must have known what was coming because there was no fear in his eyes at all."[44]

Crewmembers watched their bomber continue its erratic descent, then fall to Earth at the tiny village of Souhozem, Bulgaria, 150 miles south of Ploesti. Bulgarian troops told captured crewmen that Kingsley's body was found on *Opissonya*'s flight deck. Apparently he had been searching for a spare parachute or vainly trying to make a crash landing. In 2004 a memorial was erected to the seven Bulgarian civilians killed on the ground and the lone American who gave his life evidently trying to spare them.

Other airmen risked or lost their lives trying to save their friends, and many received the Medal of Honor. But David Kingsley knowingly abandoned any hope of survival when he gave away his parachute harness in a doomed aircraft. His decision was made with deliberation, with none of the impulsiveness of so many heroic acts. In the history of the aviation Medals of Honor, his action defines "above and beyond the call of duty."

The Forty-seventh Wing rebounded from its weather abort to revisit Romana Americana the next day, June 24. The Liberators landed more than forty hits that destroyed or damaged pipelines, canceling production for five days. But the success was costly. Some 160 planes from five Luftwaffe wings opposed the mission, including a fighter-bomber outfit with FW 190s and the frequently committed training unit JG 301. The Germans' claim of more than twenty *Abschüsse* was exaggerated, but the actual results were bad enough. Of 135 B-24s sent to Romana Americana, fourteen went down—a stunning 10.3-percent loss rate.

The next day the much-abused Astra Romana refinery finally resumed partial production. It had been shut down since early April, as follow-on strikes had scrapped the defenders' initial estimate of a two-month recovery.[45]

✪ ✪ ✪

The Second World War required industrial production on an immense scale. The inevitable combat and operational losses, like those of June 1944, had to be replaced. At month's end the Fifteenth had lost nearly 170 bombers and eighty fighters, both records. Fighter attrition that month was nearly double the May rate, evidence of increasing air combat and the greater danger of strafing well-defended targets, especially airdromes.

In Bari, Twining's headquarters tracked the command's losses throughout the campaign. Between early April and late June, the period of the Ploesti missions, Axis fighters shot down at least 240 bombers, and another 250 were lost to flak. Seventy-four other heavies were damaged beyond repair or written off in accidents.

In the same ninety-day period nearly 150 Fifteenth fighters were lost on combat missions. The ratio of fighters lost to enemy aircraft represented nearly three times the figure from January through March.[46]

The enemy's stiff resistance forced a rethinking of Fifteenth policy. The fighter groups were sent on additional sweeps—gunning for trouble aloft—and airfield strikes to smash the Jagdwaffe in its nests or as close to the branches as possible. As a result, Twining's bombers had been able to inflict growing damage on the Ploesti network, and the numbers showed results. The operating refineries' total daily processing went up and down, dropping below 1,500 tons in mid-June and staging an impressive recovery approaching nine thousand two weeks later. But where it mattered most—gasoline exports to Germany—the numbers plummeted from 135,000 tons in December 1943 to about twenty thousand in June. Export of lubricating oils and all petroleum products reflected a tightening of the flow.[47]

Ploesti was on the ropes, but the Romanian challenger had an iron jaw. There would be no single knockout punch—not Tidal Wave and certainly not the failed P-38 dive-bombing attack. Only a sustained strategic bombing campaign waged with relentless determination could succeed. And that was the goal as Italian spring turned to Balkan summer.

CHAPTER FIVE

MEDITERRANEAN SUMMER

JULY–SEPTEMBER 1944

July 1944 was like no month the Fifteenth Air Force had yet experienced. While the ground campaign along the Gothic Line 150 miles north of Rome remained static for most of the rest of the war, the air campaign kicked into "high blower"—a supercharged, relentless effort to wreck Hitler's oil and aircraft industries for good.

That summer the Luftwaffe recognized its peril. A planning assessment noted, "The greatest danger lies in the threat to the fuel supply. Here the destruction of a relatively limited number of targets would result in a complete paralysis of the Luftwaffe, all motorized units, the military and civilian means of transportation, and the Navy."[1]

Though Ploesti remained the priority, other targets attracted the unwelcome attention of the Fifteenth's bombardiers. One of the early missions resulted in an epic encounter still the subject of discussion seventy years later.

DUELING WITH THE DEVIL

On July 3 Twining launched six hundred bombers against petroleum and transport targets at Bucharest and oil storage sites at Belgrade. Escorted by more than 250 fighters, the "big friends" were nearly immune to interception.

First Lieutenant Robert J. Goebel, a twenty-one-year-old who had scored his first victory in May, led a four-plane flight of the Thirty-first Fighter Group, whose Mustangs were escorting B-24s. Responding to calls of "bogeys" over the radio, Goebel ordered his flight to drop its under-wing fuel tanks in preparation for a fight. Then he sighted "a gaggle of fifteen 109s" at twenty-six thousand feet. The lead pair of Messerschmitts already was close, just off his nose. "I think the leader saw my flight at about the same time," he wrote years later. "He had balls, I'll say that for him. The two 109s started down to attack the bombers below, or the four of us. It was a rash act, indeed."[2]

When the German leader entered a loop, he lost contact with his three partners, who accelerated down on the bombers. Goebel and his wingman followed the leader while his second section split to bracket the enemy. Whichever way the 109 pilot broke, he would be boxed in.

Goebel lined up the Messerschmitt and pressed the trigger. He was still out of range. The German was maneuvering hard, possibly using negative G, bunting the nose down. Goebel fired at least twice more without hits. "I remember being puzzled and frustrated at my inability to hit him with a solid burst." Goebel shoved his throttle forward, closing the range, but his opponent timed his breaks artfully, each time returning to the same heading—apparently for home.

Once within effective range—inside one thousand feet—Goebel finessed the controls and put his aiming dot on the 109's tail. "I fired again and was rewarded with strikes quick-flashing around the fuselage and wing roots. Then his prop wash threw me off him momentarily."

As Goebel lined up for another shot, the 109's canopy came off. The pilot followed, quickly opening his parachute. "I could plainly see him suspended beneath it," Goebel recalled. "A dark, toy-like figure, swaying gently as he floated down."[3]

Recognizing a rare opportunity, Goebel turned his armament switch to the "camera and sight" position, tracked the German in his gun sight, pressed the trigger to active his camera, and was rewarded with proof of his victory. Goebel then passed close by, raised a hand in a chivalrous gesture, and broke off to regroup his flight for the trip home.

It cannot be known for certain, but Bob Goebel had likely defeated the world's third-ranked fighter ace. Erich Hartmann, a twenty-two-year-old lieutenant in JG 52, was leading eight Messerschmitt 109s that day. With two and a half years of combat, he was credited with more than 260 aerial victories, nearly all against Soviet pilots. Known as "The Black Devil of the Ukraine" for the nose markings on his aircraft, he had fought Mustangs before, and while he respected them, he did not fear them.

A 1970 biography of Hartmann claims that he ran out of fuel and was forced to jump with Mustangs on his tail. His chute had barely opened when he heard a high-performance engine. He looked around and saw a Mustang descending toward him in an apparent gunnery pass. Hartmann's guts turned to ice—both sides occasionally fired on parachutes. He saw his fiancée's face. The Mustang flashed past, very close. Hartmann glimpsed a gloved hand raised in salute. He registered "an ugly face," then the American was gone.

Erich Hartmann survived, returned to combat, and ended the war with 352 credited kills—the highest score in the history of aerial combat. He endured a brutal decade of Soviet captivity after war before returning to Germany and to flying. He died in 1993, widely admired in the West.

Despite the Mustang escort, ten B-24s went down, including five from the 376th Group attacking Giurgiu. A radio operator, Sergeant Bill Giambrone, recalled,

> We were near the target when it happened. All of a sudden five or six fighters came at us from about 12:00 out of the sun. It all happened so fast, we really didn't have any time to react. I had just left the radio compartment for the waist. They shot us up real quick and number four was smoking badly. All of a sudden the plane was in a dive. I don't have any idea what happened up front. I grabbed my chute and crawled up the floor pulling myself to the hatch. [Sergeant J. L.] Morgan had just opened it so he could take pictures at the target and hadn't even had time to mount the camera in place. I got to the hatch and started to pull myself out when all of a sudden I was sucked out and it was real quiet. I finished hooking my parachute and pulled the ripcord. I didn't know if anyone else was out until I hit the ground.
>
> I was captured immediately. George Morrison was there and he had broken his ankle. They took me over to the crash site awhile later. The plane didn't burn when it hit. The others were all laid out in a row and I really couldn't look. I didn't have any shoes on so I did take someone's though I'm not sure who, as I couldn't recognize them. I figured he wouldn't mind, as I needed them. It was tough to figure these were my buddies only a little while before.[4]

BLECHHAMMER

In June 1944 AAF targeteers focused their sights on the enemy's synthetic fuel industry. Germany's own petroleum sources could supply less than 10 percent of the Wehrmacht's requirements, so the Reich had to turn to conquered nations like France and to allies in the oil-rich Balkans.

The best source of synthetic fuel was bituminous coal. While most synthesized fuel was inferior to that refined from crude oil, fuel derived from bituminous coal was suitable for aviation. For automotive gasoline, brown coal was adequate. The Luftwaffe required huge quantities of high-octane fuel, and from at least 1938, Germany began producing greater amounts of synthetically derived gasoline. The output was considerable, more than tripling in the next five years.[5]

British and American intelligence identified the main synthetic oil plants at Blechhammer and Odertal (both in Silesia, now part of Poland), Brux (Czechoslovakia), and Ruhland (near Dresden). These plants accounted for 70 percent of all the synthesized fuel and nearly all the aviation gas produced within the Fifteenth's range.

Blechhammer ("sheet metal hammer") was a two-part industrial complex in the eastern region of Silesia. Blechhammer North and Blechhammer South were similar sized facilities less than two miles apart. Each measured roughly one and three-quarter miles long by three-quarters wide, or 1.3 square miles—ample targets for heavy bombers. The complex was operated largely by slave labor under SS jurisdiction. Dozens of labor camps dotted the area, supporting the chemical and petroleum industries and repairing the near-constant bomb damage. Prisoners considered unable to work usually were sent nearly fifty miles away for extermination at Auschwitz.

On July 7 more than 550 bombers left their Foggia bases for Blechhammer, Odertal, and transport targets in Yugoslavia. There were twenty-five losses that day (seven of them at Blechhammer), but the most remarkable feat of airmanship took place not in hostile skies but back at the base. Returning to Castelluccio, First Lieutenant Frank McQuaid's Liberator, *Calamity Jane*—part of the 451st

Group's Forty-ninth Wing task force—experienced the fuel-feed problems that had plagued a previous mission. Number three engine, the right inboard, abruptly quit with zero fuel pressure. Then number two, on the left side, also quit.

A mile from the runway and nearly out of fuel, McQuaid and copilot Robert Nelson feathered the windmilling propellers, pulled out of formation, and began dealing with a rare crisis. McQuaid called over the intercom, "Crew to crash positions!" Then he keyed his mike and called in to the base, "Hiccup Tower, this is 665, emergency landing! I'm out of gas! Approaching from the east at 1,500 feet, coming straight in!"

The control tower replied, "Six-six-five cleared to land! Five-three-two, pull up and go around!"[6]

The other incoming bomber, instructed to abort its landing, complied with the order. *Calamity Jane*'s crew could not see the other plane, and a collision loomed. Crews on the ground gaped at the sight of a Liberator dropping away, cutting ahead of 532, which abandoned its approach. Timing it nicely, McQuaid waited to lower wheels and flaps, controlling airspeed with available power and lowering the nose. Speed bled off from 140 to 120 to 110. Then he dropped the B-24 onto the runway between two bombers that had already landed. The crew chief found fifteen gallons remaining for the operable left engine and ten for the right: a few minutes' air time.

It was an eye-watering piece of flying that no one could be trained to duplicate. Colonel Robert Eaton, the group commander whose war had begun at Pearl Harbor, allowed that not even a movie aviator could accomplish McQuade's feat.

EXPECTED OF THE CAPTAIN

On July 9 the Fifteenth returned to Ploesti as 222 heavies of the Fifth and Forty-seventh Wings struck Xenia and Concordia Vega.

The Forty-seventh crossed the mountains north of Ploesti, turned down the east slope, and attacked on a southerly heading. The Libs maintained formation during the seven-minute run from the initial point to the target, losing one plane to flak. After bombs away, the formation veered almost ninety degrees right, headed out but still under fire.

Guided by pathfinder radar, the Liberators landed nearly seventy hits on Concordia, reducing its already diminished output to less than one-third of its March level. Xenia, however, was well covered with smoke, and the Fortresses inflicted little damage.

Only six bombers were lost, but that statistic was small consolation to the crew of the Ninety-eighth Group B-24G flown by First Lieutenant Donald D. Pucket, a twenty-eight-year-old command pilot with the Pyramiders who had been in Italy only three months. Over the target, his bombardier had barely released when the plane was struck by flak. With one man dead and six wounded, two engines out, and fuel and control lines damaged, the Liberator began losing altitude.

Turning over command to his copilot, First Lieutenant Robert Jenkins, Pucket went aft to take stock. He found fuel and hydraulic fluid sloshing in the bomb bay and manually cranked the doors open to drain the liquids. Then he directed those who were still able to toss unnecessary weight overboard.

Despite its efforts, the crew could not save the bomber. About 150 miles from the target, Pucket ordered a bailout. Accounts vary, but three men were either unable or unwilling to jump, so Pucket resumed his seat and nudged the burning Liberator toward the ground. Descending in their chutes, the other crewmen watched aghast as their plane struck a mountainside and exploded.

Pucket was the second Ninety-eighth man to earn the Medal of Honor, after Colonel John R. "Killer" Kane in Operation Tidal Wave. Pucket's devotion to his crew lived on in his widow, Lorene, who declined to receive his medal unless the citation was changed. The mention of hysterical crewmen, she believed, reflected poorly on those who died on that Balkan mountainside. "Don's action in staying with his wounded crewmembers and crippled B-24," she said, "was what was traditional and expected of the captain of the ship."[7]

✪ ✪ ✪

Six days later, on July 15, the Fifteenth unloaded on Ploesti. All five wings launched 604 bombers in the greatest effort of the campaign. Only two previous missions had topped four hundred sorties. The Fifth and Forty-seventh Wings went for Romana Americana, while the other three wings targeted Creditul, Standard, and Dacia. More than 1,500 tons of bombs cascaded onto the refineries.

As always, the defenders had ample time to prepare. The smoke generators were up and running before the bombers arrived, forcing bombardiers to rely on H2X again. Photo interpreters counted 168 bomb holes at the primary target, interrupting production for two weeks.

As always, the larger picture was lost to aircrews, who counted seventeen missing aircraft. A 450th Group gunner, Hugh Jones, recorded thoughts far closer to heart: "The raid today was the clincher to this ever present enigma according to the intelligence officers. We probably will lay off the place for a whole week. As usual the flak was heavy and one of the bursts got Col. Snaith with a direct hit. He went down in flames without any chutes seen.... The fighter escort was beautiful. The MEs that were around couldn't even get near us. Ship 205 bit the Italian dust too this afternoon. It cracked up coming in the landing leg. This means five of the old crew are gone."[8] Jones's group commander, Lieutenant Colonel William G. Snaith, was the only survivor of his crew and was taken prisoner. And while the scuttlebutt about laying off Ploesti for seven days proved true, another chilling mission lay just ahead.

THE BATTLE OF MEMMINGEN

On July 18 four B-24 wings with fifteen groups were sent against airdromes, fuel, and armament factories in the Friedrichshafen area of southern Germany. The Fifth Wing's four assigned groups went for Memmingen Airdrome. Mission briefings indicated 240 Luftwaffe fighters in the target area and thirty or more along the route through northern Italy.

Two P-51 groups were delegated to escort the 112 B-17s: the 325th Checkertails and the 332nd Red Tails. The Mustangs were to take the heavies all the way to the target and back—further proof of the P-51's exceptional range. Unaccountably, the Checkertails were recalled before the bombers reached Memmingen. That left Major Lee Rayford's four Tuskegee squadrons with fifty-eight fighters after airborne aborts.

Another Mustang outfit, the Fifty-second, was detailed to provide penetration support up to the bombers' initial point at Kempten, eighteen miles south of Memmingen. It was a typical mission, requiring precise planning and execution—multiple formations from different bases aimed at merging in three dimensions at a specific point in time and space.

Winging northward, the Tuskegee Airmen spotted thirty-plus Messerschmitt 109s over the Udine area of northern Italy. The bombers had not yet arrived, so twenty-one pilots from three of the four squadrons dropped tanks, rolled over, and dived to attack. One Mustang was destroyed when struck by a drop tank, but the 332nd pilots claimed nine kills, three by Second Lieutenant Clarence "Lucky" Lester, a twenty-one-year-old Virginian. He reported,

> I saw a formation of Me 109s straight ahead and I closed in about 200 feet and started firing. Smoke began to pour from the aircraft and a little later it exploded. I was going

so fast I was sure I would hit some of the debris, but luck-ily I didn't.

As I was dodging pieces of the enemy aircraft, I saw another Me 109 to my right, all alone on a heading 90 degrees to mine, at the same altitude. I turned onto his tail and closed in to about 200 feet while firing. I noticed the aircraft began to smoke and almost stopped. I was going so fast I overran him, but noticed a blond pilot parachute from his burning plane.

"I was alone and looking for my flight mates," Lester continued, "when I spotted a third Me 109 flying very low about 1,000 feet above the ground." He dived on the Messerschmitt, triggered his guns, and notched his third victory.[9]

Lacking fuel to continue the mission, the recently engaged Mus-tangs turned back for Ramitelli. The remaining thirty-six continued north, sticking with the Fortresses. The first two groups, the Second and 463rd, flew a tight enough formation to enable close escort, but the others were widely separated.

Shortly after the Fifty-second's Mustangs departed the initial point, the Luftwaffe arrived in strength. Seven fighter *Gruppen* were airborne, and four concentrated on an unescorted bomber formation. It was a nearly perfect interception, but a Bf 109 squadron assigned to escort the FW 190s got sucked into hitting the heavies. American fighters intervened but not before 127 Germans swarmed the bombers.

Closing from the rear to point-blank range, the heavily armed and armored 190s chopped the 483rd Group to pieces. The unit reported, "The attack lasted twenty minutes and practically all passes were made from level rear and from five to seven o'clock positions. The fighter escort arrived about eight minutes after the initial attack, and was very effective from then on, despite the fact that they were heav-ily outnumbered."[10]

Fighting against the odds, the American fighters did what they could. While the remaining 332nd pilots went two and two, with one pilot killed and one captured, the other units in the area sped to the sound of the guns. The Fifty-second, already released from escort, reversed course and raced back to the bomber stream.

The First Group's Lightnings, awaiting the Forty-ninth Wing Liberators near Friedrichshafen, heard combat on the radio. They bent their throttles northwesterly, as did the Thirty-first Group's Mustangs. Arriving at Memmingen, the P-38 pilots gasped at the sight. Some counted a dozen Forts plummeting out of formation, ganged by ninety or more 109s and 190s. The Germans were pros: they made expert use of the vertical, employing "yo-yo" tactics to hit, dive out, and zoom climb for a reattack.

In a twenty-minute running fight, the two fighter groups claimed two dozen kills and probably got most of them. The Twenty-seventh Squadron's P-38s were best positioned, and First Lieutenant Philip E. Tovrea claimed three kills. Fighter talent ran in the family. The Arizonan's brother-in-law was Edward "Butch" O'Hare, a navy pilot and Medal of Honor recipient killed in a night interception in November 1943, for whom Chicago's airport was named.

Another flight leader, First Lieutenant William H. Caughlin, recalled, "I shot at least eight of them and two went down. All the Jerries that I didn't get, my flight got. Every man in my flight got at least one enemy."[11]

Despite the heroics, there was serious damage. Fifteen bombers were destroyed, fourteen of them from the 483rd Group. It tied the one-day loss record established by the Second Group during Big Week five months earlier.

The four engaged fighter groups logged forty kills against five losses, while bomber gunners claimed nearly thirty. Actual Luftwaffe casualties were twenty-eight aircraft and seventeen pilots, but in war's grim ledger, it represented a victory for the Germans.[12]

Major Walther Dahl of the Luftwaffe found himself on the receiving end of a bombing for a change. Famous as a *Viermot* slayer, the cigar-chewing group commander in JG 3 who feuded with Hermann Göring was grounded with angina. He later described hearing the approach of the bombers and the wailing air raid sirens:

> I pull on some trousers over my pajamas. My driver Matton rushes in, out of breath as the first explosions go off. The building is shaking. Damn close! We dash outside to my car, gun the engine and with squealing tires we tear off. People are running around in panic as bombs rain down. The air is filled with the sound of engines, the bark of the flak guns and the crashing of collapsing buildings. There is a small wood just off the airfield. We jump out and throw ourselves to the ground. After what seems like an eternity the sound of the bombers recedes and we drive back to the field to be confronted with some terrible sights. Dead and dying are lying around, mostly civilians. We try to help those still alive. Our accommodation blocks are in ruins, where my room was, just an enormous hole.[13]

More than fifty aircraft were wrecked on the field and some three hundred men were killed or wounded.

✪ ✪ ✪

Apparently unaware of the results of the massive July 15 mission, operations officers in Bari allotted more than 450 heavies to Romana Americana on the twenty-second.

The escort was excellent. Nearly two hundred fighters kept most of the forty-two Axis interceptors beyond range of the bombers, whose gunners claimed just five shootdowns, four by the Forty-seventh Wing. Only sixteen Luftwaffe aircraft were seen in the target area—a contrast to many previous missions. A measure of the American fighter pilots' dedication is that none claimed kills but they lost two Mustangs and a Lightning while protecting the "big friends."

The Axis defenses, however, were undiminished. Flak crews shot off 46,000 rounds of heavy-caliber ammunition, and they got hits. The twenty-six losses (5.6 percent) topped the previous Ploesti mission's record, but the harm to the Fifteenth was inconsequential.

Despite the maximum effort, only forty-five bomb hits were counted inside the perimeter. Even allowing for countermeasures, the results were unacceptable. There was only one hit on a refinery for every ten attacking aircraft.[14]

MORE SHUTTLES

On the same day, July 22, 134 Fifteenth fighters departed on Operation Frantic Three, headed east. The 306th Fighter Wing commander, Brigadier General Dean Strother, was number three in the Thirty-first Group's lead flight, behind Lieutenant Colonel Yancey Tarrant leading forty-seven Mustangs. Very few brigadier generals ever flew fighter missions, but Strother's rank could help smooth things over with prickly Russians.

Lightnings of the Fourteenth and Eighty-second Groups teamed up, the former providing top cover while the latter did most of the strafing on eastern Romanian airdromes. The Eighty-second CO, Colonel William P. Litton, had to abort early, but the group continued without him. His pilots "hit the deck" about fifteen miles from Buzau and Zilistea, executing company-front strafing attacks on several airfields. They shot five planes out of the Zilistea traffic pattern then reported a record haul: forty-one planes thought destroyed on the ground.

Meanwhile, the Fourteenth engaged airborne fighters at both targets, downing eleven. The Americans then proceeded to their Russian bases, leaving five Lightnings in the Balkan soil.

On the afternoon of July 25, Third *Gruppe* of Stuka Wing 77 was transiting to its new base at Piastow when the forty-four fixed-gear, cranked-wing dive-bombers had the misfortune to cross paths with sixty-eight American fighters.

The Thirty-first Group had just strafed Mielec Airdrome sixty-five miles northeast of Krakow and had ammunition remaining. Colonel Tarrant, being up front, got first choice and dropped three Stukas, while Lieutenant George McElroy also claimed a triple. Major Sam Brown's 309th Squadron was best positioned for what the RAF called a "Stuka party," claiming nineteen of the group's twenty-six credited kills. Even so, Brown had the narrowest possible escape: a sharpshooting Stuka gunner put a round through his canopy, scorching the top of his leather helmet. An Eighty-second Group Lightning pilot also gunned a Junkers; one squadron of nine Stukas was completely destroyed.

That day the Fifteenth Air Force fighters recorded forty-three shootdowns, the third-highest daily total of the war, with only the Fourteenth Group missing the action.[15]

The Fifteenth's second shuttle mission ended the next day, strafing more Romanian airfields en route to Italy.

But war is more than combat, and the Fourteenth Group lost its commander that month to an unforeseen cause. Colonel Obie Taylor, after commanding for ten months, was stricken with polio in June and was relieved in mid-July. He had helped turn the group around after its North African doldrums and went home an ace. He was one of an unfortunate few. Only 157 American servicemen were stricken with polio in the Mediterranean Theater throughout the war.[16]

THE COWBOYS AND CALAMITY JANE

Amid the carnage of a world war, there were occasional reminders of the combatants' shared humanity. Second Lieutenant Larry Jenkins of the Second Bomb Group was on a mission near Vienna on July 16 when his plane was hit. With flash burns to both eyes, the twenty-year-old copilot found his way to the bomb bay and parachuted to Earth, where he was immediately surrounded by three Germans. "For you the war is over," they told him. They looked at his mangled legs, and one surmised that amputation would be needed. "I didn't care," Jenkins said later, "for the pain was terrible."

Sent to a hospital near a Vienna rail yard with other wounded fliers, Jenkins experienced the air war from the groundling's view. At night the RAF dropped "Christmas tree" target markers before unloading ordnance. Just outside Jenkins's window, a flak crew dubbed "Eager Joe" boomed away with concussive 88 mm salvos.

"The sound of the bombs was terrible, and each one felt like it was funneled to my stomach," Jenkins recalled. "Food was scarce and terrible, therefore bones would not mend." A nun serving as a nurse often stayed with her charges through the bombing rather than take shelter. She considered all Americans "cowboys," and in turn they dubbed her "Calamity Jane." Despite the pounding they were taking from Jenkins's comrades, the Germans treated him according to the rules of war and even sympathetically. Jenkins's third surgeon confided that his wife and fifteen-year-old daughter had been killed by Allied bombs. Nevertheless, he dutifully continued his work until he suffered an emotional breakdown.[17]

PLOESTI AGAIN

The pace was unrelenting that month. On July 28 nearly 325 bombers of the Fifth, Forty-ninth, Fifty-fifth, and 304th Wings struck the Astra Romana and Standard refineries. Aircrews reported "at least 100" enemy fighters, but fewer than half that number actually got airborne. They were unable to shoot at any bombers, though they downed two Lightnings and two Mustangs while losing eleven of their own.[18]

Following a recommendation of the Joint Oil Targets Committee, the Fifteenth's planners aimed for the maximum effect on gasoline production. They used their entire menu of bombing methods—visual, radar, and offset technique. Eighty-three bombs hit Astra Romana, including eleven that did not explode—an unusually high 13-percent failure rate. The damage was repaired in days, and the results were not worth the cost of nineteen bombers. The 304th Wing was especially hard hit, losing ten planes. Ploesti was taking a beating but still exacting a fearsome price.

✪ ✪ ✪

July ended with a Fifth Wing attack on Xenia in which two Fortresses out of 154 were lost. First Lieutenant James Jarmon of the 463rd Group witnessed one of the losses—a B-17 flight above and ahead of his squadron. A Fortress took a direct hit and exploded, dousing the airspace below with debris and burning fuel. "I had an airplane in the formation just above me blow up on the bomb run," Jarmon remembered. "We flew through the burning gasoline and parts of that airplane. We had parts come through the nose."[19]

Bombing was disappointing with twenty hits on Concordia, now lying idle. But there was no doubt that the campaign would continue.

✪ ✪ ✪

July 1944 was the costliest month ever for the Fifteenth. It lost 333 aircraft, including sixty-eight fighters. The heavy toll followed the terrible June losses of 248 aircraft, eighty of them fighters. But with losses came some accomplishments. The Fifteenth had hammered Ploesti five times with erratic but increasingly effective results.

Yet there was a downside for aircrews. Ploesti had carried double mission credit, but in late July, its fighter defenses greatly reduced, it slipped into the single-credit column. Twining declared that double credit would be limited from then on to missions north of forty-seven degrees north latitude, skirting Innsbruck and the far slope of the Alps. Bucharest, also once a hot spot, became a "single counter" sortie. A B-24 unit later recounted, "The absence of enemy fighters over the target did not lessen the displeasure of the combat crews for the single-sortie rule. This collective displeasure was perhaps best summed up by J. F. Scroggs's crew during the post-mission debrief following the July 15 mission: 'We invite the general to visit Ploesti on our next mission—single sortie! No flak vest will be issued.'"[20]

FRANTIC FINALE

The August all-fighter shuttle mission, from the fourth to sixth, was flown at the request of the Soviets with Mustangs of the Fifty-second Group and Lightnings of the Eighty-second. The objectives on the fourth were enemy airfields well northeast of Ploesti, a distance requiring the Americans to land in Soviet territory before returning.

The Axis gunners seemed ready for the raiders, knocking down five P-38s and killing one pilot. The other four downed fighters included one flown by the Eighty-second's commander, Lieutenant Colonel Bill Litton, who had survived the Christmas 1943 massacre. With both engines afire he bellied into the ground at high speed, and his wingman glumly reported that the plane exploded. Surely the colonel was dead. Incredibly, Litton survived with serious burns. He was treated in a Romanian hospital, where doctors wanted to amputate an arm. Litton refused, warning them that Bucharest was about to surrender and threatening to have them tried as war criminals and executed. He kept his arm and returned to Italy.

Another pilot would have been captured but for the fortitude of a friend. Lieutenant Richard E. Wiltsie's plane was badly hit pulling off the target, and he radioed his plight. Flight Officer Richard Andrews replied, "Pick a good field and I will come in after you." As he headed to a likely field, Wiltsie took more hits, including a grazing wound to the head. Ignoring the blood on his face, he plunked his doomed fighter onto its belly and slid to a stop. As he jumped out, he tossed in a phosphorous grenade to destroy the aircraft.

Wiltsie then watched in grateful wonder as Andrews landed across the furrows of the plowed field. A small dogfight erupted overhead, as 109s tried to strafe the would-be rescuer, but First Lieutenant Nate Pape dropped one and drove off another. Andrews set his parking brake, climbed out of the cockpit, shucked his parachute, and helped Wiltsie up on the wing. "You fly," Andrews said. Wiltsie settled in, and the pair of airmen quickly found a way to fit into the one-seat cockpit: Andrews's right leg over Wiltsie's shoulder to clear the control column, and his left leg under the pilot's arm. It was awkward, but it worked. Guided to the Russian base, the piggyback pair landed safely. Thus ended Dick Andrews's tenth mission, which earned him a Silver Star. He was twenty years old.[21]

A Mustang pilot received the Silver Star for a similarly spectacular rescue the next month. On September 1 the Fifty-second Group was strafing targets of opportunity in Hungary when First Lieutenant Charles Wilson's plane was caught in the blast of an exploding loco-motive. He made a forced landing but was picked up by Major Wyatt Exum, a Pacific veteran flying his first European mission. They managed the four hundred miles to Manduria, Wilson's head exposed to the slipstream the entire way.

Little aerial combat resulted from 275 sorties in the three Italian shuttles—about sixty shootdowns—and the strafing results appeared marginal for the effort. The point they were making was the long reach of American fighters: more than a thousand miles from Foggia to Pyriatyn in the Ukraine. No spot in the greater Reich was beyond the reach of Allied airpower.

AUGUST OIL

August began with attacks on more oil targets, mainly alternating between Ploesti and Blechhammer. On the seventh, some 350 heavies struck Blechhammer, B-17s bombing the North complex and Libera-tors the South. The mission cost eleven bombers, while the escorts claimed twenty-three Messerschmitts, including those encountered in attacks against Yugoslavian oil and transport.

Blechhammer and other synthetic oil facilities became increasingly important in the strategic air war, and the Allies applied unrelenting pressure to any plants within range. But Romania still beckoned, and the Mediterranean air commanders, Eaker and Twining, doubled down on their efforts against Ploesti.

Following hard on an RAF mission to Ploesti the night of August 9–10 (which lost eleven of sixty-one Wellingtons, Halifaxes, and Liberators), more than four hundred bombers from all five wings went for Romana Americana, Unirea, Xenia, Astra Romana, and Steaua Romana.

The clever use of weather reconnaissance P-38s contributed to the success of the mission. Lightning pilots flying twenty minutes ahead of the bombers radioed reports back, allowing task force commanders to optimize their runs over a dispersing smoke screen. The scouts radioed updated information to each airborne wing commander who, armed with current intelligence, could select the best target for visual bombing. The plan worked. A thinned-out smoke screen permitted accurate bombing, and two inactive refineries—Steaua Romana and Romana Americana—were knocked out of business.

The Forty-seventh took over half the seventeen losses, which were entirely from flak. In fact, only three of nearly fifty interceptors got within range of a bomber.

✪ ✪ ✪

The last three days of the campaign involved a huge effort: from August 17 to 19, six thousand quarter-ton bombs were dropped on five refineries either visually, by offset methods, or by radar-directed pathfinders.

On the seventeenth, three wings put 245 Liberators over Romana Americana and Astra Romana. They scored several dozen hits on the latter refinery, inflicting serious damage to a reforming plant.

Seventeen B-24s failed to return, however, including five from the 454th Group. Quentin R. Petersen, a bombardier flying his first mission with his own crew, was one of the survivors. He recalled,

> As we turned at the Initial Point (about a minute or two from the target), I found it ominous that the box-barrage I had come to expect on these raids was absent. I'm sure that Colonel [James A.] Gunn must also have recognized that the fighters assigned to precede us to the target and drop the chaff [a sort of Christmas-tree tinsel] used to screw up radar-aiming of antiaircraft guns, had missed the rendezvous. The AA gunners below were just tweaking their sights. But what could he do? What could anyone do?
>
> The next thing I knew we were hit by the first flak we saw that day. Two of our engines were destroyed. Pieces and crew of the five leading planes passed by our craft. Recognizing that some bombs had been hit, I let ours go in salvo. With our oxygen and hydraulic system shot out, we descended to a breathable altitude, assessed the damage, and started for home alone, having fallen far behind....

Petersen later learned that because attrition had left his plane in front, when he salvoed his load so did the others—an unwanted result of the "drop on lead" policy. The ball turret gunner opined that the 454th "really blasted hell out of a wooded area." The crew bailed out over Greece, where Petersen sustained a dislocated hip. A German officer lent the American his cot for the night.[22]

The British flew their fourth and last mission of the Ploesti campaign that night as No. 205 Group dropped ninety tons of bombs on the area.

August 18 was the last large mission, sending the Fifth and Fifty-fifth Wings against Romana Americana, the Forty-seventh to Dacia, and the 304th to Steaua. The Americans dropped 825 tons on the three refineries, compounding the damage. The Forty-seventh lost five of the seven planes downed among 373 airborne.

The next day, August 19, the Fifth Wing wrapped up the Ploesti campaign. In words of a later time, the mission's intent was mainly to "bounce the rubble." The intelligence annex stated, "Final attack to finish off Ploesti and keep the fires burning.... Fires still burning when Wellingtons arrived last night and they added more."

Twining's operations staff did not think it would take much effort to finish off Ploesti. Of 854 available bombers, only 79 (9 percent) were allotted to the mission against Xenia, representing three of the Fifth Wing's six B-17 groups.[23]

Each Fortress carried eight five-hundred-pounders. The RDX explosive was fused for 0.1 seconds delay to optimize a ground burst. Xenia was the primary target and Dacia the first alternative, but the weather recon P-38s confirmed to the mission commander that visibility was good. Fourteen planes aborted or proved non-effective, leaving sixty-five to cross the target.

No enemy fighters rose to challenge the B-17s, and for once the flak gunners were largely ineffective, possibly because of chaff dispensers among the fighters. The 463rd Group took the only casualties; *Berlin Sleeper III* was the group's fourteenth loss of the campaign.[24]

The last American bomber over Ploesti was Lieutenant Milford Phillips's Ninety-seventh Group aircraft. With one engine shut down and two pulling reduced power, the plane limped off target, but the crew got home.[25]

✪ ✪ ✪

While the air campaign proceeded, the ground war broke wide open. On August 20, after increasing pressure, the Soviets smashed Romanian defenses in the northeast. The Russians' 1.3 million men and massive artillery, backed up by powerful armor and air support, could not be stopped. In a few days they seized numerous cities along

Romania's eastern border, compelling an abrupt switch of allegiance in Bucharest. Twenty-three-year-old king Michael announced that he was deposing the dictator Ion Antonescu, declared war on Germany, and concluded an armistice with Moscow in mid-September.

Meanwhile, the Soviets reached the Danube and secured the Black Sea port of Constanta. From there, little remained to impede their 125-mile advance on Bucharest and thence to Ploesti. Upon arrival, the Russians gaped at the burned, twisted metal at most of the refineries. The more astute among them realized they were viewing a power that Joseph Stalin envied but would never possess during the war.

PLOESTI EXAMINED

Shortly after Ploesti was secured, Eaker and Twining flew there for a first-hand look at their command's handiwork. On-scene evaluation showed that the four-month blitz crippled more than half of the complex's production capacity, and actual shipment was far less. The two generals were impressed with what they saw.

Most refineries showed the same grim wreckage: battered, blasted, blackened buildings and conduits, warped steel, and eviscerated holding tanks. Despite the Romanians' belated efforts, even blast walls erected around some tanks were leveled. It was a tribute to the persistence and ability of the Axis engineers and repair crews that Ploesti continued producing any oil at all. At the end, the amazingly resilient Astra Romana refinery was still producing more oil than most of the other facilities combined.

Between March (before the bombing) and late August, Ploesti production had plummeted from 269,000 tons to 84,000. The cumulative four-and-a-half-month loss of 718,000 tons represented a 56-percent reduction of potential refining capacity. The Ploesti campaign reduced August output to 10 percent of its previous high, although, as will be seen later, not all of the reduction was due to bombing. (See Chapter Nine.)[26]

The American airmen had reason for satisfaction in their work, but there was cause for concern as well. In most cases the bomber over a target scored barely one hit inside a refinery. Astra Romana, for example, the target of 437 sorties in three missions, was hit by 721 bombs, including duds. The Standard facility was attacked twice by a total of 144 bombers scoring 151 hits. Considering the typical bomb load of eight five-hundred-pounders, the Fifteenth scored roughly 12 percent against Ploesti, whose defenses—especially smoke—were highly effective.[27]

At the same time, 225 of the 804 Fifteenth Air Force bombers lost over petroleum targets (including "rough ones" like Vienna, Budapest, Blechhammer, and Ruhland) went down over Ploesti. Vienna exacted a greater toll than Ploesti because the Romanian campaign barely lasted four months, but every airman in the Mediterranean Theater appreciated the importance of Ploesti. Of the men killed at Ploesti, Twining said, "They gave their blood for Hitler's oil. They drove a hard bargain which will never be forgotten."[28]

D-DAY SOUTH

Before its last Ploesti mission the Fifteenth had other work at a far more glamorous location—the French Riviera.

Operation Anvil-Dragoon, the invasion of southern France on August 15, began nine weeks after Overlord in Normandy. The unavoidable reason for the delay was shipping. Even at the height of the Second World War, the Allies did not have enough sealift and amphibious craft to support two simultaneous landings in Europe. Nevertheless, the Mediterranean Theater commanders had considerable assets, including total control of the sea and outright air supremacy. The eleven understrength German divisions south of the Loire were supported by only two hundred aircraft. They faced an onslaught: the U.S. Sixth Army Group with 175,000 men, including French divisions, under General Jacob Devers.

The pre-invasion strategy aimed at multiple objectives: neutralize the Luftwaffe; support the assault forces on D-Day and later; and prevent or limit enemy reinforcements. The Twelfth Air Force had added missions of dropping paratroopers and working with the French resistance, the *Maquis*.

The Fifteenth attacked various targets in southern France in preparation for the landings, especially Marseille, Lyon, Grenoble, and Toulon. The Forty-seventh Wing, for example, pounded beaches and submarine pens along the Riviera, destroying six U-boats at their moorings.

The French island of Corsica, only about 150 miles from the landing beaches of Toulon, was already an Allied base. By mid-August Corsica was bristling with Anglo-American airpower: 2,100 aircraft from the Twelfth, Fifteenth, and Royal Air Forces were crammed into fourteen bases. All had been constructed or modified by the exceptionally efficient army aviation engineers prior to mid-July, despite rain and perennial shipping shortages.[29]

The Twelfth Air Force's P-47s were already on Corsica, but Eaker wanted Fifteenth P-38s to augment the buildup there. The First and Fourteenth Groups therefore flew their Lightnings 350 miles to Aghione, a dusty, dirty airstrip on the east coast. The effort required to move and support a single P-38 group was impressive. Colonel Robert Richard's First Group needed twenty-two C-47 transports laden with maintenance personnel, supplies, and spares to sustain sixty fighters for eight or ten days. His pilots settled into a ramshackle two-story building while the ground crews moved under canvas. The makeshift accommodations did not dampen Richard's spirits: "This looks like the real beginning of the real end for that SOB Hitler. We are living in an old abandoned hotel that is a real swanky Sulfur Spa (long since abandoned.) I'm living in what must have been the bridal suite."[30]

Operating six squadrons from one runway in hilly terrain posed challenges. But Corsica's hardscrabble turf offered no options, so the visiting airmen did what they could with what they had. To combat German twilight bombing raids, the P-38s began flying dusk patrols, which required night landings. On D-2, August 13, seventy-two planes tried to land after dark. Two pilots crashed in the brush, one without a scratch and the other suffering a broken jaw. Bob Richard reflected, "God was riding copilot a lot tonight."[31]

The pace of operations required continued nocturnal landings, and there were further complications. Leading a squadron one evening was Major James B. Morehead, a survivor of the brutal Pacific combat of 1942. His flight of four and another flight got down safely, but the third leader crashed on the only runway. With no other airstrips available for their gas-starved aircraft, Morehead recalled, "seven pilots [had] to bail out or force land in hilly, brushy country at night. P-38s were going down in all directions and there was nothing we could do about it since we had no heavy equipment to drag the crashed plane off the strip. Five P-38s and two pilots were lost. Miraculously, the others walked away."[32]

On "D-Day South," Twining's Foggia-area bomb groups carpeted the landing areas prior to the naval bombardment. The Allies' low casualties on most of the beaches were partly attributed to Fifteenth bombing of German shore batteries.

The airmen marveled at the amphibious spectacle arrayed below them. A particularly literary Mustang pilot escorting heavy bombers wrote, "I've never seen so many boats in all my life. The little ones left curving wakes as they darted around among the larger, slower vessels and made a picture of white crocheting on a polka-dot blue and black background."

Lightning pilots gawked at the unusual sight of Allied gliders in French pastures. One flier remarked, "They landed those things in spaces tighter than you could park an automobile."[33]

The Italian-based fighters logged thirty-nine missions that day, creating dawn-to-dark work for the maintenance crews, who always had their hands full with the big, complex Lightnings.

There was almost no aerial opposition; the visiting P-38 pilots claimed only four shootdowns from Corsica. On D-Day the First Group bagged three Bf 109s near St. Tropez, two by Captain Thomas E. Maloney, who became the group's leading scorer. Three days later the Fourteenth Group's Colonel Daniel S. Campbell dropped a Junkers 88, the last claim by the two Lightning outfits. Later the army fliers learned that the navy's carrier-based Hellcats did better, with eight victories.

Despite air supremacy, losses occurred daily. The Fourteenth lost six planes in the first two days, mainly to small arms fire and light flak. But there were other casualties, and one in particular was a heartbreaker.

On August 17, the Fourteenth's "hack" aircraft—a stripped-down B-17F—was landing with a full load. The pilot, First Lieutenant William T. Starbuck, decided to abort the approach and shoved up the power to go around. Abruptly the Fortress's nose pitched upward, perhaps because of shifting cargo that threw off the center of gravity. With the gut-wrenching feeling that accompanies the playing out of inevitable disaster, the GIs along the flight line watched helplessly as the planeload of comrades lived out their last few seconds of life.

The Fortress did all that Boeing Airplane Company had built it to do. Engines screaming, props in low pitch, and with two doomed pilots pushing forward on the controls, the B-17 fought and lost a two-front battle as drag defeated thrust and gravity trumped lift. Nose up and quickly bleeding off airspeed, the bomber stalled and fell off to the right. It disintegrated on impact. Twelve of the fifteen men on board died instantly; another succumbed in the hospital. Two survived.

✪ ✪ ✪

German transport—especially locomotives, rail lines and bridges, and motor convoys—was now the main target. The ground forces tried to coordinate with the airmen, but coordination was not always possible. Sometimes the Americans advanced more swiftly than expected without informing the air force. One flight of P-38s sighted an armored column and rolled in to attack. Just before reaching firing range, a sharp-eyed pilot recognized the Sherman tank's tall profile, in contrast to the sleeker, lower Panzer, and radioed, "My god, they're ours!"[34]

THE ORDEAL OF TOM MALONEY

Lanky, affable Captain Tom Maloney was a twenty-one-year-old Oklahoman and the First Group's leading ace. He ran his score to eight on D-Day, flying his sixty-fourth mission. Four days later, however, he began a grinding, grueling ordeal. Caught in a target explosion while attacking an airfield near Marseille, he turned for Corsica. Unable to reach the island base, he ditched his Lightning about five miles out to sea. As he recalled, "The flying characteristics of the P-38 were superb. It was gentle as a lamb ... but I immediately discovered that it floats like a crowbar."[35]

The downed ace deployed his rubber raft and slowly drifted northward in the dark back to land. After coming ashore, Maloney began walking in the moonless night. Shortly he heard a *click* followed by an extremely loud explosion—he had stepped on a mine. Both of his feet were shattered, and he suffered compound fractures of both legs. Metal shards were driven into his legs and arms, leaving large wounds that became infected. His trousers and one shoe were blown off, and his face was lacerated and burned.

Maloney lay semiconscious for three days, then spent five more reaching an estuary, where he built a crude raft. On the tenth day, August 29, local residents found him and placed him in a truck. The bouncing caused Maloney such excruciating pain that the patriotic French carried him to a paved road and summoned an ambulance.

The pilot was taken to a nearby hospital, where he endured surgery without anesthesia to remove some of the metal splinters. He lapsed in and out of consciousness until the night of September 1, when he opened his eyes to a magnificent sight—an American medical officer, who gave him a sedative. Tom Maloney slept pain-free for the first time in nearly two weeks.

Originally shipped to Tunisia, Maloney recuperated enough to be flown to Naples. Doctors there intended to amputate both of Maloney's legs, but the airman sought the intervention of his CO, Colonel Robert Richard. Whatever Richard said, it worked: he saved the legs of his top shooter, who was walking again at war's end. But Maloney was not fully rehabilitated until 1947.

✪ ✪ ✪

The two Lightning groups flew just over a thousand sorties from Corsica, losing two dozen P-38s and nearly as many pilots before the Germans were beaten down. Operational losses far outweighed combat attrition toward the end. The Foggia fliers began returning to Italy on the eighteenth. "Home today," Bob Richard recorded in his diary, "—our combat losses were four men, two of which we know are all right, and nine airplanes. Two more were killed this morning forming up after takeoff. No excuse for these things."[36]

MORE OIL TARGETS

With the Allies firmly ashore in southern France, the Fifteenth returned full time to the oil campaign. On August 22 more than 320 Liberators went to Vienna, 125 struck Blechhammer, and nearly 170 Fortresses attacked Odertal.

The Luftwaffe was waiting.

Like experienced big-game hunters, Gotthard Handrick's southern watch controllers read the American spoor correctly. They called up nine fighter *Gruppen*—some 220 aircraft—and concentrated more than half on the *Viermots*. At selected places the Messerschmitts and Focke-Wulfs were able to penetrate the escort and get among the bombers with telling results. Twenty-eight heavies were downed or scrapped (the heaviest toll since Vienna on June 26), including thirteen from the Blechhammer task force.

Fifteenth fighters claimed fourteen of the twenty-one German and Hungarian losses. The accumulated casualties among Colonel Heppes's "Puma" group now forced his remaining 109s out of combat for a month.

A German enlisted pilot, Willi Reschke, recalled his unit's attack:

> I was flying on the far left side of our own formation, and during the breakthrough to the bombers my wingman, Private Angermann, and I were engaged by P-51s. We had long since dropped our tanks, and at that altitude—above seven thousand meters—the Bf 109G-6 gave its best performance, equal to that of the P-51. We were held back only by our numerical inferiority. We worked hard to keep our *Rotte* [two planes] together. In such air battles—fighter against fighter—minutes seemed like hours, and instinctive reactions were required. We had learned to judge success by mere survival.[37]

The bloodletting continued, but even in multi-use facilities, life was focused on local affairs. When the Second Group lost nine of twenty-eight planes on August 29 over Czechoslovakia—including an entire squadron—most of the Ninety-seventh Group across the field at Amendola was unaware of the disaster. Said one Ninety-seventh gunner, "Hell, I never heard a word about it until after the war."[38]

Despite unrelenting losses, there were some exceptional results. Bridges probably were the toughest targets in World War II; they were extremely narrow, affording almost no margin for error. Often they were attacked by fighter-bombers, which could dive to low level with greater accuracy than level bombers, but most targets worth bombing are worth defending, and losses rose proportionately.

The best way to bomb a bridge was diagonally across its length, optimizing chances for a hit, whereas a perpendicular approach required saturation bombing. But on August 30 the Forty-seventh Wing obtained spectacular results against a rail bridge at Cuprija in central Yugoslavia. Three groups attacked the span with the 376th dropping one-tonners, putting 95 percent of the bombs within 1,000 feet of the target. The 98th and 449th employed thousand-pounders to complete the bridge's destruction. The wing history concluded, "Bombardiers, who regard bridges as difficult and unsatisfactory targets, were very happy over the results."[39]

OPERATION REUNION

August ended on the best note possible when hundreds of Fifteenth airmen began returning from captivity in Romania. Some had been listed as missing in action. The senior American flier held in Romania was Lieutenant Colonel James A. Gunn III of the 454th Bomb Group. His Liberator had been downed over Ploesti on August 17, and he was sent to the Allied officers' compound in Bucharest. Though the prisoners were not generally mistreated, they described conditions as "appalling."[40] When Romania changed sides on August 23, most of the guards fled in terror before the advancing Russians. The Luftwaffe, upset by the abrupt reversal of alliance, began bombing Bucharest. Gunn eventually made contact with Romanian officers with enough initiative and authority to organize the repatriation of American fliers to Italy—and to request the Fifteenth to attack the proximate German airfields.

Among the Romanians was a fabulous character, thirty-eight-year-old Captain Constantin Cantacuzino, commanding the Ninth Fighter Group. Born a prince and favored with movie-idol looks and a magnetic personality, "Bâzu" was one of those rare men who excel at everything. He had led the Romanian hockey team, set an automobile speed record from Bucharest to Paris, and won the national aerobatic championship. An international sportsman, he considered aerial combat the ultimate competition. Since 1941 he had downed nearly forty Soviet and American aircraft.

One of Europe's finest fliers, Cantacuzino also cut a wide swath on the ground. He adored women (he was reportedly married four times) and, according to a colleague, had his pick "from countesses to cooks."[41]

Lacking direct communication with Twining's command, Cantacuzino conceived an innovative approach. He suggested that Gunn cram himself into the fuselage of the prince's 109 for the flight to Italy. After discussing the plan—Cantacuzino was multilingual—Gunn consented.

On the afternoon of August 27 Bâzu Cantacuzino throttled his Messerschmitt southwesterly, his passenger unable to bail out in event of trouble. The Romanian navigated with a hand-drawn map that Gunn provided, aiming for landfall near Foggia. The 109 was adorned with a hand-painted American flag lest Fifteenth fighters draw the wrong conclusion.

The two fliers made it. Upon landing, the curious pair was driven to Bari, where planning for an airlift began immediately. "Operation Gunn" began five days later.

The Americans knew little of some airfields around Bucharest, however, and required Cantacuzino's assistance. He was willing to lead the first rescue mission, but needed an airplane. While visiting the Thirty-first Group's base at San Severo, he allowed a P-51 pilot to fly his Messerschmitt, with unhappy results. Requiring a replacement, he was offered a Mustang. After a brief cockpit checkout he took off and put on an eye-watering aerobatic demonstration. Said one admiring Thirty-firster, "He landed the Mustang as if he had flown it all his life."[42]

Escorted by Lieutenant Colonel William A. Daniel and a wingman, Cantacuzino (U.S. call sign "Funnel") flew to Popesti to arrange for the airlift. It did not take long. While the Americans circled overhead,

Cantacuzino worked his princely magic, then fired two yellow flares indicating all was well. The two airborne pilots then raced home with the word: Operation Gunn—renamed Reunion—was on.

Fortresses of the Second and Ninety-seventh Groups were modified to carry twenty returnees in good health or ten patients on litters. From August 31 to September 3, the Fifth Wing shuttled B-17s between Foggia and Bucharest, returning with more than a thousand Allied airmen. Each airlift was escorted by fighters in case the Luftwaffe tried to intervene, but no hostiles appeared.

The process went with barely a hitch: 1,166 freed POWs returned to American control, nearly all Fifteenth men. Returnees included 235 from the Forty-seventh Wing, more than any other.[43]

A B-17 pilot, Captain Charles E. Crafton, recalled the excited spectacle at Popesti:

> While we circled the field, we could see a line of men formed on the ground in groups of about twenty.... We taxied up to the men and they began waving and shouting in their joy to see us.
>
> The crewmen, some held prisoner for over a year, were dressed in motley uniforms of all descriptions. Some sported German helmets, German and Romanian uniforms, long and wicked looking knives, fancy belts, scarfs, colorful pants and shirts. Some had long beards but apparently all were in good health. One sergeant ... lugged a complete German machine gun and another was carrying two unopened boxes of German hand grenades.
>
> Romanian cigarettes, which they had purchased in prison camp canteens, were thrown to the ground or given to curious soldiers, and cases of American cigarettes were opened and eagerly smoked. Twenty airmen were loaded in each B-17 and started to taxi again, being on the ground for eighteen minutes.[44]

Arguably America's greatest airman, Major General Jimmy Doolittle established the Fifteenth Air Force in November 1943 and was then transferred in January 1944 to command the Eighth in England.
Courtesy of the National Museum of the United States Air Force

America's senior Mediterranean airmen, Major General Nathan Twining of the Fifteenth Air Force and Lieutenant General Ira Eaker, commanding the theater's Allied air forces. *Courtesy of the National Museum of the United States Air Force*

Teamwork wins the war. Lockheed P-38s fly top cover for the 461st Bomb Group's B-24 Liberators.
Frederick A. Johnsen

Wearing a flak vest, helmet, goggles, and oxygen mask, a B-24 waist gunner stands ankle-deep in expended .50 caliber cartridge cases.
Joseph Springer

A "Mickey" ship of the Ninety-seventh Group, early 1944. The distinctive radar dome in place of the ball turret provided blind bombing capability.
William N. Hess

This B-24 crewman expresses gratitude for a safe landing despite a huge flak hole in the Liberator's wing. *Frederick A. Johnsen*

Pilots of the 332nd Fighter Group—the Tuskegee Airmen—at a briefing for a bomber escort mission. *Courtesy of the National Museum of the United States Air Force*

Gathering of the Checkertail Clan, newly equipped with P-51D Mustangs in mid-1944. *William N. Hess*

Lieutenant Donald Pucket of the Ninety-eighth Bomb Group received the Medal of Honor for remaining with his doomed B-24 when some crewmen were unable or unwilling to bail out during a July 1944 Ploesti mission. *Author's collection*

Soviet personnel were avid consumers of Western publications such as *Yank* magazine, despite official disapproval. *Courtesy of the National Museum of the United States Air Force*

Four P-38 Lightnings of the Fourteenth Fighter Group in step-down formation, 1944. *William N. Hess*

Colonel William "Billy" Daniel briefing some of his Thirty-first Group Mustang pilots before a mission, 1945. *William N. Hess*

The flight line at San Severo in "sunny Italy" was carpeted with deep snow in early 1945. *William N. Hess*

Captain Leslie Caplan, 449th Bomb Group flight surgeon, credited with saving hundreds of American prisoners in German hands near the end of the war. *Laura Caplan*

Friendly enemies: Lieutenant Colonel James Gunn and Romanian captain Constantin Cantacuzino after their cramped flight in a Messerschmitt 109 from Romania to Italy. *Guy Aceto/Aviation History*

The Messerschmitt 262 jet fighter opposed many Fifteenth Air Force missions in the war's closing months. This "turbo" of Jagdgeschwader 7 landed out of fuel at Zurich on April 25, 1945. *Donald Caldwell*

The Fifteenth's only Berlin mission targeted the Daimler-Benz tank works on March 24, 1945. This strike photo shows bomb impacts from the 301st Group, attacking from 27,500 feet. *Courtesy of the National Museum of the United States Air Force*

The Fifty-second Fighter Group celebrated V-E Day by arranging Mustangs with individual code letters for the occasion. *William N. Hess*

Face of a survivor. Sergeant Bill Hess of the Ninety-seventh Bomb Group, veteran of Ploesti, Vienna, Blechhammer, and other "tough ones," and a POW who returned home at age twenty. *William N. Hess*

While raucously gleeful reunions were held on bases around Foggia, the Mediterranean air war entered a new phase.

CHAPTER SIX

OTHER PLAYERS

1944–1945

Weather scouts, Photo Joes, Droop Snoots, Yugos, and Carpetbaggers—there was far more to the Fifteenth Air Force than bombers and fighters, and seventy years later most of the other players remain largely unknown. Yet they all had their own intriguing stories to tell.

SCOUTING THE WEATHER

The Fifteenth's chief adversary was not the Luftwaffe or any of the other five Axis air forces. It was the weather. And the battle was continuous, often waged at altitudes previously considered unrealistic for military aircraft. Weather was the crucial element with which air operations constantly had to contend, even in "sunny Italy."

Especially in sunny Italy, as it turned out. Contrary to expectations, the Mediterranean weather proved worse than that of cold, rainy, fogbound northern Europe for the duration of the Fifteenth's operations.

Jimmy Doolittle recognized the problem as soon as he established his command in November 1943. A few days later he formed the Fifteenth Air Force Weather Detachment under Captain Eugene E. Churchill, which reported to headquarters' meteorological officer for coordination with bombing mission planning.

Churchill had five combat-tested P-38 pilots supported by twenty-two experienced Lightning mechanics. Their goal was to improve upon the method of scouting the weather employed since early 1943—usually an impromptu affair, with individual bomb groups sending out reconnaissance planes ahead of the formation. It was an inefficient process, as a mission still could be aborted on the basis of en-route reports.

Churchill explained the new method: "Instead of sending a hundred bombers on a flight that might be wasted, a fast fighter plane is first sent over the target to take a look at the weather and report back. There was nothing wrong with the idea itself but it took months of experimenting before it really paid off."[1]

The fliers knew that Allied "weather guessers" were not to blame for the typically inaccurate assessments. Their information ended when their scouts reached hostile airspace, sometimes still hundreds of miles from the target. Sending advance scouts made sense, but communications problems, changing weather, and limited assets conspired to thwart many missions. As Churchill said, "The freakish movement of air masses across the Alps frequently resulted in a complete about-face in the weather within an hour or two."[2]

The specialists flying P-38s proved their worth almost immediately. Mission aborts were reduced within a week of the weather detachment's organization on November 3. By the end of February 1944 Churchill's men were credited with saving fifteen missions that likely would have been scrubbed or recalled.

On February 13, First Lieutenant Walter Pittman took off from Bari's rutted airfield, launching the first Fifteenth Air Force mission to Rome. He returned three hours later. No bombing was attempted that day, but the concept was proved: the weather detachment could be relied upon.

Meanwhile, the Fifteenth was growing. Jimmy Doolittle had departed in January, and Nate Twining saw the need for more weather reconnaissance. Since November the force had grown from five bomb groups to nine, with more inbound. That meant multiple missions requiring more weather information.

Help was on the way.

✪ ✪ ✪

Originally an Arkansas National Guard unit, the 154th Reconnaissance Squadron had entered combat in North Africa in January 1943, mainly flying P-39 Airacobras. Along the way it became the first American unit to fly the Allison-engined P-51 Mustang in combat. Finally the squadron fetched up in Algeria, embarking for Italy in January 1944.

Upon arrival at Naples in early February, Major Joseph Whitwell's squadron learned that it would join the Fifteenth Air Force. The newcomers settled into Bari, where they remained for the rest of the European war.

Pilots appreciated the new P-38s, and were briefed on their upcoming missions. Sorties would last three to four hours, mostly above twenty thousand feet. Pilots and ground crews could expect 6:00 a.m. takeoffs to provide pre-bombing coverage of targets in Italy, France, Germany, Austria, Yugoslavia, Hungary, and Greece. Later Romania was added.

Whatever the geography, the weather was constant. A P-38 pilot recalled, "Over Europe at 25,000 feet and above, my outside air temperature gauge read minus 35 centigrade (-31° Fahrenheit). My intake air temp going into the carburetors read minus 20 degrees

(-4° F) and lower. The cockpit temp gauge read minus 10 degrees (+14° F) because it couldn't go any lower. We had people wearing three pairs of gloves who returned with frostbite. Our turbo coolers had three quarters of the intakes blocked off and our carburetor temps were still far below zero."[3]

Like every other aspect of air warfare, weather scouting evolved technically and operationally. From straightforward missions simply reporting visibility and winds at the target, the 154th developed more sophisticated procedures, working closely with its "clients," the heavy bombers. The scouts would lead bombers by thirty minutes (up to seventy-five miles), providing updated info on weather conditions approaching and over the target.

Weather recon flights fell into three categories. Most common were "general area missions," in which P-38s launched on a staggered schedule over the next day's flight paths. With full route coverage spanning hours, staff planners had a good idea of likely conditions for the forthcoming missions. The same information was useful to the Royal Air Force for that night's operations.

"Target checks" were launched before the bombers' scheduled takeoff. Weather scouts provided updates on conditions not only along the route but in the target area as well. If necessary, the mission could be canceled or diverted to secondary targets, saving fuel as well as airplanes and crews.

Finally, in especially heavy weather, the 154th probed clouds and storm fronts for a way through or around the worst conditions. The scouts radioed cloud cover, icing conditions, and winds aloft—vital information, especially for fuel-starved bombers homeward bound from a deep penetration mission.

"Recce" pilots were necessarily multi-taskers. Apart from flying a complex airplane, they had to do their own navigation, communication, and observation, all the while evaluating the weather and reporting it accurately. Most flew with a clipboard strapped around one thigh with a form for recording desired data. A map grid enabled the

pilot to identify areas of troublesome weather and to define the location, orientation, and progress of a front. Specifics included cloud
base and height, wind direction and velocity, and temperature in two-
thousand-foot gradients. Visibility, precipitation, icing, turbulence,
and contrail levels also were noted.

Meanwhile, assets arrived slowly. By early March the 154th had
only seven operational aircraft. To save weight, most weather recon
P-38s reduced their armament to two .50 caliber machine guns, leaving room for an additional radio and, sometimes, a camera. At
month's end Lieutenant Pittman, who had been first over Rome,
photographed the proposed route from Foggia to Budapest, using a
K-24 camera installed by the squadron engineering shop.

The recce pilot's greatest assets were speed and altitude, but some
encounters with the enemy were inevitable. In late March, Lieutenant
Robert Zirkle was intercepted by Messerschmitt 109s, one tackling
him head on. Zirkle recalled, "Noting that the tracers from the Me
were passing below me, I raised the nose of my plane to keep above
his fire. As the Me approached, I stalled my ship and dropped down
so one of my belly tanks hit him. The enemy plane spun out of sight
and I saw a parachute open."[4]

Nonetheless, the Luftwaffe and Italian Air Force were persistent.
In late March they chased down two weather scouts over northern
Italy on consecutive days, killing one pilot. But it was no easy task
for the defenders, requiring an astute radar controller to discern a
blip's likely course, then position fighters for the intercept. At high
altitude a P-38, with its turbos thrumming, was seldom an easy mark.
An alert pilot was always watchful, and he could trade altitude for
airspeed to evade the threat. If, however, the defenders forced the
quarry to turn away, the controller could issue a cutoff vector to
complete the fatal geometry.

Few of the twenty-eight Lightnings lost by the 154th fell to enemy
action. The large majority succumbed to weather, including high
winds over the Alps, mechanical malfunction, or pilot vertigo. The

squadron's eighth and last fatality occurred four weeks before the war ended when a second lieutenant prematurely retracted his wheels on takeoff for his first mission.[5]

SNOOPING PLOESTI

On April 5, four 154th pilots provided pre-attack scouting for the first Ploesti mission. Another event three days later, however, aroused more excitement: "Another red-letter day—the first bottle of ice cold Coca Cola in eighteen months is issued by the PX!"[6]

Weather scouts were not fully integrated into the Fifteenth's operations until the late spring. The 154th absorbed the original Weather Reconnaissance Detachment in May 1944, resulting in the 154th Weather Reconnaissance Squadron (Medium) under Captain James H. Fuller.

Single-ship flights gave way to four- and six-plane missions integrated into the Fifteenth's field orders, not only for on-scene reports, but for radio-relay flights beyond range of most VHF sets. On Ploesti missions, recon pilots referred to each refinery by an assigned identification number. Any defenders eavesdropping on American radio channels, therefore, could not easily discern the target of a particular bomb wing, though AAF investigators later learned that the defenders often guessed correctly on the basis of a few initial points. As in football, offensive predictability worked in favor of the defense.

In longer-range missions, reliable communication became more important. First Lieutenant Russell Field Jr. tested an improved very high frequency radio in July, achieving an effective range of nearly four hundred miles. The older equipment was good to no more than two hundred miles and usually required radio relay flights. Captain Albert Adell and Staff Sergeant Forrest Clark boosted a standard VHF radio to long-range VHF "by finagling parts, remaking old ones, and modifying new ones." Their expertise and diligence paid off, and the experimental set received nineteen endorsements up the AAF food chain from Bari to Dayton, Ohio, home of the Wright Field test section. The radio men were subsequently decorated for their contribution.[7]

The August 10 field order contained a cautionary note for fighters: "Watch for lone P-38 weather ship preceding bombers into target area by 20 min., remaining during bombing and preceding bombers back to base."

Radio procedure was standardized for Ploesti missions: "Hello Firtree leader, this is Retain. I say again, this is Retain. Over." After each transmission the weather pilot paused for questions before repeating or updating his information. At that point the bomber leader broadcast an authenticator. Two weather aircraft would orbit some fifty miles from the target—usually west—prepared to relay information from 154th pilots over Ploesti to the inbound bomb wing.[8]

Following hard on the RAF night mission of August 9 (eleven losses from sixty-one bombers), more than four hundred planes from all five of Twining's wings went for Romana Americana, Unirea, Xenia, Astra Romana, and Steau Romana. Weather recon P-38s flew twenty minutes ahead of the bombers, radioing updated information to each airborne wing commander. Armed with current intelligence, the COs could select the best target for visual bombing.

It worked. A thinned-out smoke screen permitted accurate bombing. Concordia Vega was smothered beneath 210 bombs, bringing production to a halt. Two inactive refineries—Steaua Romana and Romana Americana—were knocked out of business.

August 17 was the first "special assignment" at Ploesti, providing continuous coverage of five targets. The field order stated, "Three P-38 recon a/c will cover Ploesti area in three periods. First a/c will contact 47 Wg leader bet 0930 and 0935. Second a/c will contact 49 Wg leader bet 1000 and 1005.... Information transmitted include direction and force of surface wind and smoke and assigned NBR [number] of target or targets which can be attacked visually. Wg leader will decide which target he can attack and will take proper heading to respective IP." If communication could not be established or was lost, the wing commander decided which alternative target to attack.

The scouts were back the next day, six aircraft reporting in clear voice from a point over Ploesti: cloud cover, cloud height, direction and approximate velocity of ground wind and smoke screen, and visible targets by assigned numbers. The mission annex added, "Weather pilot will identify himself to bomber wing leader by beginning and ending with his VHF call sign, each recon plane having two report periods fifteen minutes apart. All recon aircraft be prepared to report ten minutes before scheduled first time."[9]

When the Fifteenth flew its last Ploesti mission on the nineteenth, the weather scouts again led the way. Several months later General Twining affixed the royal-blue streamer of the Distinguished Unit Citation to the 154th's guidon. The citation specified the unit's excellent work in the last three Ploesti missions.

✪ ✪ ✪

The joint nature of the Mediterranean air campaign was more evident in September, when twenty-three RAF and Canadian fliers in de Havilland Mosquitoes were assigned to the 154th. Constructed out of plywood and known as "the wooden wonder," the Mosquito was designated F-8 in American service and made a superb recon aircraft. Its twin Merlins—the same engine that powered the Spitfire and Mustang—yielded speeds over 400 mph, rendering it nearly invulnerable to interception by conventional fighters. With a two-man crew to handle the workload, the Mossie was an international favorite.[10]

Additional new equipment arrived as the year wound down. In November experimental tail-warning radar was installed in some P-38s to alert pilots to unseen threats. As German jets became more active—and more aggressive—a high-speed attack from the rear was a serious concern.

In December the squadron received some Droop Snoot P-38s with radar bombsights to brief heavy bomber crews on H2X imagery. Intended to simplify navigation through almost any weather, the timing was either good or poor, depending upon one's perspective. The squadron diarist explained,

> What with a piss-poor breakfast and the prospect of a morning's routine work down on the line, we rise on the Christmas morning and can yet sense no difference in the day. Down on the airfield we dispatch our first radar-equipped P-38 on an operational flight. As the delicate radar equipment becomes "ineffective" shortly after the plane leaves base, pilot [William R.] MacVittie and radar-navigator [Thomas J.] Watson are not able to put the "droop snoop" though its paces.
>
> Dinner was a surprise. Major William R. Dinker, the new CO, arranged for the officers to serve the enlisted men turkey dinner and all the fixings. Guest of honor was Louise the Red Cross lady, prompting some men to nudge their dining partners none too gently. Earthy GI language drew an admonition, "Pipe down, there's a woman here!"[11]

For many men of the 154th, it was their third Christmas overseas.

The winter of 1944–1945 was one of the coldest in recent years. The Foggia fields often were carpeted with snow, but missions continued with their now accustomed help from the weather scouts. Operations were erratic through much of January, but on the twenty-fifth First Lieutenant Robert V. Clifford flew to Bruck, Bavaria, on the squadron's one thousandth weather mission since joining the Fifteenth.

More missions followed. On March 12, 1945, the 154th supported the heaviest attack ever launched by the Fifteenth: 1,667 tons of ordnance on Vienna's Florisdorf refineries. Three days later three pilots logged the squadron's longest mission—seven hundred miles north to Dresden. The Lightnings led the heavies to the initial point barely ten minutes beyond the city, still smoldering from a round-the-clock pasting by Anglo-American bombers supporting a Soviet offensive.

Despite attrition, by mid-April the 154th achieved its peak strength with twenty-four aircraft. It was almost an embarrassment of riches, considering the shortage of Lightnings a year before. Near the war's end, Fifteenth Air Force's A-3 (operations) officer stated that the weather recon unit "had slashed at least six months from the length of the war in the Mediterranean by making it possible to carry out continuous bombing strikes and thus thwart the German efforts to repair damage to key factories and military installations."[12]

PHOTO JOES

No air force can function without accurate intelligence, and Twining's command relied on a variety of sources for targeting information. At the upper levels, Anglo-American code breakers monitored enemy communications for both specific information and overall trends in their attempts to predict future capabilities. Unit movements, aircraft production, and fuel supplies were all frequent subjects for electronic eavesdropping.

More immediately, however, the Fifteenth needed target folders with current photos of vital facilities such as the Ploesti refineries and Messerschmitt plants in Augsburg and Vienna. Combining decrypts and overhead imagery, intelligence analysts provided mission planners and bombardiers with detailed information.

Enter the Fifth Photographic Reconnaissance Group. Originally part of the Twelfth Air Force, the Fifth Group had flown in Tunisia under Lieutenant Colonel Elliott Roosevelt, the fourth of President Franklin Roosevelt's six children. The group moved to Italy in late 1943 and was based at San Severo, north of Foggia.

The group was reassigned to the Fifteenth Air Force on October 1, 1944. The transfer brought Twining's command to the full complement of twenty-one bomb groups, seven fighter groups, and one photo group authorized by the War Department a year earlier. Fifth Group headquarters moved to Bari on October 11, where it could coordinate directly with the strategic arm of MTAF, reducing response time to daily intelligence flights.

The primary photo recon aircraft were the F-4 and F-5 variants of the P-38. Between them, Fifteenth and Twelfth Air Forces owned about sixty photo Lightnings, spanning the Mediterranean Theater.[13]

The CO was an unusually experienced officer, Lieutenant Colonel Wilbur Stratton, an Oregonian who had joined the Marine Corps before the war and flew combat with the First Fighter Group. After a stretch as the First's operations officer, he was selected to take over Fifth Photo.

Stratton's command was composed of two Lightning squadrons with another inbound. On April 20, 1944, however, Luftwaffe bombers from southern France had attacked a ninety-ship convoy off Algiers, bound for Bizerte. A torpedo struck the SS *Paul Hamilton*, setting off her cargo of explosives. Under a boiling mushroom cloud the transport sank with all 580 aboard, including most of the Thirty-second Photo Squadron. Another transport and a destroyer also went down in one of the Luftwaffe's last consequential anti-shipping missions.

Most of the Thirty-second's non-flying officers survived on another vessel, but when they debarked in Naples, the unit had to rebuild from the ground up. The squadron became operational again only in mid-November, benefiting from pilots and planes transferred from other units and some de Havilland Mosquitoes.

Like Wilbur Stratton, some photo pilots were transfers from fighter units, and many pursuit fliers were dragged into the new job with the proverbial door knob in each hand and skid marks on the floor. But the large majority of Photo Joes soon appreciated the importance of their assignment and enjoyed the independence that came with their mission. One newcomer, who resented leaving his P-38 with four machine guns and a cannon, changed his mind when he saw the fruits of his work. After his first mission, his commanding officer took him to the shop to watch his film being processed. The flier recalled, "I'd never seen a photo lab. But there was an army brigadier general and a British air vice marshal looking at the wet negatives, then laying on missions from a field telephone. Wow!"[14]

There was more to a photo recon unit than airplanes and cameras, however. Initially the Fifth totaled some 1,150 officers and men performing a multitude of specialized jobs. For instance, Stratton owned the Fourth Photo Technical Squadron and an engineer company that produced topographic maps and mosaics and maintained a print library.

For maximum efficiency, each squadron was permanently assigned to a geographic area. Toward war's end the Fifteenth Squadron photographed eastern Germany and the Balkans. The Thirty-seventh Squadron filmed eastern Italy, central Austria, and Germany. And the long-delayed Thirty-second covered most of Italy, central Germany to western Austria, and part of France.

The group usually flew four missions a day with a "time over target" between noon and 1:30 for the best sun angles. A typical schedule for early October has sorties photographing bridges in Italy and Yugoslavia, a Trieste rail yard, a marshalling yard in Zagreb, and airdromes in Greece.[15]

Photo planes typically flew at twenty-five thousand feet or higher, depending on atmospheric conditions. Pilots avoided altitudes that produced contrails, though they were unavoidable if the ambient temperature was lower than forty degrees below zero Fahrenheit.

Even with heat ducted from two high-performance engines, the Lightning cockpit could be a bitterly cold place to work. Lieutenant Tom Follis described the well-dressed recon pilot:

> Whenever we were going on a mission we wore many layers of clothing not only to keep warm at 30,000 feet … but also for survival in case we were forced down in the snowy Alps. The long wool underwear that I had been forced to buy earlier was now very welcome. On top of all the clothes I had put on, a baby blue electric flying suit was added. This suit had small electric wires similar to those in electric blankets and was helpful in the cold weather even though it did tend to burn elbows and the rear end while other parts of the body were still cold. This suit made me look like an oversized four-year-old ready for bed on a frigid night. Two pairs of gloves helped keep hands from freezing. All these layers of clothes did create a problem when it came time to relieve oneself after several hours in the air. The relief tube in the cockpit had the annoying habit of freezing up at high altitude and spilling the contents over the pilot's hands.[16]

Over the long johns, electrically heated suit, wool uniform, and fleece-lined leather flying suit, the pilot struggled into his mae west and, once seated, his parachute harness. To sustain himself in the thin air and to communicate with the rest of the world, he wore a leather helmet with oxygen mask, earphones, and polarized goggles. He was an airborne contradiction: pudgy and semi-immobilized yet capable of four hundred miles per hour.

The AAF preferred a photo scale of 1/10,000, requiring missions flown at twenty thousand feet over the target using cameras with a twenty-four-inch focal length. At thirty-five thousand feet, the desired scale required a forty-inch lens. Weather or tactical conditions, however, sometimes confined photo pilots to lower altitudes. Mission heights of five thousand and six thousand feet dictated twelve- and six-inch focal lengths, respectively. At those altitudes the Photo Joe was within range of medium flak, and his mission became a roll of the dice. The RAF called low-level missions "dicey shows," leading to the Americanized term "dicing missions."[17]

Often one camera was not enough. Oblique shots were best for showing initial points to bombardiers, but two twelve-inch forward obliques proved more useful, slanted at seventeen and thirty-five degrees. The optimum trimetrogon configuration employed two K-17 oblique cameras with six-inch lenses for side-looking coverage mated with K-17 and K-18 vertical cameras mounting twelve- to twenty-four-inch lenses.[18]

No time was wasted when the photo flier returned. A pilot inbound to San Severo radioed ahead, giving the code word "tool kit" to alert the operations office that he was landing with imagery onboard. As soon as he shut down, technicians unloaded the negative reel from the Lightning, and the pilot received his chit from the squadron operations officer, good for a free drink in the club.

Prints were developed off rolls of negatives, sometimes delivered to the interpreters' hut still damp. Eleven photo interpreters bent over stereo-optic scanners, examining the prints with patient, practiced eyes. Specially trained to look for minute clues, the "PIs" sought anything that might give a clue about new facilities, recent repairs, or other changes. Even a shadow could be the tipoff.

After a preliminary exam, the interpreters selected the most promising photos and subjected them to more detailed scrutiny. The second-pass pictures were placed under glasses on long legs, giving a focal length that produced a three-dimensional effect.

The 3-D photos were combined with a written report on the target, time, and location and offering a preliminary analysis. The package then went to Fifteenth headquarters, where another team of interpreters compared the day's imagery with previous reports. A steady flow of information was available to planners and targeting officers who determined whether a specific refinery, factory, rail yard, or airfield was worth another mission. Photographic damage assessments made it possible to estimate the rate of repair of almost any target and, by extrapolation, to discern near-term enemy production and even intentions.

Targets of continuing interest were photographed at intervals of three, seven, or fourteen days, depending upon their priorities, though "special jobs" could be assigned anytime. Timely intelligence produced results. On October 13 the Thirty-second Squadron surveyed Seregelyes Airdrome in central Hungary, where interpreters noted an increased number of aircraft—as many as seventy. The next day the Fifty-second Fighter Group descended on Seregelyes and an adjacent field with notable success. Post-mission coverage determined that twenty-nine planes were destroyed and about two dozen damaged at a cost of two P-51s.[19]

Recon pilots became professional paranoids, always assuming somebody was stalking them. One Photo Joe explained,

> Speed was our only defense. The P-38 could generally outrun any of the Germans' airplanes, in both a shallow climb or a dive. One day a group of Messerschmitt Bf 109s jumped me, and I outran them to the coast. I think I made 500 mph, going downhill. But I hit serious turbulence, and thought the airplane was going to come apart. The main spar between the engine booms and the gondola popped a bunch of rivets. When I got back it was a wreck, and they junked the airplane. The crew chief told me (jokingly) that I'd pushed on the throttle handles so hard I'd bent them.

The bottom line was, "The most survivable photo-recon pilot was the one who was the most scared."[20]

Droop Snoot P-38Js had begun arriving in the summer of 1944. Lockheed technicians in Britain replaced the fighter nose with a Plexiglas enclosure into which a small bombardier could squeeze himself behind a sight. The intent was to use Lightnings as level bombers with the conventional aircraft to "drop on lead" when the Droop Snoot toggled its load. The concept was greeted with ambivalence: bombardiers had a spectacular ride with unrivaled downward visibility—and precious little chance of abandoning ship in an emergency. Droop Snoots, however, could provide radar imagery to enhance photo coverage of targets for attack in darkness or heavy weather.

✪ ✪ ✪

The Luftwaffe did not allow photo flights to pass unchallenged. Between mid-November 1944 and early April 1945, Messerschmitt 262 jets made twenty-nine attacks on F-5s, taking down one Lightning on December 2, when a 262 dropped out of the overcast sky, jumping a recon flight north of Munich. The interceptor killed Lieutenant Keith W. Sheetz, and though an escorting P-51 scored hits on the jet, it escaped.

Sometimes photo pilots snapped pictures of more than factories or railroads. A Thirty-second Squadron pilot, Lieutenant Smith, was intercepted by a Messerschmitt 262. Turning with the turbo fighter, Smith got a favorable angle on the jet and snapped some photos. They were invaluable: the first aerial imagery of the Luftwaffe's latest threat. Smith's initiative was rewarded with a Distinguished Flying Cross.[21]

During the winter of 1944–1945, as many as six Lightnings or Mustangs began to escort F-5s. The Fifth was conducting its own war against enemy jets, as photo missions monitored more bases and factories. In mid-February, strikes on the jet hatcheries were based on Fifth Group imagery. In one mission, twenty-two jets were destroyed and twenty of sixty-two counted at Regensburg were damaged.

Occasionally, when a mission plan turned sour, photo pilots took the initiative. On March 20, 1945, Captain James E. Emswiler encountered heavy clouds in his assigned area over central Germany. Computing that he had enough fuel to spare, he diverted northward to Berlin, photographing targets in the southern portion of the capital. His initiative earned him a well-deserved Silver Star.[22]

Long after the war, Emswiler expressed the thoughts of thousands of combat veterans when he wrote to his local newspaper,

> Senator Bob Dole in his autobiography asserts that the only heroes from World War II were those who were killed. In a recent TV ad, Bob Felder, famous Cleveland pitcher, claims that the only heroes were those who didn't come home. Does this mean that Audie Murphy who won every medal that the Army gives was not a hero? Or that all those awarded a Purple Heart for wounds received in action cannot claim to be heroes? As a pilot, I made 56 flights over Germany, including several over Berlin, and was awarded the Silver Star, a Distinguished Flying Cross and 11 Air Medals. If some of the masses of flak that were shot at me had hit my plane and killed me, would that have made me a hero? But based on the above criteria, because I was able to evade the flak and thereby lived, I can make no claim to the title.[23]

From the time the Fifth Photo Group joined the Fifteenth in October 1944 until V-E Day in May 1945, it logged 1,873 missions, losing eight pilots in combat or accidents. The recon flights yielded 15,700 "pinpoints" (specific photo targets), with 332,000 negatives producing 809,000 prints. The imagery was included in 1,700 reports forwarded to Fifteenth Air Force headquarters.[24] The statistics, however, hardly convey the Photo Joes' contribution to the strategic air campaign. The mechanics on the flight line, the pilots who usually flew solo sorties hundreds of miles through hostile airspace, the lab techs who processed the film, and the bleary-eyed analysts who stared at thousands of pictures—the members of the Fifth Photo Group fought the Mediterranean air war in relative obscurity. But headquarters at Bari knew their value—and so did the Luftwaffe, which tried hard to stop them.

THE YUGOSLAV DETACHMENT

Outbound from Wiener Neustadt on May 24, 1944, an exiled Yugoslav pilot flying a B-24 with the 376th Bomb Group, Captain Vojislav Skakich, was hit by flak. Flight engineer Bodgan Madjarevic was killed, and other crewmen were wounded. Skakich's controls were damaged, forcing him to engage the autopilot. The trick worked—he coaxed the limping Liberator six hundred miles back to his base at San Pancrazio, in the heel of the Italian boot.

Circling the field, Skakich wondered if he could land on autopilot. It looked doubtful, and the group commander, Lieutenant Colonel Ted Graff, ordered him to bail out. The pilot refused—he had wounded aboard. Most of the hydraulic system was useless, so the crew lowered flaps and wheels manually. Alternately engaging and disengaging the autopilot, the flight deck crew lined up with the runway and established a steady descent. Upon touchdown the two pilots stood on the brakes, bringing the wounded Liberator to a lurching stop at the end of the runway. Men watching from the flight line erupted into cheers. They had witnessed another exceptional feat of airmanship from the Yugoslav Detachment, one of the more unusual components of the Fifteenth Air Force.

In April 1941 the Yugoslav Royal Air Force was overwhelmed by the Luftwaffe as Germany conquered the country in eleven days. Many Yugoslav fliers fled to Greece and Egypt, seeking employment with the British. In Washington the Yugoslav ambassador requested assistance from President Roosevelt. After Pearl Harbor, the United States was allied with the Yugoslav government in exile, and Roosevelt granted the ambassador's request. He pledged four B-24Js and offered to train four crews.

Over the next few months forty candidates were selected and brought to America. They began training in December 1942 and completed their course in October 1943. Though remaining in Yugoslav service, they wore U.S. Army uniforms on detached duty with the AAF. During the commissioning ceremony at Bolling Field outside Washington, the president said, "May these planes fulfill their mission under your guidance. They are built for two great objectives. The first is to drop bombs on our common enemy.... The second is to deliver to your compatriots in Yugoslavia much-needed supplies. Remember always that we are comrades in arms."[25]

The four Liberators crossed the Atlantic, proceeding to Dakar, Casablanca, Tripoli, and Cairo. In November, the detachment joined Colonel Keith Compton's 376th Bomb Group in Tunisia. Assigned to the 512th Squadron, the four bombers became numbers twenty through twenty-three, bearing the Serbian cross and roundel in addition to the AAF's star and bars. The 512th's diarist noted, "It was quite an honor to be chosen from all the squadrons of the group as hosts for these American-trained nationals of Yugoslavia, and we have done everything possible to make them at home."[26]

The detachment flew its first combat mission in mid-November, attacking a German airfield in Greece. Soon the group moved to Italy, settling at San Pancrazio. On the second mission, November 24, two detachment bombers accompanied the group to Sofia, Bulgaria. Liberator number twenty-two was cut down by enemy fighters, though the full crew (including an American) survived as prisoners. The detachment's Yank colleagues offered heartfelt sympathy, but the Liberandos were old hands. They had seen loss before and got on with the war.

More heartache followed. On December 23, Liberator number twenty-one, flown by Major Dusan Milojevic, was shot out of formation by Luftwaffe fighters over Germany. No parachutes were seen, and no survivors turned up. Despite the losses, the surviving members of the Yugoslav detachment served dinner to their squadron mates on January 7, 1944—Christmas Day in the Serbian Orthodox calendar.

Yet 50-percent losses took a toll. In early March three fliers decided to join Josip Broz Tito's Communist guerrillas in Yugoslavia, while another simply walked away, never to be seen again. The remaining Yugoslavs consolidated into one oversized crew, taking turns flying missions. On March 24 number twenty nearly collided with an oncoming formation in heavy cloud. A gunner abandoned ship and, upon return to base, another man quit. Four British-trained Slovenians filled some of the gaps. By the summer of 1944, attrition and rotations home left the detachment's fliers the most senior crews in the squadron.

Having been warmly welcomed by the AAF, the Yugoslavs offered a gesture of thanks. On October 3 Captain Skakich presented wings of the Yugoslav Royal Air Force to Twining, Brigadier General Hugo Rush of the Forty-seventh Wing, and Brigadier General Charles Born, Fifteenth operations officer. The next month, however, amid continuing uncertainty in Yugoslavia, four detachment fliers chose to join Tito. Two Slovenians opted for Trieste.

The remaining fliers completed their tour in early 1945. Having nowhere to go—other than Yugoslavia, which had no air force—the men elected to stay in Italy. Without regular pay for over a year, they hopped a flight to Cairo to settle their British accounts, then returned to San Pancrazio, which they found deserted. The 376th had rotated home, leaving the now-orphaned Yugoslavs on their own. For several weeks they wandered like nomads from base to base, ignoring Tito's demand that they join him. In August the remaining men were inducted into the U.S. Army, and finally in October eleven boarded the remaining "pink bomber" (still bearing its North Africa camouflage) and flew to America.

Once "home," the detachment fliers fought another battle—to attain American citizenship. At length they prevailed, becoming U.S. citizens in July 1947. Six made careers in the newly independent U.S.

Air Force, two retiring as full colonels: Vojislav Skakich and Milosh Jelich.

Nowhere in the Second World War was the meaning of "allies" better illustrated than by the Yugoslav Detachment of the Liberando bomb group.

SPECIAL MISSIONS

The lights were dimmed on the Liberator's flight deck as the four Pratt & Whitney engines droned through the Balkan night. The pilot and copilot had dimmed the instrument lights to preserve their nocturnal vision as they flew at a low level over some of Europe's most mountainous terrain.

The twenty-one-year-old navigator sat at his chart table in the nose, behind the front turret, facing aft. He was accustomed to reading a map backwards from the direction of flight, and looking to his right for a view out the left side of the aircraft was second nature. He double-checked his "howgozit" track for the dead-reckoning course, and, satisfied that he was reading the wind drift accurately, he pressed his intercom button. "Ten minutes."

The twenty-four-year-old pilot squirmed in his seat—he had been sitting in the same position for almost two hours—and mentally prepared himself. He visualized the geometry of the situation: the B-24 approaching the drop zone from the southwest, ready to turn east-southeast for the best approach down the designated valley. Dropping bundles of weapons and supplies was no different from dropping bombs—range errors always exceeded lateral error. Better to drop short or long rather than left or right with hills on either side.

On the navigator's "hack," the pilots eased their bomber into a standard-rate turn. Settled on the run-in heading, the pilots and the nose and top turret gunners scanned the darkness for the expected signal. The waning quarter moon cast faint, harsh shadows across the landscape where hills obscured much of the terrain.

"Two minutes," the navigator called.

The time ticked off, each second with a beginning, middle, and end. Too long an approach gave the Germans and their Fascist partners time to anticipate the destination. Too short and the crew might miss a last-minute checkpoint.

"Lights ahead. One o'clock." The nose gunner caught the blinking signal. Marshal Tito's Partisans had heard the approaching bomber and held their signal as long as they dared.

In the rear of the aircraft other fliers prepared to drop a precious cargo, human and otherwise. Several stout canisters went out the hatch, containing weapons, ammunition, and supplies. Moments later two "Joes"—OSS agents—leapt into the dark void, their camouflaged parachute canopies blossoming quickly. Both men were on the ground in less than a minute, warmly greeted by their new comrades. Between them, the Serbs and the Americans would concoct a troublesome brew for the occupiers of Yugoslavia.

The navigator's work was not yet done. In fact, his task was not finished until the plane's base was in sight. "Come right, one niner five." The youngster knew that a smart mission planner always took a different route back than the track inbound. A southern dogleg would make it more difficult for the enemy to detect a target that was nearly defenseless against interceptors and vulnerable to flak.

✪ ✪ ✪

The mission was called Operation Carpetbagger. It was a British concept, dating back four years—the aerial phase of Winston Churchill's plan to "set Europe ablaze" with commando raids and guerrilla forces far behind enemy lines.

The Eighth Air Force launched the American contribution to Carpetbagger in 1943, dropping tons of leaflets with information and propaganda for the civilian populations of northwestern Europe. But the "nickeling" missions (so called after the British term for leaflets) evolved into full-fledged Carpetbagger operations, inserting agents of the Office of Strategic Services—both "Joes" and "Janes" who gathered on-site intelligence or worked with French *Maquis* resistance forces.

Two Carpetbagger squadrons were attached to a regular B-24 group, and by D-Day two more special operations ("spec ops") outfits were formed into a provisional bomb group. Among them they had more than forty Liberators, eventually being assigned to the 492nd Bomb Group.

By the summer of 1944 the situation in northwestern Europe was much changed as Allied armies pushed the Germans ever eastward. With less clandestine work to be done, some assets were transferred southward.

The 885th Bombardment Squadron was activated at Blida, Italy, in April 1944 under Colonel Monro MacCloskey, a stern former artilleryman from West Point's class of '24. Flying B-17s and B-24s, the squadron performed Carpetbagger operations throughout the Mediterranean Theater. Its operating area extended from France to the Balkans, and the special-ops airmen quickly discovered the theater's challenges; in their first full month they completed only forty-five sorties of seventy-two launched, a success rate of 64 percent. The reasons were many: poor weather, difficult night navigation, and failure to contact the intended recipients on the ground. A partial solution was found in the Eureka navigational beacon provided to resistance cells, permitting the aircraft to pinpoint the friendly forces.

The raw numbers were impressive. A fully loaded Carpetbagger bomber carried six thousand pounds of supplies, six or more four-thousand-leaflet nickels, and one or more agents. In 692 Balkan sorties, the squadron delivered eighteen agents and 2,900,000 pounds of weapons and supplies. One mission went to Germany (two agents and nine hundred pounds) and nine to Austria, with four agents and 7,830 pounds.[27]

Some cargo was decidedly nonstandard. In one instance the 885th delivered carrier pigeons from Corsica to southern France. Only four birds were known to reach their destinations, as wartime rationing left Corsicans hungry for protein.

Before the Allied landings on the Riviera, the 885th launched a major effort. On the night of August 12–13 the squadron sent eleven B-24s to the Rhone Valley and along the coast, navigating beneath a moonless sky to drop 33.5 tons of supplies, 225,000 leaflets, and eighteen agents. It was a stellar performance, bringing the squadron a Presidential Unit Citation.

In October 1944, the 885th moved from Blida to Brindisi in southeastern Italy, sharing a field with British and Polish B-24 squadrons. The special operations crews supported resistance forces in Yugoslavia, Greece, Hungary, Czechoslovakia, France, and northern Italy—nearly the entire Mediterranean Theater. It was a huge task for such limited assets. But help was on the way.

With Allied armies advancing throughout northwest Europe, special operations units had less to do. Therefore, in December the Eighth Air Force's 859th Squadron got "the word," which was received with mixed emotions. The squadron diarist recorded,

> In the early part, there were rumors circulating that the outfit would move to Italy to continue the Carpetbagging operations into Eastern Europe. Everyone's morale at that time had reached a low point, but with the advent of the rumor ... morale in both the ground and flying personnel raised itself to a level which, while not the highest, at least gave some indication of the squadron's attitude during the period of operations inactivity. No weight was passed on the rumor until about a third of the month had passed. At that time training for bombing at high altitude was discontinued and preparations and plans for the move were formulated.[28]

On December 17—the forty-first anniversary of the Wrights' triumph at Kitty Hawk—an advance echelon of fourteen officers and thirty-two enlisted men departed Britain for Brindisi, sixty miles up the coast from Bari. The balance of the squadron followed in fifteen C-47 transports while maintenance men flew in their assigned B-24s. The medical department had room only for minimal supplies: some aspirin tablets, sleeping pills, and half a gross of condoms.[29]

It was a memorable flight, permitting the aircrew and passengers to gawk at the Eiffel Tower in Paris and the Coliseum in Rome. But the sight-seeing ended abruptly. The 859th's tent area was found to be uninhabitable, and it took several days to correct the problems. Some one hundred officers and nearly four hundred enlisted men needed accommodations, so fliers spread sand and gravel, laid boardwalks, erected a shower, and built an acceptable latrine. Then they started flying.

As the Fifteenth prepared to combine the two squadrons into a special operations group, the 859th's first missions launched on December 29 with six sorties, including the CO, Lieutenant Colonel Leonard M. McManus. All completed their missions over Yugoslavia, drawing congratulations from Colonel MacCloskey of the 885th, who was supervising Carpetbagger missions in the area.

Two days later—New Year's Eve—six Liberators took off for Italian destinations. Four sorties failed because of weather, mechanical problems, and lack of "reception committees" at the appointed drop zones. The squadron nevertheless resolved that "the months to come would add a new record to our chapters of Carpetbagging and Supply Dropping."[30]

The Italian climate proved obstinate. The 859th spent nearly half of January on the ground but averaged nine sorties each flying day.

✪ ✪ ✪

In late January the two spec-ops squadrons formally became the Fifteenth Special Operations Group under Colonel MacCloskey, who had sent the initial congratulatory message to the 859th. Relations between the two squadrons, however, were strained. The 859th men complained about MacCloskey's heavy hand. Once he became group commander, the former commander of the 885th Squadron was seldom seen on the 859th's turf.

The 859th, moreover, considered the 885th's operating area—mainly southern France and western Austria—"milk run" territory. The 859th, by contrast, had "plenty of room—the eastern slopes of Austria plus Yugoslavia, Albania, the rough box canyons of the Alps, Moravia, Montenegro, etc." The 885th, nevertheless, had previously covered all the Mediterranean Theater's spec-ops territory by itself.[31]

One veteran's recollection of Colonel McCloskey was, "We terrified him." On a rare tour of the 859th's compound, he dressed down the gate guard for sloppy procedure, ordering the GI to shoot at the next person who failed to stop when challenged. With that, the group commander visited the newly constructed pine outhouse.

The next visitor was an elderly Italian woman returning some laundry. She spoke no English and had no way to respond when challenged. Seeing the guard draw his pistol, she turned and fled—toward the privy. Following orders, the guard squeezed off a round which, as intended, missed the old woman but, not as intended, struck the outhouse. The .45 bullet punched through the fresh wood, passing between the colonel's knees, lodging in the throne and sending splinters into the colonel's exposed thigh. "The medic happily reported that blood had been drawn, although there was some regret that the barrel of the .45 had not been a trifling to the right in its aim."[32]

The 859th CO, Leonard McManus, decided to keep the same guard post because otherwise an errant bullet might strike the squadron day room.

In March 1945 the Fifteenth Special Group was redesignated the 2641st, apparently because there were not 2,640 other *special* groups in the AAF. Both spec-ops squadrons continued flying as before but with greater coordination as Germany withdrew from the Balkans. In a sixty-day period in early 1945, the group flew 209 successful sorties to the Balkans and 152 in Italy, dropping nearly thirty-five tons of "nickels."[33]

February brought much improved weather, permitting 240 sorties, but tragedy struck on the ninth when First Lieutenant Robert W. Maxwell's Liberator disappeared over Yugoslavia. Though new to the squadron, his crew was capable and well liked. "A depressed feeling of sorrow for him was felt in this squadron for quite some time."[34]

The group received a Distinguished Unit Citation for missions into northern Italy's Po Valley the night of February 17–18. In twenty-six days that month, it delivered thirty-four agents and one thousand tons of supplies, weapons, and ammunition. In 486 attempted sorties, the crews made 354 successful drops, or about 14 per day. The 72-percent completion rate would have been higher if intended recipients had responded to aircrew attempts to contact them at the drop zones.

As Allied armies slogged northward, the Carpetbaggers required fields closer to their new operating areas. They sought bases on the Tyrrhenian coast, opposite Corsica. In late March 1945 both squadrons moved four hundred miles north to Tuscany, settling near Rosignano, south of Pisa, at a Twelfth Air Force transport and bomber base. Accommodations were much improved over the squalor of Brindisi. The airfield featured a large castle, which became squadron and group headquarters, and morale picked up in the pleasant surroundings. Operations resumed on April 1. Meanwhile, the first crews to complete Italian tours rolled out, encouraging those still flying.

And there was flying aplenty. The special operations group flew multiple missions daily, dropping supplies to units ahead of the advancing Fifth and Eighth Armies in the Po Valley, and night missions resumed for resistance forces in Austria and Czechoslovakia. But the job was costly, as the 859th lost three crews that month. One pilot, Captain Walter L. Sutton, was on his second European combat tour. Replacements arrived from regular B-24 groups and were integrated into the squadron after training in Carpetbagger operations.

At month's end Leonard McManus completed his tour and was relieved by Captain Albert Baller. Missions continued during the first week in May, which brought joyous news—Germany capitulated in Italy, and two of the missing 859th crews were reported safe and en route to the United States. Most of the third crew returned from captivity, having fetched up in France.

Two weeks later the squadron vacated Rosignano, alighting at Gioia del Colle, west of Bari, and encamping on a dusty, barren baseball field. "There was no joy at being back in southern Italy," the diarist complained.[35]

✪ ✪ ✪

The agents dropped behind enemy lines included native Germans and other Europeans (often Jewish refugees) willing to work for the Allied cause. Secrecy was paramount. Pilots and navigators were not permitted to meet their passengers and seldom saw them. Only the jumpmasters in the rear of the aircraft had personal contact with the agents and knew them only by a *nom de guerre*. The agents' apparent courage was genuine, as capture inevitably brought torture or worse. Sergeant Frederick Mayer was betrayed by a shady contact in Austria. Stripped naked, he was flogged with a whip while insisting he was an innocent Frenchman. Finally confronted with his betrayer, he employed cool logic to convince his captors that the war was ending, and not favorably for Germany.[36]

✪ ✪ ✪

At its height, the 2641st consisted of thirty-four aircraft flown by forty-eight crews, and in its active period—January to May 1945— seven planes were lost and thirty-five fliers killed. (Losses of the two squadrons prior to forming the group were not included.) During the last thirteen months of hostilities, the 885th alone logged some 2,800 sorties, dropping 501 agents, 4.7 million tons of supplies and weapons, and 177.6 tons of leaflets. More than 1,260 flights went to Italy and 831 to France, with the balance spread among the Balkans, Czechoslovakia, Austria, and one to Germany.[37]

The Carpetbaggers did their job and did it well, often under perilous conditions at night and in mountainous terrain.

BRINGING THEM BACK ALIVE

Though only marginally a Fifteenth Air Force operation, the sustained campaign to retrieve downed fliers from enemy territory benefitted thousands of Twining's men.

In 1944 and 1945, Balkans operations centered on Yugoslavia, mainly supporting Marshal Tito's Communist guerrilla army, the Partisans, who afforded a large, well-organized opposition to Axis forces, including rescue and return of downed Allied airmen.

Foremost among Tito's rivals was General Draža Mihailović, who established a liaison office in Italy. Twining was advised by the theater commanders to avoid any sign of favoritism between the competing Yugoslav leaders, leaving it to the Office of Strategic Services to handle the touchy internal feud. Mihailović's largely royalist Chetniks offered a conservative foil to the Communist Partisans. For several months the Allied Mediterranean command tried to remain neutral, but the British eventually leaned toward Tito and severed relations with the Chetniks in May 1944. Nevertheless, Mihailović's forces continued to support the Allied airlift.

As the air war progressed that summer, Eaker's command recognized that a growing number of Strategic Air Forces fliers remained at large in the Balkans—as many as 1,100. Previously the Twelfth and Fifteenth Air Forces' escape and evasion sections had dealt with the situation as best they could, usually employing methods developed by the British. In January 1944 the OSS had dropped two officers into Partisan territory to meet with Tito and make arrangements. The meeting was eminently successful: Tito ordered Partisan units to cooperate with the Americans, especially with Lieutenant Eli Popovich, an engineer. He oversaw construction of a clandestine airfield north of Drvar in western Bosnia and Herzegovina. Other fields followed.[38]

Then in July, Eaker proposed to the Mediterranean Theater commander, General Maitland Wilson of Great Britain, that a unified airlift be established to return downed fliers to Allied control. He proposed a unit of perhaps twenty men, including medical personnel, to expedite their recovery. "It is clearly understood that the activities of this American unit will be non-diplomatic and non-military," Eaker wrote. "It will be devoted entirely to rescue purposes; its activities will be coordinated with the (RAF) Balkan Air Force." Eaker had consulted with Wilson's American deputy, General Jacob Devers, and diplomatic representatives, "all of whom agree with me that the project is feasible and necessary."[39]

Eaker's letter led to establishment of the Air Crew Recovery Unit (ACRU) at Bari, reporting to MAAF headquarters but administered by Twining's command. Thus began Operation Halyard. Most of the airlift was provided by a C-47 group from XII Troop Carrier Command, but coordination between the two air forces generally was efficient.

Eaker's handpicked leader of ACRU was a remarkable officer. Colonel George Kraigher had flown for Serbia in the Great War, later worked for Pan American Airways, and helped establish Pan Am's wartime African service. Because of his ties to the Partisans, he narrowly escaped capture when Germans attacked Tito's headquarters in May 1944. He and the marshal piled onto a C-47 flown by a Russian crew, alighting at Bari to continue the war.[40]

Airfield construction was key to the operation. Lacking heavy equipment, the Yugoslavs used hand tools and ox-drawn wagons. Usually working at night, the guerrillas downed trees, leveled terrain, and provided security. That summer there were sixteen or more landing strips in Partisan territory, each capable of handling C-47 Skytrain transports.

Halyard quickly became a multinational operation, involving the Army Air Force and OSS; major Yugoslav factions; the Royal Air Force and Special Operations Executive, as well as American rangers. Coordination was essential, so communication was at a premium. Reliable radio contact between OSS field teams and Bari was established in August, and thereafter the ACRU became increasingly active. From early August to late December, the ACRU flew seven evacuation missions from three Chetnik-controlled airstrips in Serbia and Bosnia, mostly from Pranjani. Of the 417 evacuees, 351 were AAF and RAF personnel.[41]

In August, however, the Allies formally recognized Tito as leader of the Yugoslavian resistance and dissociated themselves from Mihailović. Throughout most of the rescue period Twining recommended that aircrews opt for Partisan rather than Chetnik areas, as there was greater opportunity for rescue and evacuation in areas under Tito's control. But at least a few fliers had semantic problems. One B-17 gunner, looking down at the Bulgarian mountains, declared, "If we have to bail out I sure hope we find some of them Protestants."[42]

A Fifteenth man who spent two weeks with the Partisans described his experience with a co-ed guerrilla force:

> Nobody thought anything about it. They are all considered
> soldiers together and all are governed by the same strict

rules. While you're fighting as far as sex is concerned—
absolutely nothing doing. If a fellow disobeys and gets a
girl in a family way they just take him out and shoot him.

One of the cutest Partisan girls I met was a soldier girl
who came to one of the parties they threw for us. It was a
party every night after we got into safer territory. She had
killed I don't know how many Germans and so they had
made her a lieutenant. She wasn't sixteen yet.[43]

By October 2, 6,941 Allied airmen had been evacuated from the
Balkans, including 1,088 from Yugoslavia, about three-quarters of
them from Partisan areas. Partisans in Slovenia returned 303 American
and nearly four hundred British fliers, along with others. As Twelfth
Air Force transports cycled in and out of Balkan airstrips the total of
AAF men returned from Yugoslavia alone grew to approximately
2,400.[44]

Not every downed flier was eager to return to Italy. The Thirty-
first Fighter Group's Fred Trafton was known as a free spirit, a flight
commander who "directed traffic" in combat. On April 23, two days
after making captain, he claimed three planes to make ace, but he was
downed and wounded. The New Hampshire flier was rescued by
Partisans including a female guerrilla who spoke no English but didn't
have to. Trafton later credited her with telepathic powers, and she
"took real good care of him." On two occasions Trafton was ordered
to board a C-47 taking Americans to Foggia, but he declined the offer
for obvious reasons. Finally, in late July, as his friends later noted,
"girlfriend or no girlfriend, third time was the charm."[45]

Not all downed airmen were flown to safety. Among the exceptions
was Tom Rowe, a Chicagoan with a troubled conscience. Though married with two daughters, he was unhappy wearing the uniform of a
doorman at the Palmer House. In 1942 his wife conceded that he should
exchange hotel livery for olive drab, so he enlisted in the army. His
ambition to become a paratrooper clashed with the needs of the service,

and he became an expert aircraft mechanic. That rating put him in the top turret of a B-24 as a flight engineer in the 461st Bomb Group at Cerignola. Upon arrival, Lieutenant Robert Crinkley's crew was told that the men should consider themselves already dead.

The crew's fourth mission was Blechhammer. On November 20, Crinkley's Liberator ate a load of flak and, separated from the group, diverted to Yugoslavia. After bailout the crew reassembled and was scooped up by Partisans. The Americans were granted an audience with Tito himself, who asked, "Did you bomb Berlin?" The fliers were trying to explain about Blechhammer when they were told that the marshal knew no other English.[46]

Unlike most fliers, who were airlifted to safety, Crinkley's men were succored by British operatives with a boat. Boarding the undersized yacht at Zara (today Zadar), the Americans had a scare when a cruiser passed close by during the night, but it turned out to be British. The clandestine boaters made port the next morning at Ancona, an RAF base. The fliers were impressed to note a bar complete with sofas but enjoyed the hospitality only briefly before being flown to Bari. Tom Rowe was treated for a flak splinter in a leg but recovered to join another crew and, wounded again, completed his tour. At war's end he was in charge of military prisoners in a stockade previously run by a corrupt officer who used his position to work the black market.

By April 1945 there were thirty-six landing sites and 322 drop zones in Partisan areas, and at war's end some 125 ACRU personnel worked in Partisan territory. ACRU teams rescued 5,718 Fifteenth Air Force fliers from Yugoslavia and eleven other nations including northern Italy. It was a remarkable feat, representing one-fifth of all AAF fliers reported missing in the theater. Additionally, many of Tito's wounded were airlifted to Italy.[47]

The successful completion of Operation Halyard and related missions attracted little notice, even after V-E Day. But to thousands of Mediterranean Theater airmen, the clandestine airlifts from enemy territory represented salvation on angels' wings—even the olive-drab airfoils of Douglas C-47s.

CHAPTER SEVEN

AIR SUPREMACY

SEPTEMBER–DECEMBER 1944

Axis power withered in the Balkan heat that summer of 1944. Romania capitulated in August, Bulgaria in September. Internally fragmented, Slovakia was largely occupied by German forces in September. Only Hungary remained allied with Germany until the following spring.

As summer waned, morale rose in the Fifteenth Air Force, especially with the retrieval of lost friends. In mid-September the Forty-seventh Bomb Wing launched Operation Freedom, the return of some combat crewmen from captivity in Bulgaria.

Though a member of the Axis, Bulgaria had maintained relations with Moscow. The Soviet conquest of Romania, however, placed Russian troops on the Bulgarian border, and Stalin declared war on September 5. Unable to oppose the Red Army, Sofia forsook the Axis three days later in favor of an alliance with Moscow.

There was little understanding in the West of Bulgarian sympathy for Russia. Within living memory—the late 1870s—czarist armies had driven Ottoman occupiers from Bulgaria, freeing the nation after 475 years of Turkish rule, setting the stage for full independence in 1908.

When the Russians overran Bulgaria that summer, the Fifteenth Air Force immediately laid plans to retrieve some three hundred men from captivity. It was a smaller operation than the rescue of Allied personnel from Romania but still required logistical support. Planning for Operation Freedom was conducted at Bari, mainly under Colonel Reuben Kyle, the Forty-seventh Wing chief of staff.

Despite the distances involved, Kyle accepted British assistance in Africa. His planners organized an interim airlift to Egypt before returning the former prisoners to Italy. On September 15 Kyle led six B-24s from each of the wing's four groups to Cairo. He took along seven correspondents and photographers to cover what promised to be an emotional event.

In Cairo the liberated men were processed for return to Italy. They were deloused, issued fresh clothing, and received medical exams. The wing historians recorded, "The best food was spread out for them, but all of these failed entirely to eliminate from their faces telltale lines of suffering and long imprisonment."

After two days in Egypt, the evacuees traveled by ambulance to the flight line, where they climbed aboard the Liberators. Observers noted an aura of solemnity rather than joy. "Though they were going home, it was hard for these men to forget the mistreatment, the illness and the unmentionable filth of their prison camps in Bulgaria. Some were too sick to be moved; others were placed aboard on litters and others hobbled."[1]

Landing in Italy, the survivors gaped at their reception: Lieutenant General Twining and wing commander Brigadier General Hugo Rush amid photographers, reporters, bands, and Red Cross personnel, along with hundreds of AAF well wishers. "Repatriation of these prisoners was considered a personal triumph by the Forty-seventh Wing," said the history. "Their incessant bombing which paved the way for the Russian victory was rewarded with the rich prize of seeing some of their old buddies again, safe and on their way home to civilization."[2]

With Romania in Russian hands and the Ploesti campaign at an end, most of the Luftwaffe was removed. After June, only two groups of JG 77 remained in Italy and the Eastern Mediterranean, and one group of JG 53 remained in Hungary. Hungarian fighters and Fascist Italy's remaining units augmented the Luftwaffe but not enough to affect the Fifteenth. The attrition charts at Bari reflected the reduced fighter opposition. From 171 aircraft lost to enemy action in August (the fourth-highest monthly total of the war), the Fifteenth's known combat losses dropped to sixty-eight in September. Bomber losses to Axis fighters almost disappeared, dropping from ninety-one in August to seven in September. The near absence of aerial combat meant that Twining's airmen mainly faced antiaircraft fire, everything from 20mm automatic weapons up to 105mm artillery. In the last four months of 1944, the Fifteenth lost twenty-one bombers and fighters to enemy aircraft but 339 to antiaircraft guns.[3]

✪ ✪ ✪

As the Germans withdrew from the Balkans, Allied airpower concentrated on communications targets in order to impede the retreat. On September 2 the Fifteenth lost ten fighters over Yugoslavia, including seven Lightnings from the First and Fourteenth Groups. It was the third-highest one-day toll of fighters during the war—all lost to ground fire.

The First Group lost two pilots near Belgrade, but Lieutenant Arthur Hoodecheck evaded. The Fourteenth lost two, including Lieutenant William T. Church, flying his seventy-fourth mission. The squadron diarist commented, "Fine fellow. We are down to nine P-38Js now."[4]

The reason for the shortage was ordinary attrition and aircraft stranded after the shuttle missions. Pilots were flown to Russia to fetch the Lightnings back to Triolo, while other fliers were ferried to Britain to obtain replacement aircraft.

The Thirty-firsters launched a devastating attack on rail, road, and river traffic on September 2. They began with all three squadrons sweeping in line abreast—a wall of noise blending the authoritative moan of Merlins under high power with perhaps eighty machine guns per squadron pounding half-inch bullets into Axis steel. The group left three P-51s behind after busting thirty locomotives, two dozen trucks, and assorted transport, including barges. The Mustang jockeys also downed an unfortunate pair of Junkers transport planes that crossed their path.

Many fighter pilots relished "loco busting," as nearly all European locomotives were steam-driven until the 1950s. The explosive effects of .50 caliber on steam engines were far more satisfying to pilots than catching a rare diesel train "that just sort of died on the track."[5]

✪ ✪ ✪

Meanwhile the bomber war progressed, with occasional diversions courtesy of the enemy. Before an early September mission, fliers at Celone Airfield were enjoying "Axis Sally," the turncoat American broadcaster from Maine. Mildred Gillars had come to Germany in 1934 seeking career opportunities in broadcasting or music and decided to stay with her fiancé when the war began. While covering the 1936 Berlin Olympics she had met Frank A. Kurtz, an American who had won an Olympic bronze in swimming in 1932. Now he was Colonel Kurtz, the stern and capable commander of the 463rd Bomb Group, which was the sixth and last B-17 unit to join the Fifteenth, beginning operations at the end of March.

One of the group's navigators was a twenty-year-old Minnesotan, Robert C. Clemens, who had arrived in Italy that June. Years later he recalled, "In early September I flew Fifth Wing lead with Colonel Kurtz. We listened to Sally's broadcasts because she played the latest popular music of the era. That day she broadcast that the Germans knew where we were going to bomb (Budapest) and they would shoot down Frank Kurtz 'and that young, pink-faced navigator from Minnesota.'"[6]

On September 5 the group put twenty-eight B-17s over the target with poor results, but Sally's threat proved hollow: all 463rd aircraft returned to base. It was one of Kurtz's last missions, as he completed his tour a week later. In March 1945 he took command of Kirtland Air Base, a B-29 training facility near Albuquerque. It was a more important assignment than it appeared: Kirtland provided operational support for an undertaking called the Manhattan Project.[7]

"BLACK HAMMER"

After Ploesti dropped off the target list, Fifteenth bombers spread their ordnance across other petroleum facilities throughout the Reich. That fall a frequent destination was Blechhammer (which Allied fliers nicknamed "Black Hammer"—not a translation, as the name actually means "sheet metal hammer"), some 160 miles north-northeast of Vienna (in western Poland today). It was a long mission—1,260 miles round-trip from Foggia.

Divided into two large compounds designated Blechhammer North and South, the complex reportedly had the potential to produce half a million tons of synthetic oil annually. It had first been struck in June, then with increasing frequency. Defended by one hundred or more heavy antiaircraft guns, Blechhammer began taking a steady toll of Fifteenth bombers.

The Fifth Wing returned on September 13 while Liberators hammered other petro-targets, including Odertal and Auschwitz. Twenty-five bombers had been lost already at Blechhammer, including a dozen B-17s, so the Fortress crews knew what to expect.

Nine heavies went down that Wednesday, the hardest hit group being the veteran Ninety-seventh, which lost five planes.

Flying a nearly new B-17G was First Lieutenant Bruce D. Knoblock, a twenty-eight-year-old Wisconsin native. On the bomb run, navigator Lieutenant Leon Cooning, flying his twenty-fourth mission, exclaimed, "Look at that damned flak!" The sky was speckled with bursts—the proverbial get-out-and-walk-on-it variety.

One of the waist gunners was Sergeant William N. Hess, a young Louisianan flying his eleventh mission (sixteenth credit) with the 340th Squadron. He had joined the crew at age eighteen and, because he looked even younger, he became known as "Junior." On the Blechhammer mission he had just turned nineteen. He was unhappy that he had been issued a worn, dirty parachute pack because his regular chute was being repacked. Ordinarily he let his pack dangle by one snap from his harness but now he left the replacement on the floor, doubting that he would need it. An 88mm battery put a shell into the sweet spot, hitting one Fortress in the bomb bay. The squadron was carrying RDX bombs that day, a more volatile explosive than TNT. The flak shell detonated the ordnance in one of the three Flying Fortresses in Hess's flight. The B-17 evaporated in the explosion and crippled two others in the formation.

Later there was speculation that the group's high squadron dropped bombs on the low squadron, but it is unlikely that the bombs would have fused in time to produce a huge explosion. Whatever the direct cause, two of the three planes in the flight were quickly lost, one with no survivors, the other with five.

In the exposed left waist position, Bill Hess was knocked unconscious by the fragments and concussion. While struggling to keep the plane level, Knoblock called for an intercom check. One of the gunners said, "Junior's dead, sir."

Knoblock turned easterly, hoping to reach Soviet forces in Romania. But after perhaps a hundred miles the crippled Boeing gave out.

The pilot rang the bailout bell and the crew began abandoning ship. By then Hess had regained consciousness but he was still dazed. When he raised himself from the aluminum floor the steel plates fell from his shredded flak vest, and he noticed his helmet on the deck with a fist-sized dent. He picked up his dirty replacement chute, snapped it to his harness, and staggered to an exit. Followed by the copilot, he grasped his rip cord and leapt into space.

Hess descended to earth southeast of Krakow, alighting in a small wooded area with deep ditches running throughout. They provided welcome cover, as he heard the buzzing whine of supersonic objects snapping overhead. Some German soldiers had seen his parachute and, with a rough idea of his location, began taking long-range pot shots. After all, ammunition was cheap and plentiful, and diversions few.

The Louisiana teenager ducked and dodged through the trees, making good progress away from the threat. Then, in reduced visibility, he walked into three men wearing gray. They wore coalscuttle helmets and carried Mauser rifles. Bill Hess was a prisoner.

Two of Knoblock's crewmembers evaded. The radioman, specially trained to monitor German frequencies, got away clean. The copilot, reportedly with only one mission behind him, had beginner's luck. He fetched up with a heroic Polish family willing to conceal the American, but he got cabin fever. After three months he wandered into town and was scooped up.[8]

END OF THE AMERICAN SUMMER

1944 was the year of the "American summer" in Hungary, though the Fifteenth Air Force, flying from Foggia, was also known as "the Italians." In September Twining's bombers struck Budapest and related targets eight times, prompting the Hungarian Air Force to expand the Puma fighter group into a wing totaling six squadrons. Hungary's limited assets were focused eastward against the Soviets, however, and Magyar Messerschmitts engaged American aircraft only five times from September through early November.

The Hungarians benefited from radar warning of U.S. formations coming from Italy and did not take off until the attackers crossed the Yugoslavian border. Climbing away from the raiders to gain precious height, the Messerschmitts relied on ground controllers to vector them onto the "Italians." A Bf 109 pilot, Lieutenant Mihaly Karatsonyi, was credited with five American aircraft that summer, but he recalled, "I could see the handwriting on the wall and I knew we were going to lose the war when I watched helplessly as over 1,200 American bombers and fighters flew over Hungary. What were we to do with only forty of us in our tired old Me 109s? It was the beginning of the end for the Pumas during that dreadful summer of 1944."[9]

After Romania's capitulation most of Twining's Lightnings flew dive-bombing and strafing missions, but the Hungarians remained wary. "The P-38s were well respected by us because of its tremendous combination of four .50 caliber machine guns and one 20mm cannon in its nose," Karatsonyi explained. "We adopted a hit-and-run tactic with the Lightnings because if you stuck around and tried to fight them, you might end up outmaneuvering two or three, but there were always a dozen more lurking in the shadows, waiting to latch onto your tail."[10]

On October 12, in dogfights around Lake Balaton, the Red Tails' 302nd Squadron claimed nine kills, three by First Lieutenant Lee Archer, while the 52nd and 325th Groups downed nine more. The Checkertails and Red Tails each lost a P-51, both credited to Hungarians. Thereafter Fifteenth aircrews rarely saw a white-crossed Messerschmitt, as Balkan aerial combat diminished to almost zero.

OCTOBER FLAK

On October 13 the Fifteenth put up two aerial task forces: 620 Liberators to Vienna and 250 Fortresses against Blechhammer, screened by a total of some four hundred fighters. The Americans lost thirty-two planes, including six fighters shooting up railroads. All the losses were attributable to flak or ground fire, as only a handful of FW 190s engaged, and they never bothered the bombers. It was Twining's biggest loss since Vienna in late June, and rarely again did the opposition down twenty planes in a day.

As Axis fortunes waned that fall, the Germans withdrew additional forces from the farther reaches of their empire. The situation cut both ways for Allied airmen—they enjoyed greater latitude on the peripheries but faced more concentrated air defenses in the Reich itself, especially antiaircraft fire.

One of the legendary weapons of the Second World War was Germany's fabled 88mm antiaircraft gun, which doubled as a fearsome tank killer. "Flak" was Teutonic shorthand for *Flugzeugabwehrkanone*. In its most common form, the Flak 36/37 (first deployed in 1936 and 1937) fired a twenty-pound shell as high as thirty-five thousand feet. Its bursting radius of thirty feet could kill or cripple a four-engine aircraft. The improved Flak 41, appearing in 1943, was produced in modest numbers (556 versus 20,754 for the Flak 18/36/37) and used only in Germany.

Deployed in four-gun batteries, the 88s fired "pattern barrages" of rectangular boxes into the path of a bomber formation. With one of the guns tracking the targets by optical predictor or by radar, the others easily duplicated the readout on each mount. The aiming problem was solved by an exercise in spatial geometry based on known values: target height and speed, initial velocity of the shell (2,700 to 3,000 feet per second), and time of flight to the desired altitude. After that, the exercise evolved from marksmanship to probability theory.

The gun's design was optimized for a high rate of fire: upon discharge the recoil stroke automatically opened the breech, ejected the empty casing, and cocked the gun. The loader dropped the next round into the loading tray, slammed the breech shut, and stood ready for the next round. The assistant loaders kept a conga line of grunting, sweating soldiers passing the ammunition, if not quite praising the Lord like their storied Allied counterparts.

A well-drilled gun crew of ten to twelve could sustain fifteen rounds per minute—one shell every four seconds. Expert crews approached twenty rounds in sixty seconds. It took anywhere from four thousand to nearly twenty thousand shells to down a bomber. Fortunately for Allied airmen, the Germans never perfected proximity fuses, which detonated a shell when the miniature transmitter sensed a target. Otherwise, kill ratios would have improved even more.[11]

The other heavy antiaircraft weapons were the 105mm Flak 38/39 and 128mm Flak 40, together accounting for some 5,300 tubes between 1939 and 1945. The latter were especially effective, rated at three thousand rounds per bomber kill, as opposed to about fifteen thousand for 88s.[12]

Axis fighters posed the greatest threat to the Fifteenth during its first eight months. But from June 1944 onward, flak took an increasing toll: throughout the year the Fifteenth Air Force attributed nearly seven hundred bomber losses to enemy fighters and 950 to AA guns.[13]

The Germans' success in downing Allied bombers, however, came at immense cost. That summer the Luftwaffe flak arm deployed 662,000 troops and nearly half a million auxiliaries, including old men, boys, women, and even fifty thousand Russian POWs—in all, more than one-third of the Luftwaffe's 2,890,000 personnel.[14]

✪ ✪ ✪

The bombing campaign received most of the attention, but other Mediterranean operations continued apace, including the little known Operation Manna. From October 14 to 16, the Eighty-second Fighter Group escorted six British missions against Megara Airdrome, west of Athens. It was a truly joint operation, conducted by the RAF Balkan Air Force and Twelfth Air Force troop carriers, with Fifteenth Air Force fighters.

On the sixteenth a low ceiling forced the C-47s towing Waco gliders to fly below two thousand feet, affording the P-38 pilots a close-up view of a rare sight. But there was an exception. Lieutenant Roy Norris's lucky number was eighty-two: he had been a glider infantryman in the Eighty-second Airborne Division before going to flight training and on to the Eighty-second Fighter Group. He recalled,

> After the "gooney" birds and gliders had landed, our group proceeded west, to an island to land for refueling. [The island was Vis, forty miles off the Croatian coast, a sometime Tito headquarters.] Now, knowing of this refueling stop, I had placed all my ration cigarettes on the right side of the cockpit. They covered the emergency hydraulic pump and valve. On landing each P-38 was positioned next to several 55 gallon drums, which contained gasoline. The pilot was to fill the tanks while a man hand pumped from the drums. This man wore an open shirt and shorts made from burlap! His shoes were in shreds. With no place to trade my cigarettes, I gave them to the man. The British officer in charge of the refueling "chewed" me out, something fierce! He said, "I made this man rich!" After refueling, we flew back to Vincencio, our home base.[15]

A LONG WAY TO DEFECT

There was another "joint operation" at about the same time, though certainly unsanctioned. It involved the only American pilot to defect to the enemy in World War II, and he took the long way round the world to do it.

First Lieutenant Martin J. Monti, age twenty-three, was raised in a large Catholic family in St. Louis by an Italian father and German mother. Before the war he was heavily influenced by Father Charles

Coughlin, the "radio priest," who developed a large isolationist, anti-Communist audience.

After receiving his army wings as a flight officer, Monti was commissioned and sent to the China-Burma-India Theater. But he deserted from Karachi, hitchhiked to Egypt, and arrived at the Foggia complex in October 1944. From there he got to Pomigliano north of Naples, where he passed himself off as an Eighty-second Group pilot. He cadged a photo-recon Lightning from a service squadron and flew north to a small field near Milan, under Fascist Italian control. He landed and announced his intention of joining the Wehrmacht to fight the Soviets. At first the Germans were understandably skeptical of the defector. But he convinced his new allies of his desire to join the crusade against communism and became a propaganda broadcaster known as "Martin Wiethaupt." Furthermore, he enrolled in the SS as an *Untersturmführer*, equivalent to second lieutenant.

After V-E Day Monti surrendered in his black SS uniform. Tried for desertion in 1946, he received a sentence of fifteen years at hard labor but gained a parole in just one year with the peculiar condition that he re-enlist. He had worked his way up to sergeant in 1948 when the FBI learned of his collaboration in disseminating Nazi propaganda. He stood trial for treason and was sentenced to twenty-five years. Like most wartime criminals, he was released early and gained a parole in 1960. He died in 2000, not quite eighty.[16]

THE SECOND WINTER AT WAR

The Foggia rainy season began in mid-September, but the next month brought serious problems. Veterans of the winter of 1943–1944 knew what to expect. Heavy, persistent rain canceled many missions, and on others the pilots struggled up through low cloud decks, seeking clear air between layers. All too often the fliers encountered solid clouds, sometimes extending above the operational ceiling of their aircraft.

In October the Fifteenth Air Force issued minimum requirements for the winterization of tents. Each tent floor was to be covered with brick, tile, lumber, or gravel, with walls of adobe-like "tufti," or lumber, at least eighteen inches above ground level. Wing commanders had discretion over uniforms, and most, like Colonel William L. Lee of the Forty-ninth Wing, issued woolens to replace khakis. Supply ran behind demand, however, and weeks passed before all enlisted men received the heavier uniforms.[17]

Though the Fifteenth had been operating at full strength since May, some adjustments were made that fall. In October, Brigadier General Charles Born, formerly Twining's operations officer, became deputy commander of the Fifteenth. Simultaneously, Brigadier General James A. Mollison took over XV Air Service Command.

Also in October, Brigadier General Dean Strother established XV Fighter Command, an arrangement similar to the Eighth's. He turned over the 306th Wing to Brigadier General Yantis H. Taylor, who now ran the four Mustang groups, while Colonel William R. Morgan took the three Lightning groups in the new, subordinate 305th Wing at Torremaggiore. It made sense. With different logistic and maintenance requirements, the Mustang and Lightning groups benefited from having their own administrative echelons. The new command structure lasted until war's end.

FIGHTERS IN THE FALL

The hunting thinned out for Mediterranean fighter groups, which officially claimed 151 aerial kills in August. The next four months produced a total of only 150.[18] The era of the ace was ending. The Fifteenth never developed the kind of "ace race" that characterized the Eighth, but the top guns kept score nevertheless. The Checkertail Clan's Major Herky Green held the lead with eighteen victories (three before joining the Fifteenth) when he rotated to Bari headquarters in September. Close behind was the Fifty-second Group's best shooter,

Captain John Varnell, with seventeen victories in nine weeks from late May to early August. He was hot, scoring twelve of his kills in just five encounters. Twenty-two years old, he jumped from second lieutenant to captain in about six weeks. He also ended his tour in September. Among those left in combat, the leader was Captain John Voll of the Thirty-first, with thirteen black crosses on his Mustang. He still had combat time remaining.

✪ ✪ ✪

Losses to Axis fighters nearly dropped off the chart: some groups flew fifteen missions or more during October without sighting a single enemy aircraft. But flak remained potent. On the October 4 mission to Munich, for instance, the sixteen attacking bomb groups lost fifteen planes. Hardest hit was the 461st, which put twenty-six Liberators over the marshalling yard at 23,700 feet. During the bomb run, Munich's practiced flak gunners shot seven planes out of formation, but the remainder performed superbly, dropping 70 percent of their bombs within a thousand feet of the aim point. It was one of the finest performances ever recorded in the Mediterranean Theater. Lieutenant Colonel Philip R. "Spike" Hawes led the survivors back to Toretta, where ground crews noted damage to all nineteen planes.

Despite the general disappearance of Axis fighters, the skies could still hold surprises. Escorting bombers to Munich on October 29, the Eighty-second Group's Ninety-fifth Squadron picked up an apparent straggler, a single P-51B. The olive-drab Mustang sidled up to the Lightnings, whose pilots were unconcerned, as sometimes P-51s flew a roving escort, though almost never solo. "He appeared to be just a friendly P-51 pilot, rather lonely,"[19] reported one of the pilots.

After breaking escort the Lightning pilots descended to ground level to expend their ammunition in strafing. One P-38 had taken hits and was limping outbound on one engine, accompanied by five others. First Lieutenant Eldon Coulson and his wingman assumed high cover, protecting the other four from a "bounce" from above. The mystery

Mustang suddenly reappeared, southeast of Linz, but it was no longer passive. It approached as if making a gunnery pass, so Coulson and his partner turned into the stranger. The P-51 broke off but returned for more runs. Each time the P-38s met the apparent threat.

Finally the Mustang emerged from low clouds, tracking toward the damaged Lightning. Coulson called, "Here comes that Mustang again!" The interloper was closer than before, pressing its run. Then it opened fire from ridiculously long range—perhaps four thousand feet. Coulson reacted immediately. He tracked the offender in his sight and pressed the button for all four machine guns and the 20mm cannon. In a beautiful full deflection shot, the armor-piercing incendiary rounds flickered and flashed the length of the Mustang's fuselage, knocking it into a spin. The P-51 crashed, inverted, in a fireball on a mountainside.

Back at base, Coulson was closely questioned over a couple of rough days. Headquarters finally confirmed that there were no friendly losses for the time and place of his encounter with the mystery Mustang, and he was awarded an official victory. "Also, intelligence reported there may be two or three more P-51s the Germans might be using, and for us to keep on guard."[20]

Fighting enemy-flown American aircraft was one thing. But the unpredictability of war could take events in another direction entirely.

A NOVEMBER TO REMEMBER

Unlike the Eighth Air Force, which allotted two Mickey aircraft to each B-24 group, the Fifteenth adopted an "all or nothing" approach in 1944. "Red Force" units received four radar pathfinders and flew most missions against major industrial targets. "Blue Force" units generally bombed visually, attacking targets closer to home. By one analysis, Twining's crews did better radar bombing than their RAF counterparts, recording an average miss distance of two miles. Thus, the Fifteenth B-24s were doing "twice as well or half as poor."[21]

That fall Twining also began sending as few as three Liberators to precision targets in poor weather. For instance, selected crews from each squadron of the 464th Group were trained at night, employing "Mickey" gear in preparation for daylight blind bombing. Standing orders prohibited the Mickeys from bombing in clear skies, to preserve valuable assets.

The group's first such operation was flown November 3, despite heavy rain, against a rail yard in Munich. First Lieutenant August Lechner's crew was first off that morning, with two others departing at ten-minute intervals. Climbing into a frigid sky, Lechner's B-24 acquired a coating of ice while penetrating two fronts before getting "on top" at twenty-two thousand feet. Upon reaching the initial point, the fliers nervously looked for the Luftwaffe. Munich inevitably put up a strong defense, but not so much as a flak burst marred the air. Copilot Donald Baker even wondered if the navigator's dead reckoning was accurate. The radar bombardier toggled his load in unaccustomed serenity. Then the rear gunner opened up on the intercom. The second Liberator, a mile or so astern, was flogging its way through a maelstrom of flak. Lechner and Baker realized that, being first over the target in uncommonly bad weather, they had surprised the defenders. The 464th logged two more Mickey special missions that month, and several more before V-E Day.[22]

Around the same time, a respected opponent left the scene. One of the Fifteenth's last encounters with Hungarians occurred on November 5, when some 720 bombers screened by 335 fighters converged on the Florisdorf refinery in northern Vienna—the greatest effort the Fifteenth had yet launched against a single target. Elements of six Luftwaffe fighter groups scrambled, but many were too late to intercept, leaving the defense to seven German and four Hungarian squadrons. The planes that could attain a favorable position tried to dent the massive force of some five hundred Liberators.

Three Hungarian Messerschmitt pilots claimed one B-24 each, while another collided with a Mustang. The raiders lost a total of five bombers and two fighters. But the Puma wing buried four Bf 109 pilots, the last casualties against "the Italians" from Foggia.

The American fighters notched ten kills, six by the Checkertails. On the withdrawal First Lieutenant Oscar Rau's flight leader jumped several 109s over Lake Balaton. In a prolonged rat race, "Ockie" Rau shot one bandit off his leader's tail then performed the same service for his wingman. Over the next twenty minutes he added two more to earn a Distinguished Service Cross in his only combat.

THE LEGEND OF CURLY EDWINSON

Colonel Clarence T. Edwinson commanded the Eighty-second, one of three P-38 Lighting fighter groups in the Fifteenth Air Force. The thirty-two-year-old flier had been a standout athlete at Washburn College in Kansas, where he was compared to the legendary Red Grange as a running back. Winged in 1936, Edwinson became an instructor and later served as an observer in England during the Battle of Britain. He flew in Alaska before assuming command of the Eighty-second in August 1944, unusually experienced with nearly four thousand flying hours.

On November 6 the group supported a Soviet advance in eastern Yugoslavia. The first day's mission went well, and the Russians asked for a repeat performance the next day. The Eighty-second teamed with the First—124 Lightnings strafing briefed objectives and targets of opportunity around Yugoslavia. In the target area, one squadron of the Eighty-second jumped on a motor convoy, destroying several vehicles, and though a P-38 fell to flak, the badly injured pilot was rescued by Partisans.

Leading his twenty-seventh mission, Edwinson then took most of two squadrons to shoot up some locomotives and another truck column. Almost immediately the top-cover pilots spotted unidentified aircraft taking off from Nis, about sixty miles from the Romanian border. The erstwhile strafers crammed on full power, clawing for altitude. So did the single-engine fighters from Nis, variously identified as 109s, 190s, or Spitfires. One of them abruptly pulled up and fired at the trailing P-38. The Lightning crashed and exploded, killing Lieutenant Phil Brewer. Lieutenant Kenneth Katschke rolled in, drew a bead on the assailant, and fired. His aim was good: the hostile fighter went down spinning. Just before it crashed Katschke glimpsed the insignia—a red star.

The Eighty-second Group was fighting Russians.

Other P-38 pilots also recognized their opponents as Yakovlev fighters and hollered a radio warning. But some of the Soviets remained aggressive, and when one shot at a Lightning, Lieutenant John Blumer flamed it. The fight continued unabated, two more Yaks dropping away. Another Lighting pilot was killed—Lieutenant Sid Coulson, who had downed a German-flown Mustang barely a week before.

Lieutenant Tom Urton got a Russian's attention by wagging his wings in a don't-shoot gesture. Some of the Yaks repeated the motion. Meanwhile, Curly Edwinson's flight had its own set-to, sparring with an aggressive Russian. Following some spirited maneuvering, a Lighting pilot gained position and hosed the Yak with machine gun and cannon fire. It made off trailing smoke. Finally Edwinson and the Soviet leader sidled up to each other, wagging wings. The Russian was Captain Aleksandr Koldunov, a twenty-one-year old Hero of the Soviet Union. The fight had ended.

Back home at Vincenzo, pandemonium reigned. An international incident had to be explained. Soon an explanation emerged: the Lightnings had attacked some fifty miles from the briefed target, mistaking one valley for another. After shooting up the first convoy, the P-38s had attacked a second. They destroyed some twenty vehicles and killed several Russians, including a general.

Three Lightnings had been lost—one to flak—and three Yaks had gone down with two pilots dead. The loss of a Russian corps commander drew a furious response from Moscow. The Soviets demanded that the U.S. chiefs of staff "severely punish those responsible." A rumor circulated that the American flight leader was to be executed.[23]

The geopolitical fallout was predictable. A secret report issued by Mediterranean Allied Force Headquarters on November 25 quoted Eaker's preliminary investigation, which went to the Joint Chiefs in Washington and to Major General John R. Deane, head of the U.S. Military Mission to Moscow. The summary stated in part, "The request for the strafing came through Balkan Air Force, based on the needs for air effort to trap and destroy the Germans trying to move north through Yugoslavia. Two groups of P-38s of the 15th AAF were assigned to the strafing; all squadrons except one strafed the assigned area."[24]

The summary stated that between August 18 and November 7, the Fifteenth had flown thirty-seven missions supporting Soviet units and guerrilla forces in Yugoslavia and Hungary without untoward incidents. Eaker's report, clearly sympathetic to Edwinson, noted the colonel's extensive flying experience while emphasizing the difficulty of low-level navigation at high speed over numerous valleys. The Soviet column was only ten or twelve minutes, for a P-38, from the intended target. "There is a startling similarity," the report noted,

> between the map appearance of the briefed target and the actual target strafed. (Map used was British 1 to 500000 Europe Air Shkedra (Scutari) sheet corrected through January 1942.)
>
> Upon return to base the top cover leader was equally as positive as to the identification of the point where strafing began and only when gun camera film was developed did it become established that the wrong road had been attacked. The respective roads are roughly 55 miles apart.
>
> All pilots will readily understand how even one as experienced as Colonel Edwinson, flying on the deck in such

rugged country, under frequent flak attack as he was, could make a mistake of 10 minutes in navigation.[25]

After three months in command, Curly Edwinson was hastily transferred stateside, where his career proceeded unimpeded.

✪ ✪ ✪

On November 16 the Thirty-first Group's John Voll was a twenty-two-year-old captain. He had tied Sully Varnell's seventeen-victory record and was one behind the 325th's Herky Green, who had been transferred to Twining's operations staff.

The red-striped Mustangs found little opposition during the escort to Munich, and Voll turned back with radio trouble. Alone ten miles southeast of Aviano, he spotted a Ju 88 on a reciprocal heading, dived, and gave chase. The Junkers was fast, but the Mustang was faster, and Voll reeled it in. But before it splashed, the bomber obviously hollered for help. When he glanced up, Voll saw a mixed formation of black-crossed fighters, 109s and 190s. The fight was on.

For the next five minutes John Voll fought for his life. He had three things going for him: his cool head, his hot hands, and a Mustang named *American Beauty*. The Germans outnumbered him twelve to one, but they got in each other's way, offering the Ohio triple ace repeated opportunities. In a hard-fought, gut-wrenching combat, he hit eight, being certain of two Focke-Wulfs and a Messerschmitt.

When he landed at San Severo, the young veteran threw up from the delayed release of tension. Then he slid off the wing, dropping to his hands and knees, wracked by dry heaves. Voll was credited with four destroyed, two probables, and two damaged, the last time he scored. He flew *American Beauty* the last time in December and rotated home, the Mediterranean Theater's ace of aces with twenty-one kills.

That month the Thirty-first's new commanding officer was Lieutenant Colonel William A. Daniel, a thirty-year-old Tennessee flier. In an accelerated rise typical of wartime, he had been promoted from captain to major to lieutenant colonel in barely a year. A career fighter pilot, he had arrived in April with an exceptional 2,900 hours flight time. After eight months with the group staff he moved into the top slot. His subordinates were nevertheless well disposed: pilots valued up-front leaders, nurturing the good ones and sometimes ignoring the others.

Billy Daniel was a good one: short and slight with a perennial grin, as if he knew something was about to happen, and the troops quickly took to their pipe-smoking CO. Despite his experience, however, he had trouble getting on the score board. One of the squadron commanders, burly Captain Sam Brown, took him under his wing. He got results. Daniel bagged two Bf 109s on a late May mission, adding one each in June and July. Newly promoted to full colonel in March 1945, he made ace the hard way: downing a jet late that month.

DECEMBER DENOUEMENT

As the year ended, the Fifteenth's fighters were sent on more and more ground-attack missions. The Mustang groups occasionally pulled off some spectacular strafing, as when the Checkertails claimed sixty-three "grounders" in Serbia on September 8 and thirty-seven in western Hungary on October 21.

P-38s were flying more dive-bombing missions, leaving much of the escort work to Mustangs. The Lightning carried a good load—two thousand-pounders on occasion. Lieutenant Gale Mortensen of the Fourteenth Group said, "You wanted to start high enough to look around but you couldn't get too steep because the P-38 accelerated pretty fast." A high dive speed meant unpleasant G loads on pullout—often more than six times the force of gravity. The navy's purpose-built bombers typically dived at seventy degrees, but they had speed brakes to retard airspeed. Not until the L model did Lockheed provide dive recovery flaps.[26] In dive-bombing, most misses were "short" or "long" rather than left or right, so pilots had to experiment until they found the technique that worked best for them. One flier said of dive-bombing, "Easier than I thought with no flak coming up."[27]

✪ ✪ ✪

By mid-December 1944, the Luftwaffe was so scarce that intelligence officers were hard-pressed to cover the enemy fighter portion of mission briefings. For the strikes against the Odertal and Blechhammer refineries on the seventeenth, aircrews were told to expect "no more than fifteen single-engine aircraft in the area, flown by students from a local operational training unit."[28] Contrary to expectations, however, the Forty-ninth Wing encountered unusually heavy fighter opposition—the Luftwaffe would defend its fuel sources even if other targets were left unprotected. Flying against Odertal, the 461st Group was partly dispersed in heavy weather with just five of twenty-six planes reaching the target. South of the initial point, the main formation was struck by an estimated fifty 109s and 190s. They were from Lieutenant Colonel Walther Dahl's JG 300, trained in all-weather flying and based in central Germany to reinforce Reich air defense where most needed.

The timing could hardly have been worse for the Americans. Because of the distance flown, the B-24s' ball turrets were on "standby" status to reduce drag and save fuel, rather than lowered into position ready to fight, depriving the formation of one-fifth of its defensive firepower. They also had to do without the ball turrets' gyroscopic lead-computing sights, the most accurate available on bombers.

In a fifteen-minute shootout, the group was subjected to 20mm fire and rockets. The intelligence officers' dismissive briefing notwithstanding, the Germans flew "skillfully, aggressively, and persistently." They attacked in pairs from the rear quarter with low breakaways. It was an effective tactic: with few ball turrets deployed, nine bombers were shot down and a tenth ditched in the Aegean, with nearly a hundred fliers killed or missing. The 461st gunners claimed two dozen shootdowns—probably not far off the mark—but the losses were staggering.[29]

The bombers had to drop through the undercast and couldn't see the results. As the depleted formation pulled away, Captain Marion C. Mixson checked the survivors when a German voice cackled in his earphones. Using the correct call sign, the Luftwaffe pilot taunted, "Where is the rest of your formation?" With that, he laughed and signed off.[30]

The Germans' glee was short lived. Though twenty heavies were lost to all causes during the day, the Thirty-first and Fifty-second Group Mustangs nosed through the weather to stampede all over the *Sturmflieger* and trample them in the Silesian dust, claiming twenty-eight destroyed while losing two. On the nearby Blechhammer mission, Fourteenth Group Lightnings bagged five for three pilots captured. In all, Jagdgeschwader 300 wrote off forty fighters with half the pilots killed and several wounded.[31]

The Odertal-Blechhammer mission sustained the worst losses to enemy fighters in the post-Ploesti period. The fifteen bombers hacked down by the armored Focke-Wulfs represented more than half the Fifteenth's casualties to interceptors for the last four months of 1944.

Yet another threat emerged on the return leg. The 485th Group overflew the "oil triangle" in southwestern Hungary, about 120 miles south of Vienna. Upon return to Venosa, Lieutenant Colonel John T. Atkinson told debriefers that six Liberators were damaged by exploding "rockets" fired from the ground while the formation cruised at twelve thousand feet. Ten days later a Second Group gunner, Sergeant Melvin McGuire, observed something similar over Wiener Neustadt. A guided surface-to-air missile (SAM) drew a bead on his B-17 but veered away, apparently after losing tracking.[32]

Both incidents might have involved the *Wasserfall* (waterfall) missile, arguably the only one of Germany's experimental high-altitude

SAMs that might have been operational. Twenty-six feet long and weighing four tons at launch, *Wasserfall* was propelled by a binary fuel to 1,700 miles per hour. With radio and radar guidance, its 520-pound warhead was expected to destroy or damage multiple bombers in a formation. However, the Luftwaffe abandoned its SAM program in early 1945 to concentrate on the proved Me 262 fighter and the low-tech He 162 jet interceptor.[33]

Acknowledging the growing threat, the AAF dispatched two new Lockheed fighters to Italy: sleek, futuristic P-80 Shooting Stars. Supported by Lockheed technicians, the Wright Field test pilots arrived in December 1944, flying their jets against First Group P-38s at Lesina to perfect tactics of prop fighters against Me 262s. The Shooting Stars cost about $110,000—big money in 1945 but not much more than a P-38.

✪ ✪ ✪

With few enemy fighters coming within shooting range of bombers, many groups began flying with one waist gunner instead of two. The nine-man crew exposed fewer airmen to the routine dangers of wartime flying than the ten-man crew did, but it saved only about 200 pounds—an inconsequential weight compared with the twenty-eight tons of a loaded Liberator.

The crew reduction was unpopular with gunners. The change not only broke up close-knit teams, with the waist gunners alternating missions, but it extended the period to complete a combat tour. Aerial gunners arriving in Italy that summer expected to finish their tours in as little as three months, but after the change it could take five or more, depending on the targets assigned. The elimination of double credit for Romanian missions also contributed to the extension.

Yet most crews remained tight, despite the inevitable differences in backgrounds. A 461st Group navigator had been a master brewer, studying in France and Germany before the war. When drafted, he was earning a fabulous salary: $25,000 per year (the equivalent of about $330,000 in 2013). In the same crew a waist gunner had been head of a garment workers' union and refused a commission, preferring to maintain solidarity with the proletariat.[34]

Enlisted men could not complain that officers avoided danger. Four of the ten men in a heavy bomber crew were officers. About half of the AAF personnel exposed to death or capture, including fighter pilots, were therefore officers. The historian Stephen Ambrose computed that more than twice as many air force officers were killed than in the rest of the army combined.[35]

LIVING THERE

Most of the Foggia complex had been subjected to heavy bombing when occupied by Italian and German forces. But American engineers had moved in and, with Yankee know-how, had transformed the rubble into useable facilities with astonishing speed and efficiency. Conditions steadily improved, and by the fall of 1944 the muddy, semi-primitive airfields of late 1943 had been transformed. Tents were heated with an avgas-fueled barrel. Then wood frames with a tent top replaced all-canvas enclosures, with four men per tent.

The Americans ate more bread and pasta, and enlisted men who spoke Italian engaged in weekly trading with civilians.

Most bases boasted baseball, basketball, and volleyball teams. Though providing diversion and an outlet for youthful energy, athletics could inflict casualties. Lieutenant Gale Mortensen, a Fourteenth Group P-38 pilot, caught a hot grounder that broke the tip of one finger.

✪ ✪ ✪

Despite the type of mass production that the United States alone ever perfected, few aircraft were identical beneath the paint. Two bombers in the same squadron with sequential serial numbers could have different "personalities." One might be down for a variety of

reasons so often that it became a "hangar queen," eventually canni-
balized for parts. The other might fly fifty or even a hundred missions
without an abort, one of the cherished "up birds" that carried more
than its share of the load. Some units routinely flew more sorties than
the others. The Ninety-ninth Group at Tortorella had four of the five
"flyingest" B-17s—three with more than 120 missions each.[36]

Such records were due to the slavish devotion of ground crews.
Mechanics and other technical specialists took enormous pride in their
work, often approaching the obsessive-compulsive. The opportunity
to work on so exotic a machine as a four-engine bomber or a racy
fighter seemed too good to be true. For some crews, the flying crea-
tures of steel, aluminum, and rubber could take on the characteristics
of a beloved pet. A 450th Group pilot recalled that he "never went
out to the flight line at any hour of the day or night that the mechanics were not out there working. These mechanics were the most dedicated people I ever saw. They'd break down and cry when their plane
went down. It always seemed they thought there was something else
they could have done to make the plane more airworthy."[37]

A rough sampling of aircraft mechanics revealed that many—perhaps most—grew up with a love of engines. No country but the United
States, where automobiles were an established way of life by the
1930s, could have produced such a vast pool of talent. George
McGovern praised the crews: "We couldn't have kept anything as
complicated as a Liberator functioning very long without their superb
attention."[38]

Relying on decades of experience, the AAF organized its maintenance crews in a pyramidal structure. A squadron's topkick NCO was
the line chief, a career professional who usually worked equally well
with human and mechanical material. His subordinates were flight
chiefs, usually master sergeants, responsible for three flights of three
bombers. In turn, each aircraft had its own maintenance squad, a crew
chief normally with three mechanics and technicians under him. The
best depiction of a flight mechanic was Harry Carey's performance as

Master Sergeant Robbie White in the wartime movie *Air Force*, which followed the adventures of a B-17 crew in the Pacific. Vastly experienced, all knowing, alternately tough and cajoling, the character represented the generation of men who kept 'em flying.[39]

The four squadrons in each bomb group were expected to meet or exceed the unit's quota of aircraft for each day's flying—twenty-eight to thirty-six bombers, more or less evenly divided among the squadrons, on a typical mission. When the word descended through channels from Bari headquarters to the bomb wings down to the groups at the operating bases, everyone turned to. The term "maximum effort" implied an extraordinary undertaking, but most missions probably required the maximum number of bombers airborne to put as much ordnance on target as possible.

With an unrelenting work schedule, something had to give. Men on the flight line might work round the clock without rest, and sometimes the best opportunity for some sack time was during a mission. The six to eight hours that the bombers were airborne could be precious to bone-weary men too tired to drag themselves back to their tents. Many just slumped where they were out of the way, unconcerned about noise, traffic, or hunger.

Then they got up and started over again.

✪ ✪ ✪

Personnel drove operations as much as available aircraft, with attrition and replacement vying for superiority. Throughout 1944 the Fifteenth's ratio of bomber crews lost in combat or accidents to those completing their tours was at near parity: about 1,500 each. After the Ploesti campaign, however, the Fifteenth continued growing at a steady pace. August was the first month in which more crews rotated out than were killed or captured, and from September to year's end the ratio was 1.6 crews "retired" to each crew lost. Even better, from September to December the Fifteenth saw a net gain of six hundred bomber crews. By the end of 1944, therefore, with a steady flow of replacements, Twining finally had enough aircrews to maintain the desired mission schedule. That month the Bari personnel office counted two crews for each bomber.[40]

Sometimes a bomber returned to base without a full crew. On December 13, for example, a Blechhammer mission inflicted thirteen losses, the heaviest toll that target ever extracted from the Fifteenth, with three missing that day from the 464th Group.

Another 464th Liberator took a serious hit as First Lieutenant David R. Epley's crew had one gunner killed and two wounded. Though Epley and copilot Noel A. Wood landed their damaged Liberator at Pantanella, the ball turret gunner was absent. The radioman, Sergeant Darwin Carlson, reported, "After the ship received a direct hit through the left side, I started to open the escape hatch near the tail turret. Sgt. Davis was to my right while I was trying to open the hatch. After realizing the ship was not going down, I looked around, and Sgt. Davis was not present. The lapse of time from when I started to open the hatch, and saw that Sgt. Davis was missing, was fifteen seconds at the most. It is my believe [sic] that Sgt. Davis, thinking the ship was on its way down, did bail out through the hole blown on the left side of the ship." Sergeant Robert R. Davis was later reported to have died of wounds.[41]

✪ ✪ ✪

The Fifteenth attacked Blechhammer at least ten times between mid-October and the end of the year. The AAF dropped more than seven thousand tons of bombs on the two facilities, and the wrecking job was largely complete at the end of 1944. By then the Fifteenth's influence was felt far beyond the Mediterranean Theater.

On December 16, nearly eight hundred miles north of Foggia, two hundred thousand Germans supported by six hundred tanks and 1,600 artillery tubes smashed into a quiet American sector in the Ardennes Forest of France and Belgium. Seeking to divide the Allies and drive to Antwerp, the critical Anglo-American supply port, three

German armies began a four-week slugfest impelled by their desperate need for fuel.

At the end of the Battle of the Bulge—Hitler's desperate last effort in the West—hundreds of German vehicles were abandoned. Relatively few had been destroyed or damaged; most had run out of gasoline. In the grim ledger of war, the Fifteenth's Ploesti missions, and the petroleum bombing generally, had paid a major dividend.

HOLIDAY SEASON IN ITALY

On Christmas Day, 1944, the airmen were rousted from their bunks with a routine, "Everyone out! Briefing at 3:00, breakfast at 4:00." On the day of peace on earth and goodwill toward men, Liberators and Fortresses took off from Foggia that morning with full bomb loads. (The Fifteenth had flown on Christmas Day, 1943, though in far smaller numbers.)

More than 250 heavies struck the synthetic refinery at Brux, Czechoslovakia, and the marshalling yard at Weis, Austria, while 145 others strewed ordnance across rail targets in Austria and Germany. The defenders were equally willing to continue hostilities that Wednesday, as flak over Brux came up "heavy, intense, and accurate." Five B-17s went down, including the one hundredth loss for the Second Group.[42]

Five Liberators were shot out of the sky near Innsbruck, including a 376th Group aircraft. Sergeant Bill Barton followed his friends out the exit and experienced an eerie contrast to the noisy, flaming violence he had just left. Upon parachuting onto the snow-covered ground he was approached by an elderly man with two children. Satisfied that the unarmed American was no threat, the Austrian motioned, "Kommen, kommen."

The trio led Barton to a house where he was offered a chair and a shot of schnapps. The Frau provided a bowl of Christmas cookies followed by soup and meat. "We tried to converse with an English-German dictionary," Barton recalled, "but about then the police arrived from the town below." As the guards led him out, the lady of the house asked, "You Catlic?" Barton said he was, to which she replied, "Dominus vobiscum." "The Lord be with you" could not have been a more appropriate wish.[43]

Many units experienced both war and Christmas. The 451st bombed the Wels marshalling yard southwest of Linz without loss while the base chaplain held a Christmas service that morning. The First Fighter Group not only served turkey and trimmings, but ice cream for desert. For sweet-starved airmen it was "Manna from heaven."[44]

✪ ✪ ✪

New Year's Eve 1944 was observed in various ways at various bases. Undoubtedly the most raucous celebration was at Foggia Eleven (Vincenzo), where two fighter squadron commanders "proceeded to most thoroughly shoot up the camp." That was bad enough, but the miscreants put .45 caliber rounds through the Eighty-second Group commander's tent. Colonel Richard A. Legg's "roommate" was Lockheed tech rep Richard "Stumpy" Hollinger, who allowed that he "just about bought one."

Dick Legg was somewhere between tolerant and indulgent toward his COs. He issued reprimands to Majors Thomas C. Kelly and Robert M. Wray, prompting Kelly to quip that he expected the paper to ruin his prospects for making general. The army bureaucracy had its own priorities, however, and Kelly's promotion to light colonel arrived hours later as a New Year's Day present. His unindicted co-conspirator, Bob Wray, also pinned on silver oak leaves before long.[45]

✪ ✪ ✪

The war continued with missions on the four days following Christmas, at a cost of forty-four aircraft, including sixteen bombers and two fighters, over Blechhammer and Auschwitz on the twenty-sixth. The latter proved the last major strike against the notorious oil refinery.

Five days after Christmas, Major Roy Nelson's weather office reported a low-pressure system building off the east coast of Italy. With the detailed analysis beloved of meteorologists, the "weather guessers" noted ample moisture from ninety thousand square miles of the Adriatic and increasing temperature differences along the air mass boundaries, causing a greater pressure gradient that brewed increasing winds. The lower pressure at the center of the emerging storm generated stronger vertical action, creating precipitation that threatened to turn rain into snow. That meant grounding the Fifteenth Air Force.

New Year's Eve arrived on a near-blizzard wind with driving snow that discouraged much celebrating. Mostly the fliers and support personnel huddled in their billets or crowded into officer's and enlisted men's clubs, enjoying whatever seasonal festivities the USO, Red Cross, or Salvation Army could offer.

At Bari, Twining's operations office calculated that it ended the year with 2,174 bomber crews and nearly 1,100 fighter pilots. The airmen would have ample work in the dawning new year.[46]

CHAPTER EIGHT

MISSION ACCOMPLISHED

JANUARY–MAY 1945

Airmen at Foggia Main and the surrounding fields awoke on New Year's Day, 1945, to find their corner of "sunny Italy" under a light blanket of snow. It had begun falling the day before, driven on a brisk wind. There would be eight more days of snow that month, and it would continue sporadically until early March.[1]

The weather rendered Salsola inoperable, forcing most of the First Fighter Group from Foggia Number Three. On January 8, a year to the day since moving from Gioia del Colle to Salsola, the air echelon moved to Vincenzo, southeast of Foggia. The pilots bunked with their Eighty-second Group counterparts while ground crews set up tents across the field, an inconvenient arrangement but workable. One First Group pilot recorded, "Things were crowded but cramped but the

82nd folks went out of their way to accommodate us." Elements of the First remained at Vincenzo until mid-February.[2]

Poor weather kept most Fifteenth aircraft on the ground except the persistent scouts of the 154th Weather Reconnaissance Squadron. Finally, on January 4, after five days of no offensive operations, weather cleared sufficiently to launch 370 heavies against rail targets in six northern Italy cities.

The next day, Twining got some four hundred heavies airborne against Yugoslav transport targets. With the formations dispersed by heavy clouds, some individual approaches were made to Zagreb's marshalling yard, but a 90-percent cloud cover foiled all but one of 112 Liberators.

Lieutenant John Panas, a 461st Group radar operator in Captain David Johnson's crew, recalled, "We arrived at the target at 23,000 feet and to our dismay found the target had 90 percent cloud coverage.... We were supposed to use the Norden bombsight on this target. Because there was no flak or fighters in the area, we made three passes hoping for a break in the weather. On each pass I was using my radar to spot the target for the bombardier, but the clouds never cleared. On the fourth run I told the pilot and bombardier that I would take over because I had a good fix on the target. We managed to drop our bombs on the assigned target at long last."[3]

Partially augmenting reduced bomber operations, P-38 groups flew more Droop Snoot missions that winter, using the modified Lightning's plastic nose with bombsight on high-level formation attacks. The Eighty-second Group's aircraft received shackles for as many as six five-hundred-pounders or five bombs and a drop tank.

One of the group's Droop Snoot crews was rated among the best. Lieutenant Walter Zurney had pulled some strings to get out of B-24s and into P-38s. A mechanic before the war, he had served as crew chief for then-Lieutenant Bob Baseler in Panama. Zurney cornered his old boss, now a colonel and former CO of the 325th, at 306th Fighter Wing headquarters. With B-24 credentials, Zurney was named the Ninety-seventh Fighter Squadron's "Droop Snoop" pilot and teamed with First Lieutenant Fred Gong, previously a lead bombardier with the 483rd Group. Gong, likely the only bombardier of Chinese descent in the Fifteenth Air Force, exclaimed, "Walt flew the plane so steady I just couldn't miss."[4]

But there were bound to be gremlins. The same day as the B-24s' abortive Zagreb effort, the Eighty-second sent a Droop Snoot mission to Doboj, Yugoslavia. On takeoff one pilot accidentally toggled his five bombs from three hundred feet, trashing his hundred-thousand-dollar Lightning in the blast. Bombing results were deemed "lousy" mainly due to heavy clouds.

The Eighty-second tried its hand at level bombing again on January 21, lining up forty-three Lightnings behind the Ninety-fifth Squadron's Droop Snoot. The "Snoop" caught fire and crashed on takeoff, however. Pilot and bombardier escaped, and though sabotage was suspected, the mission proceeded. The high-level fighters claimed hits on the Fiume refinery, a rail yard, and harbor facilities.[5]

In the first month of 1945, Fifteenth fighters claimed just nine aerial kills, all by the 325th, mainly around Vienna and Regensburg. The Checkertails' January sharpshooter was Second Lieutenant Edward L. Miller, who on the twentieth bagged three of the four long-nose 190s the group claimed. They were his only victories of the war—by 1945 fighter pilots had to maximize each opportunity.

January seemed like a bust. Bombing missions left the ground on only seven days, and one of those missions was ineffective. The Fifteenth attacked both Blechhammers, Oswiecim, Brux, Odertal, and Austrian targets, often with good results and light losses. But four years of experience had taught bomber men the need for persistence— frequent restrikes were necessary to knock a target out of business permanently. The Fifteenth, after all, had needed four months to shut down Ploesti.

✪ ✪ ✪

In mid-January the First Fighter Group had begun planning for a complex mission conducted under strict security. Detachments were sent to Gibraltar and points east through the Mediterranean to provide air and sea escort for unidentified Allied VIPs. The flights met no resistance but incurred losses: two pilots lost in accidents over Italy.

Maintenance support for the operation was stretched across a 1,500-mile route, from Gibraltar to Athens. One February morning in Greece, mechanics used hammers and wrenches to knock ice off the P-38s' wings. In spite of a ground fog, the Lightnings got airborne on schedule to escort two eastbound C-54 transports. Upon completion of the mission, the group received a congratulatory radio message from the British foreign secretary: "Mr. Eden wishes to thank the Lightning pilots for their splendid effort."[6]

The airmen had played a small but crucial part in the historic conference at the Soviet Black Sea port of Yalta, which safely concluded on February 11. There Roosevelt, Churchill, and Stalin completed plans for World War II's end game and the postwar division of Europe. The First Group's Greek detachment learned that the two returning Skymaster transports carried General George C. Marshall, the army chief of staff, and Admiral Ernest J. King, the vice chief of naval operations.

The Lightnings were back in Italy on the nineteenth, and the First Group was reunited at Salsoa. Suitably dried out, the base boasted perhaps the largest theater in the Fifteenth Air Force, sure to draw top-level USO acts.

✪ ✪ ✪

Weather continued to affect operations in February, and when bombing missions got airborne, 80 percent required radar. Persistent Foggia fog and violent winds over the Alps confined Twining's heavies to mostly "local" missions in northern Italy until the fifth, when the on-again-off-again efforts against strategic targets resumed.

Though enemy fighters were scarce, the Luftwaffe still could turn up. In early February there was another episode like the 82nd Fighter Group's encounter with the rogue Mustang the previous October, this time involving the 455th Bomb Group over Austria. A stray B-24 bearing the 304th Wing's black diamond joined on a wingman in one of the 455th's boxes. No radio contact was established, and the lead pilot grew suspicious that the stranger was operated by the Luftwaffe, providing flak batteries with the formation's altitude and airspeed. He ordered every gunner who could bring his sights to bear to open fire. Turrets swiveled and waist gunners unlimbered their single mounts. As .50 caliber rounds began slicing though the thin air, the intruder banked away, reversing course.[7]

A strong effort on the fifth destroyed more oil storage at Regensburg with small losses. Two days later, however, revisiting petroleum facilities around Vienna and Bratislava, the heavies found antiaircraft crews on top of their game. The group's Red Force found "absolutely perfect bombing weather" over Vienna, as did the Blue Force over Bratislava. The American bombardiers enjoyed unobstructed views, but so did the Luftwaffe gunners. Because of heavy, accurate flak, "our bombs were strewn over half of Austria and Czechoslovakia," one of the airmen complained. Upon the survivors' return to Castelluccio airfield, the mechanics surveyed eighteen Liberators with visible flak holes. "The sheet metal crews could only shake their heads and get the tin snips ready to cut more patches."[8] The day had been costly: two dozen bombers fell to flak, including six Liberators from the 451st Group.

On February 13, hundreds of Liberators and Fortresses did a thorough job on Vienna, striking ordnance depots, storage yards, train repair shops, and marshalling yards, destroying or blocking rail access in much of the city. By month's end the capital was nearly paralyzed, and Allied targeteers reckoned that the nearby Moosbier-baum chemical-refinery complex was 50-percent destroyed. Similar targets were attacked at Graz, while other task forces flew to Hungary and Yugoslavia.

The Fifteenth could go anywhere it chose within range of Foggia, but not without paying a toll to the *Flakwaffe*. February combat losses were double January's, with more than one hundred bombers and nearly forty fighters written off, only two by enemy aircraft.

Priorities had changed. In early 1945, two-thirds of Twining's heavy bomber missions were directed at transport targets, and one-third to oil. In February, aircrews flew tactical missions against railroads in northern Italy, Austria, and southern Germany. The debate between the Oil Plan and the Transport Plan of early to mid-1944 had been resolved as petroleum production continued to decline. The Wehrmacht was running out of gas.

TURBO TROUBLE

Officially it was the Messerschmitt 262 *Schwalbe*, or Swallow, the world's first jet fighter. To the pilots privileged to fly it, the shark-nosed interceptor was "Turbo," for its twin jet turbine engines. With a top speed nearly a hundred miles per hour faster than piston-engine fighters, the 262, along with the Me 163 rocket fighter, V-1 cruise missiles, and V-2 ballistic missiles, represented the cutting edge of German technology.

When the Luftwaffe's young fighter general Adolf Galland first flew the jet in early 1943, he famously reported, "It was as though the angels were pushing." But technical and bureaucratic delays kept the jet sidelined past the point that its stunning performance could make a difference.[9] The revolutionary Swallow had gone operational in the summer of 1944, and Fifteenth pilots had glimpsed fast, high-altitude contrails during missions over southern Germany. Twining's fighters had first sparred with 262s in December, getting within firing range on only three occasions. On December 22 two Thirty-first Group pilots on photo escort combined to down a Turbo, but thereafter the jets remained immune until late March.

By early 1945 the 262 was becoming known, and its threat to bomber formations was genuine if limited. Armed with a potent battery of four 30mm cannon and two dozen rockets, the Turbo could handily destroy any bomber flying. Of some 1,400 built, perhaps no more than fifty were operational at once, and thanks to Hitler's interference, many were diverted into service as *schnelle Bomber*, fast bombers.

The Eighth and Fifteenth Air Forces responded to the new jet-propelled threat by trying to smash the eggs before they could hatch. One of the Fifteenth's first efforts took place on February 16, when some 260 B-24s pushed through marginal weather to a Messerschmitt plant at Regensburg. The German armaments minister, Albert Speer, had begun constructing underground plants safe from Allied bombs, but time ran out. From late February through March, perhaps ninety 262s were destroyed on the ground at Leipheim and Obertraubling in Bavaria. Forced to disperse the precious assets, in some places the Germans used stretches of the Autobahn as makeshift runways, hiding the jets in nearby trees.

In the spring of 1945, the Fifteenth typically launched seven hundred to eight hundred heavies and four hundred fighters almost daily, frequently targeting Turbo hatcheries. The jets opposed them whenever possible, engaging Allied aircraft on twenty-one days in March, including every day from the fifteenth to the twenty-fifth. Turbo units claimed some 115 American bombers during the month—clearly an exaggerated figure, and even if valid, insufficient to affect the war.

Still, the jet pilots kept flying as long as kerosene and ammunition lasted. Galland, with a better grasp of strategy than his masters, had recognized that the war was lost in 1941. But he and his *Kameraden* possessed a sense of heady fatalism. Oberleutnant Herbert Schlüter spoke for many: "This was an extremely difficult time for us. The daily strain was hard to take. We were on the defensive and were 'the hunted.' For this reason I was happy to be transferred. Finally, we would have the chance to fly a superior aircraft and show the 'Amis' how we could do it better."[10]

The Fifteenth encountered 262s in strength for the first time on March 22 while bombing the Ruhland synthetic plant again. Jagdgeschwader Seven launched twenty-seven jets from Parchim, 160 miles to the north, and got results. Led by two-hundred-kill major Theodor Weissenberger, the aggressive 262 pilots ignored the flak zone, flashed past the Mustangs, and tore into the Fifth Wing, downing at least seven Forts. The 483rd alone lost six. The Second Group reported eight Me 262s attacking the formation with one B-17 shot down in exchange for a jet credited to three gunners.

Staff Sergeant Alfred Novak said, "I saw B-17 number 440 attacked by an Me 262 which came in from six o'clock low, firing 20mm [sic]. It received a direct hit between No. 1 and No. 2 engines and caught fire. The aircraft appeared out of control and in a roll. The wing then fell off and the aircraft continued in a dive. I couldn't follow it all the way to the ground because of fighter attacks. I observed no parachutes." Only the tail gunner survived.[11]

LAST BATTLES

March was rough on the First Fighter Group. Ten pilots were killed, captured, or missing, including the commanding officer and his number two. The deputy CO, Lieutenant Colonel Charles Thaxton, went down on the fourth but was found by Partisans. He returned in early April, temporarily assuming command. Upon being hospitalized, Thaxton was relieved by Lieutenant Colonel Milton Ashkins.

March 31 was the group's worst day of the year: five losses, including three killed; one evaded; and the commanding officer captured.

Strafing along the Austrian-Hungarian border, the twenty-nine-year-old Texan colonel Arthur C. Agan parachuted from his burning aircraft and was nabbed by Germans just short of the Russian lines.

ACE IN A DAY

On March 14 the 325th Group escorted Liberators to Nové Zámky, Czechoslovakia. First Lieutenant Gordon H. McDaniel, a Tennessean with one previous victory, was descending from twenty thousand feet when he encountered the fighter pilot's dream: a formation of eight or more "bogies" strung out in front of him, with altitude and position to his advantage. "We were in an area where anything could happen," McDaniel related. He was worried that the strangers might be Russians so he proceeded with caution.

"I closed up behind the last plane, about 150 feet from him. There was no doubt about it—they were Jerry planes. The guy directly ahead of me had a big white three and a black cross on the side of his plane." McDaniel ordered his flight to shuck its drop tanks, then he attacked.

Working from back to front, McDaniel lined up several FWs in sequence, closing unseen on four of them. The first exploded in his face, and he got within about thirty yards of another before the obviously green German realized his peril. In moments McDaniel ran his score from one to six, becoming the third and last Fifteenth Air Force ace in a day—one day after his twenty-first birthday. When he looked around, McDaniel saw only his wingman—the second section had dropped out with mechanical problems.[12]

Eleven other Checkertails also scored that day, including Captain Harry Parker, beginning his second tour. He claimed a double, and now with thirteen kills, he was the leading Fifteenth ace remaining in combat.

★ ★ ★

Though fighter interceptions of bombers had dropped nearly to zero, flak only increased. As the Reich's borders were compressed, its defenses necessarily became concentrated. On March 23, the 465th Group joined a fleet of 157 Liberators sent to bounce the rubble of the Saint-Valentine tank factory. Austrian airspace already was notorious, but Saint-Valentine lay fifteen miles north of Linz, known as "a flak hole" and "one of the greater areas of hell."[13]

Lieutenant Robert Carlin, later a successful artist, recalled:

> We could see the target clearly as we turned to start the bomb run. It was a biting clear day, and intensely cold at 26,000, all making for flawless visibility. Black boiling curls appeared at once. We were eleven minutes from the target and already the shells were exploding around us. They were huge, meaning they were close. The flak those days was so bad that we were being forced to split the mission. The first wave would suppress the gunners, hopefully allowing the second wave to approach and bomb with greater accuracy.[14]

Enough was enough. The flak was so dense that some four-burst patterns overlapped, loud enough for crews to hear over the drone of four powerful engines. With some planes taking heavy damage and flak splinters bouncing off others, the lead bombardier dropped sixty long seconds from the planned release point. Almost immediately the formation took evasive action. "Radio silence ended as we broke into a hard right turn," Carlin said. "Down steep, hard right. We leveled off only to find more flak awaiting us. Hard left, and dive. Able Box dropped beneath my vision. The horror of sliding into them ripped me in sudden panic. They appeared again, but it was an effort to release the steel grip I had on the yoke."[15] The day's operations cost seven Liberators.

The next day the Fortresses went to Berlin.

TARGET BERLIN

By March 1945 the Eighth Air Force had been attacking Berlin for a full year; they hit the German capital twice that month. The Fifteenth had not had that privilege, and a look at the map shows why. The city lies 570 miles from London but nearly eight hundred miles from Foggia. Nevertheless, grand strategy called for a diversionary strike against Berlin by the Fifteenth as part of Operation Plunder, the Allied crossing of the Rhine, three hundred miles to the west, on March 23–24. Twining sent his six B-17 groups, while fifteen B-24 groups attacked jet bases in Neuberg and Munich, as well as other targets in Czechoslovakia.

Though Berlin had been bombed about 350 times since 1940, high priority targets remained. One of them was the Daimler-Benz tank factory, whose defenses were proportionate to its importance. Briefers noted nearly four hundred heavy flak guns in the area with AA batteries spread along the ingress route. Some 250 piston-powered fighters were thought to be based within range of the factory, with perhaps forty Me 262s available.[16]

In March the Luftwaffe scrambled a mere 220 fighters against Fifteenth Air Force missions—one-sixth of the number launched the previous August. But everyone knew that the *Jagdflieger* would oppose a major strike at the Nazi capital.[17]

Brigadier General Charles W. Lawrence's wing put up 169 Fortresses, but eleven "boomeranged," returning to base with mechanical problems. The rest of the task force cruised north in good weather—good for bombing and good for the Luftwaffe to locate the heavies. From the Alps onward the sky was unusually clear.

The escort plan called on all four Mustang units and a Lightning group—thirteen squadrons in all—leaving two P-38 outfits to cover the B-24 missions. More than 250 fighters departed Italy with 241 "effectives" reaching the target area.

Three penetration escort groups rendezvoused with the bombers at 11:45, variously remaining with the "big friends" from 12:25 to 1:20. The 325th and Thirty-first came early and stayed late, providing penetration, target, and withdrawal support for the three leading and three trailing bomb groups, respectively. The Fifty-second Group provided target and withdrawal support. Two Lightning squadrons of the Eighty-second drew penetration support, while one squadron escorted the heavies on withdrawal. The Red Tails were assigned penetration support, preceding the bombers and remaining "to prudent limit of endurance."[18]

The 325th was intended to help the bombers to the target but did not rendezvous until fifteen minutes after three other groups. Other than the satisfaction of entering Berlin airspace, the mission was disappointing for the Checkertails, who saw four jets but were unable to engage. After a six-hour mission, all pilots returned with their gun muzzles still taped over.

For Berlin, the Forts flew with full ten-man crews. Both waist gunners were needed on a trip to "Big B," which was certain to draw fighter reaction. But as usual, flak remained the greater threat. Four B-17s fell to the batteries at Brux, Czechoslovakia, about 130 miles south of Berlin. Seventy miles further on, more flak erupted as the wing motored over Ruhland, "coming up in blobs." The B-17s eased into their evasive action, trying to confuse the gunners with a seemingly random choreography that actually was well choreographed, an arabesque in three dimensions.[19]

Jagdgeschwader 7 spooled up thirty-three jets in two relays, striking the Boeing armada at Dessau on the ingress and on the southern perimeter of Berlin itself. The home team included some all-stars: Heinrich Ehrler (204 victories), Franz Schall (126), and Hermann Buchner (50).

At top speed the jets had a good 350 mph edge on the lumbering Forts. The Messerschmitts had to slow down, however, for adequate time to track a target. Mostly they attacked from behind to reduce the closure rate, affording more time for accuracy.

Five bomb groups saw enemy aircraft, only the Ninety-seventh escaping attention. Often the Luftwaffe pilots ignored the growing flak menace to close nearly to pistol distance on the Forts. Several 262s launched a dual-axis attack, some speeding in head on, while others used the bombers' contrails as concealment from astern. Ten Boeings were shot down en route or were unable to join formation, leaving 147 over the target. The Fortresses turned onto their bomb runs making 150-mph-indicated airspeed, varying from four to eight minutes from initial point to release.

The defenders concentrated on the 463rd Group, which lost six Forts—two to Turbos and another jointly to flak and fighters. Jets inflicted the 483rd's sole loss, while the Second Group lost one to flak and one combined. The 459th and 483rd also took casualties.

Flying with the Second Group was bombardier Lieutenant Ariel Weekes. Despite a high draft number, he joined the Air Corps, leading to "a love affair with the B-17." "The 262s were after us up there," he recalled. Starting the bomb run, the group's lead plane was hit and left formation. Consequently, Weekes became lead bombardier. "It went off OK," he related.[20]

In clear skies the leading bomb groups had no trouble identifying the target, thanks to a prominent arena just east of the factory. The six groups dropped 356 tons of thousand-pounders from altitudes between 25,000 and 28,300 feet, taking thirteen minutes from start to finish. Despite favorable conditions for visual bombing, the results were poor, partly because heavy smoke obscured much of the target area after the initial strikes. Two groups' performance was assessed as "not accurate," one as "half accurate," and two as "somewhat accurate." Only the Ninety-niners were rated entirely accurate with "an excellent pattern in the briefed MPI" (desired mean point of impact). The Second's bomb pattern was assessed as "good."[21]

Sergeant Lincoln F. Broyhill, a twenty-year-old gunner from Virginia who had transferred from the Eighth Air Force, got more shooting than ever that day. He was flying with the 463rd in Captain William S. Strapko's *Big Yank*. The plane bore a portrait of President Roosevelt; its radio operator, Albert Bishop, was selected to play "Taps" at the Streparone base's memorial service for FDR two weeks later.

Big Yank drew the vulnerable "tail-end Charlie" position in the formation, affording Strapko's gunners ample trigger time. As Bishop reported, "Our Red Tail fighter escort took off as soon as the Me 262s' presence was announced on combat radios.... [The jets] dived into us, firing, with flaps down at about 20–30 degrees and noses up attitude, setting up a very good target for our gunners at our slow airspeed."[22]

Alerted by copilot Lieutenant Clair Harper, the top turret gunner, Sergeant Howard Wehner, swung on a Turbo that seemed determined to ram. He held his triggers down, hammering half-inch rounds into the Messerschmitt until it pitched up and exploded about fifty yards out. Harper insisted he could see the German's face.

"Babe" Broyhill recalled,

> I saw four jets attacking a lone B-17 from another group. The B-17 knocked down one of the enemy fighters before it flew in a crippled manner towards the Russian lines. The remaining three fighters came at our plane. Two of them came right behind each other at my position. They were about 1,000 yards away when I started cutting loose with my guns. The first made a pass at 200 yards and my tracers were going right into its fuselage. Suddenly it went down in flames. The second came into my sights after the first had dropped. I kept shooting away because he was getting

into my hair. Suddenly, it also spiraled down. Upon hitting
the ground, it burst into flames. Because I had my guns
spitting lead so rapidly, they jammed.[23]

Big Yank set a record for one crew with three jets downed in a
single mission, and Broyhill took the individual title with two. The
group claimed six—obviously an error since the actual jet losses
included those to fighters, but the numbers demonstrated the intensity
of the combat.[24]

While bombers shot it out with the interceptors, four of the five
fighter groups reported jets. The Fifty-second Fighter Group engaged
only 109s. Colonel Billy Daniel's Thirty-first Group claimed five jets,
one by the CO himself, earning his ace. Riding his Mustang on the
periphery of the bomber herd, Daniel reported, "I saw the two enemy
aircraft turn into the bombers from astern, and I turned in and started
to close and fire. However, I observed four more enemy aircraft turning in. I waited for the number six aircraft to turn, then closed in on
him from about four-thirty o'clock to 500 yards and fired. No strikes
were observed, although the enemy aircraft snap-rolled and went into
a spin. I observed a parachute and four blobs of smoke."[25]

The 332nd engaged eight jets and submitted claims for three
destroyed. First Lieutenant Roscoe Brown lost one in a high-speed
dive, then climbed back to altitude and spotted four jets below. "I
peeled down on them toward their rear, but almost immediately I saw
a lone 262 at 24,000 feet, climbing at 90 degrees to me and 2,500
feet from me." Using his gyroscopic gun sight to effect, he said, "I
pulled up at him in a 15-degree climb and fired three long bursts from
2,000 feet at eight o'clock to him. Almost immediately, the pilot
bailed out—from 24,500 feet."[26]

Between bomber and fighter claims, the Fifteenth reckoned it had
shot down sixteen jets, a massacre. In truth, the Italian-based airmen
downed four. On the other side, the jet pilots were credited with ten

bombers but got only two for certain. The Turbos also claimed five fighters and likely downed three. Two Red Tails were killed while one survived and another limped to safety in Russian territory.

The actual victories over jets that day are nearly impossible to tabulate. The 463rd's gunners definitely downed one; the 332nd reported a Turbo pilot bailing out and one seen to crash. The Thirty-first saw one jet diving into the ground and reported three Germans in parachutes.

The 463rd and 483rd received their second Distinguished Unit Citations for the Berlin mission, and the 332nd its first. Tangible results of the bombing were uncertain. Postwar investigation revealed that the factory kept delivering engines for Panther tanks through April, a week before V-E Day.[27]

MORE JETS

Another jet unit entered the lineup in late March as General-leutnant Adolf Galland's Jagdverband (Fighter Unit) 44 went operational at Munich. Galland, Germany's youngest general, had run afoul of Hitler and Göring over policy and slander against his aircrews, who often lost one quarter of their number per month. He was sent off to run a bobtailed unit where presumably he would have the good manners to be killed in action as befitted a recipient of the Knight's Cross with diamonds.

JV 44 was perhaps uniquely low-key in the Prussian-influenced Wehrmacht. Galland told Leutnant Franz Stigler that anyone who could obtain a 262 would be welcome. Stigler wangled himself a Turbo and joined the club, his credentials stamped with a deep crease across his forehead. Years later he deadpanned, "That's how I learned you don't attack a B-17 from behind."[28]

On April 4 two jets whistled off the airfield at Riem to intercept P-38s approaching Munich at high altitude—a photo escort flight. The controller put the 262s on a head-on approach, and Unteroffizier

(Corporal) Eduard Schallmoser centered a Lockheed in his Revi gun sight. He pressed the trigger but nothing happened. He glanced at his armament panel, saw the safety was engaged, and belatedly flipped it off. When he looked up again, he had a windscreen full of Lightning.

The two fighters collided. The American, Lieutenant Bill Randle, felt the impact and lost control. As his P-38 dropped into a graveyard spiral, he jettisoned the canopy and went over the side. Pulling up, Schallmoser saw his opponent's parachute. The jet, with a dented right wing, got back to base.

Galland's unit claimed forty to fifty shootdowns during its brief existence—seven by the general himself. But though it had more 262s, the Luftwaffe's technology could not offset the Allies' immense numerical advantage. As the war in Europe entered its final month, operations around Foggia continued unabated.

BEING THERE

Air campaigns turn not only on the size of the fleet but also on the planes' availability. Apart from aircrews, Twining relied on some sixty-two thousand non-flying personnel to maintain the aircraft, handle ordnance, analyze intelligence, feed the men, and drive ground vehicles.

At full strength a typical heavy bomb group comprised sixty aircraft, of which fifty or more (roughly 85 percent) were operational at one time. Each plane made six to nine sorties per month. The number of sorties grew tremendously from 1944 into 1945. During the period when bombers required heavy escorts, 250 fighters might be airborne at one time. After air supremacy was achieved in the spring of 1945, fewer fighters were needed on escort, freeing others for strike missions. Days of four hundred sorties became common, and XV Fighter Command peaked at 586 on April 15, when supporting the advance of the British Eighth and the U.S. Fifth Armies.

The high standard of maintenance in the Fifteenth was never more evident than in the April 15, 1945, missions supporting Allied troops in northern Italy. An amazing 93 percent of the bombers and fighters participated—tribute to the dedication and ability of the "wrench benders" on the flight lines all around Foggia. The Thirty-first Group, for example, provided seventy-three Mustangs on three consecutive days, and none of the 219 sorties was aborted. An official summary noted, "Today's effort is the largest of World War II by the Fifteenth AF (most fighters and bombers dispatched and attacking, and the largest bomb tonnage dropped) during a 24-hour period; 1,142 heavy bombers bomb targets."[29]

Despite the focus on operations, there was more to life in the Fifteenth than bombing missions. The 460th Bomb Group, for instance, based at Spinazzola, became acquainted with the village of Poggiorsini, a pro-Communist enclave and therefore forbidden to American personnel. Less than a mile's hike from base, Poggiorsini inevitably attracted unauthorized visitors. As the group's diarist recorded, "Even though it was off limits, this did not prevent those with an adventurous spirit from going there for a number of reasons."

A British antiaircraft unit was situated near the cemetery, and with almost nothing to do, it welcomed Yanks to share biscuits, tea, and a chat. But the airmen could not always ignore the civilian population, generally struggling to survive. An unknown but probably considerable quantity of goods—clothing, food, soap, and sundries—found its way to town. Among the most prized contraband were parachute canopies, and 460th alumni like to think that some postwar brides wore silken gowns labeled "Pioneer Parachute Company."[30]

BEHIND THE WIRE

While air operations continued on a growing scale, an almost unknown battle was waged deep in Germany. It involved thousands of Fifteenth airmen in enemy hands. The German word for prisoners of war was *Kriegsgefangenen*, prompting Americans behind the wire to call themselves "Kriegies." Nearly five thousand Fifteenth fliers were known to have been captured by the enemy, and three hundred more were interned by neutral powers, mostly in Switzerland.[31]

The Luftwaffe had its own POW camps, usually divided between officers and noncommissioned personnel. Though abuse of prisoners did occur, the Wehrmacht generally followed the Geneva Convention of 1929, and the survival rate among aircrewmen known captured was over 98 percent.[32] By the spring of 1945, however, the Germans themselves were going hungry, and Kriegies inevitably felt the pinch. Conditions in the overcrowded camps deteriorated, leaving POWs increasingly cold, hungry, sick, and weak.

The 455th Group's Tom Ramey recalled,

> Prison camp life was one of cold, drafty buildings, warning wires, guard towers, lengthy roll calls in bitter cold weather, searchlights and guard dogs at night, boredom and loneliness. Escape was the binding thread that held out hope. Tunnels were dug, found by the Germans, filled in and then under the threat of death, new tunnels were dug again. From a handful of nothing but American ingenuity, POWs were able to fashion many articles to meet basic necessities of life. Humor was the thread that made life bearable and the waiting tolerable.[33]

Humor was where men found it—or where it could be made. In Stalag Luft IV at Gross Tychow, one compound had a disproportionate number of POWs from Texas and New Mexico. Many were conversant in Spanish and used their linguistic skill to foil eavesdropping guards. Sometimes the Southwesterners spoke of nothing in particular just to frustrate the jailers.

Among the fliers at Stalag Luft IV was Sergeant Bill Hess, the teenaged gunner who had bailed out of his Ninety-seventh Group

B-17 in September. He bunked with an Eighth Air Force radioman, Sergeant Alton Dryer, who had grown up in the Texas Hill Country, where German was the second language. Dryer understood nearly everything his captors said but didn't let on.

Red Cross packages arrived erratically, often robbed of coffee but otherwise usually left intact by the guards in some camps. Most packs included three pairs of socks—a valuable commodity. Somebody stole Hess's socks, leaving him with none.

The one man everybody from Gross Tychow remembered was Captain Leslie Caplan, one of five Allied doctors in Stalag Luft IV. The thirty-seven-year-old flight surgeon had flown missions with the 449th Bomb Group and been shot down near Vienna in October. He described "Luft Four" as "a domain of heroes, but from a medical standpoint it was a kingdom of illness." Faced with "patients" suffering malnutrition—some ate rats—Caplan worked wonders of medicinal improvisation. To combat diarrhea, he burned wood down to charcoal, pulverized it, and mixed the powder with potable liquids. The brew tasted horrible but those men who could force it down their throats—and keep it down—gained some benefit.[34]

"THE MARCH"

On February 6, six thousand prisoners, including about 2,500 men in Caplan's group, left Stalag Luft IV on a forced march of nearly five hundred miles westerly to escape oncoming Russians. The trek lasted eighty-six days. Eating boiled potatoes and beets, the men subsisted on fewer than eight hundred calories per day—one-fourth the American average. Caplan personally knew of seven men who died en route or under German control.

Along the way Bill Hess's feet froze, and he lagged far behind the column. A lone guard stayed with him—a German youngster about his own age. Finally Hess was spent. He collapsed in the snow, too exhausted to continue.

The German reached into his greatcoat and produced something wrapped in paper: a sandwich. He gave half to the American, now more a comrade in shared misery than a prisoner. Thankful beyond expression, Hess ate what was offered. He felt some strength returning to his body and raised himself off the ground. The guard patted Hess on the shoulder, urging, "Mach schnell," or "Hurry up."

Proceeding up the road, the unlikely pair came to a barn where dozens of prisoners were gathered for the coming night. An American officer saw them coming and shouted an order: "Pick that man up!" Willing hands raised Hess off his tortured feet and carried him inside. The officer was "Doc" Caplan. He scrounged some rags to bind Hess's bloody feet and managed to halt the hemorrhaging. But that was only part of the challenge. Many men had severe dysentery, and there were no drugs to cure it. Caplan collected enough wood to burn to ashes and concocted his trademark anti-diarrheal brew. "This should counter the poison in your system," he explained, extending a bitter but lifesaving cup to each ailing prisoner.

During the march Hess and three others unable to continue were stashed at a farm. Especially concerned about the gangrenous foot of Hess's friend Alton Dryer, Caplan convinced a German military doctor to assist him. The German, who spoke English, informed Dryer grimly, "Sergeant, I must lance the foot but I have no anesthetic, you understand?"

"Buddy" Dryer was a rugged Texan. He replied, "Doctor, you do what you have to do. Bill, you hold me down no matter what I do or say."

The doctor produced a scalpel, sliced two slits in Dryer's instep, and threaded a wire through both cuts. Then he pulled, hard. Blood, pus, and liquids spewed from Dryer's foot, and he bucked and screamed in Anglo-Saxon expletives. When the horrific procedure continued, he switched to German. The doctor momentarily stopped the beneficial torture, amazed at the American's fluent Teutonic profanity.

When the doctor was finished, he swabbed out the wound with alcohol, bound it with a bandage, and wrapped a GI tee-shirt around the bandages. Finally he looked at Dryer: "Sergeant, where did you learn to swear like that?"

"Oh, I'm from up north of San Antonio. Lots of Germans up there, sir."

Once the patient was able to hobble, an *Oberfeldwebel* escorted Dryer and Hess to a train station. The Luftwaffe sergeant was downright paternal. "He was an older man," Hess recalls, "probably in his early fifties." The German even carried one of Hess's shoes, as the gunner's frozen foot was still too swollen to wear it.

The kindly sergeant stayed with the Americans until the ride ended in an underground station in an unknown city. He sent the two cripples upstairs through scores of obviously hostile civilians, Dryer leaving a blood trail up the steps. He looked around. "Bill, I don't think we're supposed to be here." The Yanks glanced upward to find their savior grinning widely. Satisfied with his joke, he took them in tow again.

Then, with one arm around Dryer and Hess hobbling on frostbitten feet, the dutiful non-com put his charges on another train. "I cannot go with you," he said. The thought of two seeming escapees hopping a train in bombed-out Germany conjured up a variety of scenarios, none pleasant, but the fliers had no choice. Their escort placed them in a rail car. After a crowded two-day ride, they were met by guards who marched the Americans to Stalag XI-B, a multinational camp about fifty miles north of Hanover.

RAF fighter-bombers routinely attacked the marshalling yard at XI-B. Some Typhoon pilots extended their passes to fly over the camp, tipping their wings in salute to the POWs. The prisoners' morale perked up when a Spitfire chased a Junkers 88 into the ground, though soon a P-51 pilot bailed out of his crippled Mustang. He told the resident sergeants that he was a second lieutenant flying his second mission.

Word got around that Hitler had ordered *Terrorflieger* executed rather than repatriated, but few officers were willing to comply, either from ethical or practical reasons. SS units remained fanatical to the end, however, enthusiastically executing real or suspected deserters. Nonetheless, some guards opted out when the opportunity arose. Bill Hess saw one young German ditch his light machinegun in a snow bank and dash for the trees, apparently not far from his home.

The Kriegies settled in to await their fate.[35]

APRIL ATTRITION

After Romania changed sides, P-38 pilots mostly went hungry as the Luftwaffe largely disappeared from airspace available to Lightnings. So the Lockheed fighters went down on the deck, strafing far afield from Foggia. By then the Axis had ample flak, and "the light stuff" could be wicked. Airdromes, marshalling yards, and other obvious targets received additional 20 and 37mm AA weapons, as some pilots learned.

A Lightning pilot wrote, "The Germans, their firepower for the most part intact, were being squeezed, and attacking this mass, bristling with guns, was like poking a stick at a hornet's nest. Anti-aircraft fire came from every roadside and hillside. The sides of freight cars fell away to disclose heavy machine guns and anti-aircraft cannon manned for the most part by very skilled gunners. Lord knows they had had enough experience."[36]

That spring fewer and fewer strategic targets were worth a major effort. The fighters increasingly turned to transportation, sometimes joining Twelfth Air Force units. From January through May, however, nearly half of XV Fighter Command losses were attributed to operational causes; flying in weather had become almost as dangerous as combat.

Not even aces were immune, including the Fifteenth's top active shooter. The Clan's Captain Harry Parker, victor in thirteen combats, had been shot down by a P-38 a year before but returned eager for more combat. He was killed on April 2 on his 273rd mission, an escort to Brux, near Vienna. Spotting bogies beneath his squadron, he and two others dropped down to investigate and were lost from sight in the undercast, fate unknown.

That same day the Fifteenth lost its top P-38 ace, Captain Michael Brezas of the Fourteenth Group. Twenty-one years old and from Massachusetts, he had downed a dozen planes in seven weeks of July and August 1944, though squadron mates said that he got more than he claimed. But he ran afoul of AA while shooting up Magyarlad airfield in Hungary. Briefly held by the Germans, he was liberated by Russian forces, though he returned to Triolo bitter about the treatment received from the supposed allies. He told friends that if the war had continued, he would have been just as happy shooting Russian aircraft as German.[37]

On April 10, 325th guns turned nine locomotives into scrap metal near Munich but unexpectedly encountered airborne targets. Among six kills was a Ju 88 downed by Lieutenant William E. Aron of New Jersey, who became the seventy-fourth and last ace of the Fifteenth Air Force. The twenty-one-year-old went down on another strafing mission almost two weeks later. Reportedly taken from his plane by hostile Italians, his body was never recovered.

The next day, April 11, First Lieutenant Robert W. Whitehead of the Fourteenth Group had just strafed locomotives in Czechoslovakia when his flight met two FW 190 fighter-bombers of Schlachtgeschwader 10 returning from a mission. The twenty-one-year-old Hoosier lost his fight with one of the Germans, who was in turn downed by Whitehead's wingman, First Lieutenant Harry Morris, avenging his leader's death. Whitehead probably was the last Fifteenth Air Force pilot killed in air combat.[38]

The First Group strafed rail lines in southern Germany on the fifteenth, deploying its squadrons in the Regensburg-Salzburg-Munich triangle. Minimal top cover was assigned, as the group had seen only four airborne bandits since December.

The hunting was good: P-38s strafed twenty-one locomotives, destroying eleven, and riddling two dozen rail cars, including a *Flak-wagen*. One luckless Focke-Wulf pilot crossed the sights of a Twenty-seventh Squadron pilot, First Lieutenant Warren Danielson. It was his first victory and the group's last.

But the Lightnings paid for their success. Operating in a denser defense environment, the "ack-ack" fire was thick and lethal. Five P-38s were shot down, including the leaders of all three squadrons.

The concentrated defenses of northern Italy and southern Germany confounded the conventional wisdom of strafing. Ordinarily the first fighters sweeping over a target got away clean, as they usually enjoyed the advantage of surprise, while wingmen and trailing flights tended to catch the flak. But no more. When aggressive formation leaders made repeated runs on defended targets, their odds were the same as those behind them. Not even the P-38's twin engines prevented heavy Lightning casualties. That month they accounted for twenty-four of the forty-two fighter losses, the First and Fourteenth Groups losing nine and ten respectively.

The First Group's attrition continued that month, as Lightnings had to hunt at low level to find concealed targets, within range of light and medium AA guns. The toll included two squadron leaders and a flight commander near Padua-Verona on April 23. An operational summary concluded, "the damage inflicted against the losses sustained does not make this type of mission practical in Northern Italy."[39]

In fairness to the P-38, the casualties for the most part were the result simply of exposure. Since Romania's capitulation eight months before, the big Lockheeds had drawn a disproportionate share of air-to-ground missions, while Mustangs focused on escort. During April, in fact, the Thirty-first Group lost only three P-51s in combat and the Fifty-second only one.[40] Despite the losses, however, the Fifteenth's combat attrition for April was down 33 percent from March—from 112 to 84.[41]

✪ ✪ ✪

The pace of operations never slackened. Depending on weather, some groups flew eleven missions in the first twelve days. Then on the thirteenth came word from home that Franklin D. Roosevelt had died at Warm Springs, Georgia.

The news affected nearly everyone, though some took it harder than others. At Cerignola a Democrat in the officer's club was disconsolate: "The war is over. The war is lost." With that, the flier—already known as a heavy drinker—got blitzed, repeatedly diving off the bar and trusting his friends, presumably including some Republicans, to catch him. Finally the others told the offender that he could stay as drunk as he wished, but the rest of them had to fly the next day.

Among the men in the bar was a pilot from South Dakota, First Lieutenant George McGovern. He recalled, "It just struck me how close we really were. Here we were 3,000 miles from home and yet the death of Roosevelt hit that group of men awfully hard. They weren't particularly political—it's just that they hadn't known any other president."[42]

Then the fliers got on with the war.

✪ ✪ ✪

Tactical operations continued against enemy supply routes from southern Germany into Italy. On April 20 the heavies attacked bridges in the Brenner Pass and Po Valley, while P-38s bombed rail lines from Innsbruck to Rosenheim. In two days the Lightnings scored forty rail cuts and destroyed or rendered useless four rail bridges. The next day P-38s inflicted thirty-nine cuts and left three rail yards, a rail bridge, and a highway crossing destroyed or inoperable.

As opposition declined, bombing accuracy rose. The star performer of April was Colonel LeRoy Stefonowicz's 451st, which frequently put 90 percent of its ordnance within the desired thousand feet of the aim point. On the twentieth, attacking a bridge at Lusia, the bombardiers scored 100 percent—probably the only perfect score in Fifteenth history. All sixteen spans of the 590-foot bridge were down.

ENDGAME

The last losses came in batches and singles. At San Giovanni the 455th Group spoke for the entire air force. "Everyone knew the war would soon be over, and the aircrews started sweating out the last few missions, as they had made it this far, and some suspicions and anxiety prevailed about getting shot down at this stage."[43]

Fourteen bombers from a dozen groups failed to return from Austrian rail targets on April 25, as did a Carpetbagger B-24. That day the 455th "Vulgar Vultures" lost Lieutenant John Greenman's crew over Linz. Seven Liberators took severe flak damage with eleven others lightly damaged.

The group's Mission 253 was scheduled for the next day, and as usual the Liberators started their Pratt & Whitney engines. But they had barely turned their props when the providential red flare arced upward from the control tower. "April was over and so was the war in Europe," said a group history.[44]

The information was not distributed uniformly. That evening at Castellucio the softball game was interrupted with word of cessation of hostilities until further notice. The rejoicing was short lived; that night the 451st was alerted for "POM," preparation for overseas movement in two weeks. The order could mean only one thing—the Liberators were deploying to the Pacific.

✪ ✪ ✪

The last U.S. fighter victories in the Mediterranean Theater came the next day, the twenty-sixth. During a photo escort near Prague, a flight from the 332nd Group tangled with five 109s to protect a recon Lightning. The Red Tails claimed four kills, including two by Lieutenant Thomas W. Jefferson.

April 26 also brought the last fighter losses. Two Thirty-firsters were hit while strafing, and both planes went down without any sign of life: Lieutenants Ralph Lockney and Raymond Leonard were listed MIA. They were experienced pilots: Lockney had escaped from Yugoslavia in February, and Leonard had downed a jet in March.

That day the 460th Group flew its 205th mission since March 1944, launching thirty-one Liberators against tactical targets in northern Italy. Heavy overcast kept them from attacking the primary and secondary targets, forcing most planes to abort. But the six B-24s of "Able Box" made a radar run on the Klagenfurt marshalling yard, where Captain Paul B. O'Connell's *Seldom Available* was shot down by flak. All but one man safely parachuted from the spiraling Liberator—probably the last Fifteenth bomber lost to enemy action. Sergeant Edward S. Kovaleski of Southbridge, Massachusetts, was declared dead 366 days later.[45]

MAY TWILIGHT

Rumors swirled around Foggia. The Germans were surrendering. They were not surrendering. The Fifteenth was being demobilized. It was transferring to the Pacific. The uncertainty gnawed at the men—nobody knew for certain.

In the waning days of hostilities, emotions tugged in different directions. Aircrews recognized the same "last man" syndrome some of their fathers and uncles had described as the clock ticked closer to the eleventh hour of the eleventh day of the eleventh month a quarter-century before. One fighter pilot explained, "The closer they got to the announcement that the war was over, the less everyone felt like they thought they would feel. It wasn't sadness, but they were not happy either. They didn't quite know how to feel; emotions kept changing inside them, in turmoil and confusion. Everyone thought he knew how he should feel, but admitted he didn't feel that way."[46]

Some enlisted men had been overseas for three years. Long-serving units such as the 154th weather scouts, which had been in the theater since late 1942, were "nervous in the service." Men were tired of gin and juice and just wanted a quart of milk. Major William R. Dinker repeatedly tried to learn his unit's intended fate but always received the exasperated headquarters response, "Look, how can we tell you when we don't know ourselves?" One wag noted, "Don't believe all these rumors like driving to Vladivostok by jeep!"[47]

The Fifteenth Air Force's final bombing mission was to Salzburg on May Day. Battling poor weather, Lieutenant Colonel J. C. Reardon's twenty-seven Fortresses were briefed to hit the main rail station and marshalling yard. The Second Group—whose motto was "The Second is first"—was the last in combat, logging Mission 412. Heavy-caliber flak was assessed moderate and inaccurate, though two crewmen received slight wounds and another suffered anoxia. One B-17 left formation with a propeller feathered but landed at Cervia.

Reardon recognized the changed circumstances as the end of hostilities approached. His twenty-year-old navigator, Lieutenant Farley G. Mann, related, "A decision was made by Colonel Reardon, and agreed on by his crew, that we would not drop our bombs on the marshaling yards. We all knew that the war was all but over. Colonel Reardon said, 'Let's get them in the open fields,' and we dropped our bombs in what we hoped were open fields." That evening at Amendola the group commander, Colonel Paul Cullen, noted that strike photography showed no damage to the target. Though the CO appeared angry, said Mann, "I believe he was putting on an act."[48]

On May 2 men eagerly monitored radio news reports. The broadcasts were optimistic: all Axis troops in northern Italy and some provinces of southern Austria had surrendered unconditionally to the Allies. Hitler was dead and Berlin had fallen to the Russians.

At Mondolfo airfield there was more immediate news. That day the Thirty-first Group's Lieutenant Ralph D. Lockney returned from an adventure worthy of an Errol Flynn movie. Hit by flak over northern Italy on April 26, Lockney had bellied in his P-51, but no one saw him exit so he went MIA. While being held with other prisoners, he received the surrender of the German guards who laid down their weapons. But when anti-Fascist guerrillas attacked the compound, the Americans returned the Germans' rifles for the defense of all. In the ensuing shootout, the intrepid Lockney took himself elsewhere, then hitch-hiked home by the scenic route: Venice and Padua.[49]

Flight schedules were altered in the twilight between war and peace. Reconnaissance missions continued, but the only escorts were for transport runs and leaflet drops. Fifteenth fighters accompanied U.S. and British planes dropping supplies in Yugoslavia and points west and locating POW camps. Meanwhile, Europe inched closer to peace. On May 7 Germany's unconditional surrender was expected within twenty-four hours, and on several bases officers collected small arms from all but military police, anticipating celebratory gunfire when The Word came down.

The end came far from Foggia. In the wee hours of the seventh, the Western Allies accepted Nazi Germany's unconditional surrender in a school in Reims, France. The formal announcement came from London that evening, and the surrender took effect on Tuesday, the eighth. The Second World War in Europe was ended.

The Mediterranean edition of *Stars and Stripes* headlined, "It's All Over Over Here!"[50]

Most groups observed V-E Day in the air and on the ground. Speeches were delivered by squadron and group commanders amid "a lot of hell raising going on." Twining approved "Victory Flights" around Italy, an order the fliers were delighted to obey as they indulged in aerial revelry high and low. Remarkably enough, no accidents were recorded from the authorized buzz jobs.

At Bari the weather scouts noted, "VE night is marked with volley after volley of rifle fire from camps nearby. (That was a clever move to take up all our guns yesterday!) British searchlights fanned the sky with piercing blue pencils of light and nearby Yugoslav troops splash the blue-black sky with red, green, and yellow flares...."[51]

Marking the occasion, Nathan Twining issued a message to the 78,550 men of his command. "The cost to us, in men and materiel, has not been small, but with that indomitable American spirit and know-how, we have surmounted all obstacles to accomplish our mission. Many of our comrades are not here to share in this final victory, but to those gallant airmen and to the ground personnel who contributed so heavily to this record, I want to say, yours is a job well done."[52]

And so it was.

CHAPTER NINE

LEGACY

MAY 1945 AND BEYOND

T he war was over but the flying was not.

The Foggia complex still hummed with activity—proficiency flying, a few recon flights, and preparing for possible deployment to the Pacific.

But losses continued. In the Thirty-first Fighter Group alone in May and June, three pilots were killed, an enlisted man died in a vehicle accident, and two other Mustangs were damaged.[1] The Eighty-second Group wrote off three Lightnings in late May, as did the Fourteenth. When the AAF was losing nearly two hundred planes and 220 fliers a month in the continental United States, overseas losses simply represented the grim cost of doing business.[2]

Many airmen spent their leisure time counting points to determine their eligibility for rotation home, while others anticipated the return of friends from captivity. It was the Fifteenth's urgent mission to get supplies to Allied personnel held in prison camps throughout the theater. Lieutenant John Panas, a radar navigator in the 461st Group, described the satisfaction of dropping something other than bombs: "On May 10 we flew over Spittal, Austria, and dropped food and medical supplies to the American POWs who had been held there. It was a great feeling, flying low over enemy territory and knowing that the guns on the ground had been silenced forever! The Air Force had responsibility to keep our soldiers in good health until the Army Ground Forces could reach them." The Liberators—whose name was especially fitting for the mission—flew low enough to see ex-Kriegies scrambling for parcels and waving their thanks. Panas added, "When we emptied our precious cargo, Colonel [Charles] Gregory gave them a little show by buzzing their barracks at rooftop level."[3]

WAITING TO GO HOME

On V-E Day Twining's command numbered 12,468 officers and 66,082 men: 78,550 total.[4] Most had one overriding ambition, described in contemporary doggerel:

> Those who want to be a hero
> They number almost zero.
> But those who want to be civilians,
> Jesus! They number in the millions!

The same sentiment applied to families waiting at home, and the AAF wasted little time dismantling the Fifteenth. On May 9 the 485th Bomb Group started leaving Venosa, followed by four other Liberator units through month's end.

The Fifth Wing's B-17 groups were retained longer than the others. Three were assigned to the Occupation Air Force for several months, while two made up the "Homebound Task Force," ferrying troops to the United States. The other, the 301st, departed for "Uncle Sugar" in July. Eleven Liberator groups were slated for reassignment or demobilization in the States, while four were transferred to Air Transport Command, deployed as far afield as Morocco, Brazil, and Trinidad. The fighter groups returned to ConUS by the end of November, as did the recon units.

The last of the Fifteenth to depart was the veteran Second Bomb Group, which bade farewell to Foggia at the end of February 1946. On May 26, 1945, Nathan Twining departed the theater to lead Air Materiel Command. He turned the Fifteenth over to Brigadier General James A. Mollison, previously chief of XV Service Command. In August, Twining became commander of the Twentieth Air Force in the Pacific.

While awaiting transport home many men enjoyed extended leave. Some special operations airmen returned "exuberant over the beauties of Switzerland and, incidentally, *les femmes fatales*."[5]

Meanwhile, some Fourteenth Fighter Group pilots unofficially availed themselves of a B-25 parked at Triolo after V-E Day. Since no one seemed concerned, the Lightning pilots tried it out. After finding they could taxi it—the Mitchell had a nose wheel like the Lightning— some of the fliers decided on a grand tour. They hit Athens, Cairo, and Tel Aviv. In most places they circled the tourist spots: "We got a good look at the Pyramids," said Gale Mortensen. A devout Mormon, he was particularly interested in seeing the Holy Land. Ordinarily such antics would incur official displeasure, but when the miscreants finally returned their borrowed bomber, they resumed their routine, awaiting a trip home and discharge.[6]

Upon release some young veterans were addressed by an officer who intoned, "You boys had a nice war so go home and have a nice life."[7] The Fifteenth Air Force was inactivated on September 15, 1945. It was reactivated at Colorado Springs in March 1946 and joined the new Strategic Air Command. After SAC was disbanded in

1992, the Fifteenth became an air mobility task force, standing down in March 2012. Today the Fifteenth Air Force remains on inactive status.

RECKONING

Global war on an industrial scale consumed enormous quantities of men and material. The Fifteenth stood up in November 1943 with an initial cadre of 3,564 combat aircrewmen. Over the next eighteen months, those men were replaced four times, for a total 67,441. From start to finish, aircrew casualties totaled 19,529: nearly 30 percent. Today a sustained loss rate of 3 percent might shut down an air campaign as too expensive to maintain.

As of May 20, 1945, the Fifteenth's combat casualties comprised 2,703 known dead, 8,007 missing, 2,553 wounded, and 4,352 POWs or internees, totaling 17,615. The 1,900-man discrepancy between the two totals is likely due to noncombat losses.[8]

The most dangerous territory for the airmen of the Fifteenth was Austria, where almost one-quarter of their casualties occurred. Next was Italy (18 percent), Germany (14 percent), and Yugoslavia (13 percent). The Fifteenth was busiest, on the other hand, over Italy, where it dropped 30 percent of its ordnance, followed by Austria (24 percent) and Germany (12 percent). The airmen were able to drop more ordnance with fewer casualties over Italy thanks to the lower threat level in Italian skies.

Throughout its existence, 26 percent of the Fifteenth's enlisted men and 19 percent of its officers spent more than two years in the Mediterranean Theater. Non-flying personnel did not rotate home following completion of fifty credit missions, so they remained in the theater longer.

In eighteen months the Fifteenth owned 6,858 aircraft, of which 5,090 were lost or written off—nearly 75 percent. Fighters sustained the heaviest losses and recon planes by far the lightest.[9] The cost of replacement aircraft was substantial. A B-24 cost around $215,500 and a P-51 $51,500—$2.8 million and $684,000, respectively, in 2014 dollars. Planes have become vastly more expensive, however. A B-2 stealth bomber costs $1.15 *billion* and an F-15E Strike Eagle $31 million.[10]

The Fifteenth lost some 2,110 bombers, and those that survived the war did not last long after the Mediterranean warriors were dispersed. The last B-17 unit, the Fifth Bomb Group, flew Fortresses in the Philippines through 1948. Other units kept the Boeings as reconnaissance and special-mission aircraft through 1950.

The last B-24s in service as bombers apparently were based at Castle Field, California, into 1946, before the Ninety-third Group converted to B-29s.

Mustangs went to war again as F-51s, flying with the U.S. Air Force and Australian, South African, and South Korean units to 1953 and beyond. Thunderbolts and Lightnings were not retained after World War II.

FIGHTER SCOREBOARD

The 325th Checkertail Clan finished at the top of the Fifteenth Air Force with 406 victories in Thunderbolts and Mustangs, followed by the Thirty-first with 383 and the Fifty-second with 259, both flying P-51s. The Mustang was masterkill in the Fifteenth, though the three P-38 groups' opportunities had been diminished from August onward, when they were heavily committed to dive-bombing and ground attack. In the last nine months of hostilities, the First and Eighty-second groups claimed only four kills each; the Fourteenth claimed twenty-two. In that same period, the Thirty-first got eighty-two and the 325th eighty-nine. The hardy little horse from North American had the legs and the mission to continue scoring in the air.

Seventy-four fighter pilots downed five or more enemy aircraft to become Fifteenth Air Force aces. Forty-six of them scored all their kills in Mustangs, led by John Voll of the Thirty-first (twenty-one victories), Sully Varnell of the Fifty-second (seventeen), and Sam Brown of the Thirty-first (fifteen and a half). Herky Green was unique in achieving acedom in both the Thunderbolt and the Mustang, for a total of fifteen victories, in addition to three he had won previously in Twelfth Air Force P-40s.

Six Checkertails logged their victories in P-47s, while three others downed five with the P-47 and P-51 combined. Eighteen Lightning pilots made ace, nearly all in June and July 1944. They were led by Mike Brezas of the Fourteenth Group with a dozen kills.

Whatever they flew—Mustang, Lightning, or Thunderbolt—the Fifteenth's fighter pilots owned the skies of southern Europe, from France to the Balkans.

THE TUSKEGEE MYTH AND LEGEND

By far the most publicized unit of the Army Air Forces in World War II is the 332nd Fighter Group. In fact, the Tuskegee Airmen have received more coverage than any five groups in the Fifteenth Air Force combined.[11]

The Red Tails' reputation assumed mythic proportions in the 1980s, but few of the claims made for them withstand scrutiny. Despite having four squadrons rather than the standard three, the 332nd was last in aerial victories. It is true that most other groups had a head start, but even with the extra squadron, the Tuskegee Airmen ranked a distant last in kills per month in combat—one quarter of the top average. The 332nd produced no aces, whereas the other six groups averaged thirteen. It's been said that Colonel Davis did not want any stars on his team, but an examination of individual pilots' records shows that none made claims for five destroyed.

Without a unified policy from Twining, fighter groups were largely free to determine their own escort methods. In the Fifteenth, all but the 332nd adopted aggressive methods intent on breaking up German

formations before they closed with the bombers. It was sound doctrine, as the Luftwaffe had learned at considerable expense in the
Battle of Britain. Furthermore, Doolittle had scrapped Eaker's similar
policy upon taking over the Eighth in early 1944. Doolittle's decision
to loose the fighters, combined with growing numbers of Mustangs,
cut the number of bombers lost to enemy aircraft nearly in half from
January to June 1944.[12] Twining's bomb groups liked seeing nearby
fighters, as had Eaker's Eighth Air Force crews. But Doolittle realized
almost intuitively that close escort ceded the advantage to enemy
fighters, and eventually Twining came to the same conclusion.

The legend that the Tuskegee Airmen never lost a bomber to
enemy fighters was widely if naively accepted. But in 2006, air force
historians pored over every 332nd mission report and found that the
Red Tails lost twenty-seven bombers. We have no comparable figures
for other fighter groups, but going by the average of bomber losses
during the Tuskegee Airmen's time with the Fifteenth, the 332nd
escort record appears good to excellent.

The reasons for the Red Tails' low bomber losses were twofold.
The 332nd shot down relatively few enemy aircraft because it saw
fewer than the other groups, which intercepted the Jagdgruppen
farther afield. The Germans who penetrated the screens of the other
six groups, therefore, often encountered the 332nd near the heavies.

What is poorly understood is that the strategic goal was not simply to reduce bomber losses but to gain air superiority (accomplishing
the mission with acceptable losses). With the attainment of outright
air supremacy—uncontested control of enemy airspace—Fifteenth
bomber losses to fighters plummeted to nearly zero in the final months
of the war. The question of close or roving escort, therefore, was not
an either-or question. The use of both methods provided a binary that
was devastatingly effective.

Admirers have claimed that the 332nd shot down more German
jets than any other fighter group. In truth, the Red Tails were credited
with three Me 262s while the top Fifteenth Air Force jet score was

seven by the Thirty-first Group. The overall record was held by the 357th Group of the Eighth Air Force, with seventeen.

The Tuskegee Airmen might reasonably have concluded that they were not morally obliged to serve a government that discriminated against them on so many levels. But they recognized that America, imperfect as it was, represented a vastly better future for humanity than Nazi Germany or Imperial Japan. Eighty Tuskegee pilots died overseas, proving that all blood runs red. Their legacy requires no exaggeration. When it counted most, they volunteered and showed up.

BOMBING NORTH AND SOUTH

The Combined Bombing Offensive was a tripartite endeavor involving the U.S. Eighth and Fifteenth Air Forces and the RAF Bomber Command. They squeezed Nazi industry, transport, and petroleum production in a giant geographic vise, day and night, for years. There has never been a similar strategic achievement, before or since.

The contrasts between the northern and southern bombing offensives were most evident in targeting. Whereas the Eighth dropped one-third of its bombs on transport targets, the Fifteenth's share was nearly half, a difference that reflects the Fifteenth's access to vulnerable Axis communications, especially in northern Italy and the Balkans.[13] Well within range of southern Germany and Austria, the Fifteenth aimed forty-two thousand tons at the Reich's aviation industry, compared with forty-seven thousand for the Eighth and twenty-nine thousand for the RAF.

Despite the AAF's heavy emphasis on industrial plants, however, the war turned on oil: Germany continued producing large numbers of aircraft and vehicles but ran out of fuel for them. The Fifteenth was responsible for 58 percent of USSTAF's oil campaign sorties; fourteen of the sixty-six petroleum plants targeted were in Romania.

The enormous statistical evidence compiled after the war confirmed that the AAF effort (north and south) overwhelmed the RAF's contribution, with nearly 350 American attacks on petroleum targets (mostly 1943–1945) versus barely 150 British attacks throughout the war.[14] In the last twelve months of hostilities, however, the RAF finally devoted more attention to the Oil Plan. Bomber Command dropped ninety-three thousand tons on petroleum targets, compared with sixty-six thousand tons by the Eighth and forty-eight thousand tons by the Fifteenth. Analysts later concluded that nearly 20 percent of British bombs on oil targets were duds, as were 12 percent of AAF ordnance.[15]

How critical was oil? At its height, the German army was perhaps 80-percent horse- and mule-drawn; at any given moment, the Wehrmacht maintained an average of 1,100,000 animals. Near the end, new Luftwaffe pilots entered combat with about one-third the flight time of their opponents—an impossible situation.[16]

The most formidable target was the Vienna area, a transport, oil, and production hub that extracted a steady toll, topping three hundred planes at war's end. Said one bomber crewman, "You weren't really in the Fifteenth unless you'd been to Vienna." One major arrived at Panatanella in 1944 talking incessantly about the perils of the Pacific: the weather, the flak, the fighters. He even expressed a condescending opinion of the Mediterranean Theater. Flying as an observer with the 464th Group approaching Vienna, he looked ahead at a darkened sky, declaring, "Looks like a hell of a thunderstorm up ahead." The command pilot, Captain Chester Schmidt, replied, "That isn't weather—it's flak." The visitor blanched, grabbed a helmet, and regurgitated his breakfast therein. Schmidt was none too pleased when he clamped a helmet on his head during the bomb run—the one just used by the Pacific veteran.[17]

After Ploesti, the Fifteenth's third-toughest target was Munich, where at least 101 aircraft were downed. Wiener Neustadt, Regensburg, Blechhammer, Steyr, and Budapest all accounted for fifty or more planes.

Sixty years later, "Black Hammer" still had airmen's respect. A 460th veteran recalled, "The names Blechhammer, The Lost City of Atlantis, and Shangri-La all share the quality of mysticism. Blechhammer, however, was real, not fantasy. Like Atlantis and Shangri-La, you cannot find it on a map; it was not a city, or a location that is identified by that name today. Some of the ruins of Blechhammer North and South are still there, and the power plant at Blechhammer South has been rebuilt, and is in operation. While we remember Blechhammer as a synthetic oil plant, it was in reality much more than that." The 460th knew it well, with nine missions to Blechhammer South and two to the North complex between June and December, costing an average of one Liberator per trip.[18]

PLOESTI IN RETROSPECT

In January 1944, three months before the Fifteenth launched against Ploesti, the Committee of Operations Analysts predicted that the Wehrmacht (all the German armed forces) had six months of fuel stockpiled and that a focused attack on refineries would cut production by 2.75 million tons, producing "curtailment but not collapse."[19]

Allied expectations for a Ploesti campaign proved excessive. At the time, many analysts believed that shutting off the Romanian taps could largely ground the Luftwaffe. While the Germans always rose to defend petroleum targets, they had other options—notably synthetic fuel plants, which had received a high priority from the late 1930s. Coal-derived gasoline was especially useful to Hermann Göring's air force, and remained so throughout the war.

The 1944 campaign lasted from early April to mid-August and involved 5,287 Allied sorties (229 British) that dropped 12,870 tons of bombs. The cost was steep: 237 bombers (fifteen RAF) and forty-nine fighters. The latter included P-38s employed as dive-bombers.

The figure of most importance to the Luftwaffe was aviation gasoline received from Romania. The pre-campaign figure of sixteen thousand metric tons in both February and March was halved in April and May, dropping to a mere two thousand tons in June, but it rebounded to seven thousand tons in July. Total Wehrmacht gasoline exports dropped from fifty-eight thousand tons in March to twenty thousand in July, the last full month of the campaign, and twelve thousand in August.[20]

The Fifteenth's efforts produced results, but how much? A post-bombing analysis noted, "The August attacks left Ploesti in a highly vulnerable position. All but one of the larger refineries were incapable of any substantial production for some weeks or months. The single exception, Astra Romana, accounted for considerably more than half of the potential production of the next month." The survey concluded, "One successful attack on it and Standard, comparable with the successful August raids on other installations, would have knocked production down to 15% of the base level for a substantial period."[21]

American airmen were eager to connect the dots between the end of the Ploesti campaign and the severe reduction in the area's oil production. But that may be too simple a conclusion. With the Soviets steadily advancing into Romania, the Germans had little reason to exert much effort to repair the damage. Why give the enemy possession of working refineries? In any case, the question proved moot as Russian troops occupied Ploesti beginning August 30.

Despite its success, the Fifteenth made its own job unnecessarily difficult. After the Ploesti campaign, interviews with Romanian officers noted several factors that eased the defenders' burden. They included "airline operations" with predictable schedules (target times between 10:00 a.m. and 3:00 p.m.), repeating routes and altitudes. Only five areas were identified as initial points, simplifying the defenders' planning.

Emphasis on visual bombing permitted flak batteries to gain accurate altitude information by optical range finding without reliance on radar. Given the technical limits of blind bombing, however, the attackers had no alternative.

Still, despite shortcomings, the Fifteenth accomplished its primary mission. In Adolf Galland's assessment, "Raids of the allied air fleets on the German petrol supply installations was the most important of the combined factors which brought about the collapse of Germany."[22] The German armaments minister, Albert Speer, agreed, stating that oil was the primary strategic target in the war. The CBO, he added, would have been even more effective had petroleum been targeted sooner.[23]

Days after Germany's surrender, Hermann Göring was interviewed by General Spaatz and other senior U.S. airmen. The deposed marshal, who had studied French, English, and Latin in school, was eager to talk. Asked if air attacks affected Luftwaffe training, he replied, "Yes, for instance the attacks on oil retarded the training because our new pilots could not get sufficient training before they were put in the air, where they were no match for your fliers." American targeting, said the Luftwaffe, was "excellent. As soon as we started to repair an oil installation you always bombed it again before we could produce one ton." That assessment was not quite accurate, as Ploesti demonstrated, but the lingering effect of sustained bombardment was undeniable.[24]

THE MIGHTY EIGHTH VERSUS THE FORGOTTEN FIFTEENTH

In the popular memory of World War II, there were two Army Air Forces: the Eighth and everything else.

Many Fifteenth airmen felt like second-class citizens in the AAF, lamenting, "We were a poor boy outfit." The sentiment found expression in a Mediterranean Theater ditty sung to the tune of "As Time Goes By."

> You must remember this
> The flak can't always miss
> Somebody's gonna die.

The odds are always too damned high
As flak goes by ...
It's still the same old story
The Eighth gets all the glory
While we're the ones who die.
The odds are always too damned high
As flak goes by.[25]

Seven decades later MTO veterans still wonder why they were so overlooked. Undoubtedly much of the reason has to do with geography. From 1942 onward, America and the world focused on the eventual Allied landings in northern France. Long before anyone heard of "D-Day," the Soviets clamored for a second front, though the case has been made that the Combined Bombing Offensive represented a front in three dimensions for three years before June 1944. But boots on the ground were what most people looked for.

The Italian slogging match failed to grab the public's imagination. After all, Ernest Hemingway liberated the Ritz Hotel bar in Paris rather than a bistro in Rome. And despite the prize-winning reporting of correspondent Ernie Pyle and the popular irreverence of GI cartoonist Bill Mauldin, "the Med" simply could not compete with the perceived glamour of England. Perhaps a Fifteenth aerial gunner came closest to the mark when he asked, "If you were a war correspondent would you rather sip scotch in a London hotel or swig vino under canvas at Foggia?" The question answers itself.[26]

In postwar popular culture, the Mediterranean air war remained thoroughly overshadowed by the Mighty Eighth. At least half a dozen films have portrayed the British-based bombing offensive, starting with three 1948 releases: the excellent *Twelve O'Clock High*, based on Beirne Lay's novel; *Command Decision*, derived from a taut stage play; and the lightweight *Fighter Squadron*. John Hersey's solid novel became *The War Lover* (1962), followed by *The Thousand Plane Raid* (1969), a forgettable TV movie. Most recently *The Memphis*

Belle (1990) built on the fame of the wartime documentary. *12 O'Clock High* also was adapted as a television series that ran from 1964 to 1967.

Only three well-known aviation movies are set in the Mediterranean Theater—*Catch-22*, the 1970 satire based on Joseph Heller's Twelfth Air Force experience, and two 332nd Group entries, the 1995 television movie *Tuskegee Airmen* and the disappointing 2012 feature *Red Tails*.

Yet a few anomalies exist in the Eighth-Fifteenth rivalry. Every group but one in the Fifteenth received the Distinguished Unit Citation during the organization's existence. The 451st received three, and sixteen others received two each, though the 376th Bomb Group, the First and Eighty-second Fighter Groups had two previous DUCs. The Ninety-eighth was the only group without a DUC during the Fifteenth's career, but it had been decorated twice previously. In contrast, between November 1943 and V-E Day, less than two-thirds of the Mighty Eighth's groups received the DUC. The reasons for the discrepancy remain unknown. In the period ten fliers from the Eighth earned the Medal of Honor. In addition to David Kingsley's and Donald Pucket's posthumous Medals of Honor, at least twenty-eight Fifteenth airmen received the Distinguished Service Cross, the nation's second-highest decoration. Eleven of them perished and two others were captured.[27]

Most of the other numbered air forces received even less attention than the Fifteenth. The Mediterranean Theater's tactical air force, the Twelfth, was largely ignored, and its counterpart in the European Theater, the Ninth, always played second fiddle to the Eighth. From November 1943, the Ninth received two Medals of Honor, the Twelfth one.

In the Pacific the Fifth Air Force received by far the most press—no surprise given the immense ego of the Southwest Pacific commander, General Douglas MacArthur. The other Pacific Theater air forces, the Seventh and Thirteenth, were largely overlooked in the Central and

South Pacific, while the small Eleventh battled the Aleutian williwaw far more than the Japanese. The spirit of the Flying Tigers lived on in Major General Claire Chennault's China-based Fourteenth, which overshadowed the Tenth in India.

Closer to home, the Sixth Air Force spent most of the war guarding the Panama Canal Zone. The First through Fourth Air Forces were regionally based in the United States. There were no sixteenth through nineteenth, but the Twentieth conducted B-29 operations from the China-Burma-India Theater and from the Mariana Islands.

WHAT BECAME OF THEM

Bomber crews usually were grateful to survive, but some fighter pilots never got over the raw thrill and heady satisfaction of flying combat: the challenge, the comradeship, the youthful sense of purpose. For a twenty-five-year-old male who had lived at four hundred miles per hour, shooting whatever crossed his sights, peace could be dull.

Nevertheless, the huge majority of veterans, from the top down, adjusted. Ira Eaker was recalled to Washington at the end of April 1945, becoming Hap Arnold's deputy and the chief of air staff. Eaker retired in 1947 and died forty years later.

Carl Spaatz, who conspired with Eaker and Twining to bomb refineries rather than railroads, moved to the Pacific in the summer of 1945. He served in the same capacity as overall strategic air commander and witnessed Japan's surrender in September. He succeeded Arnold as the air force chief in 1946 and retired in 1948, having realized his generation's ambition of an independent air force.

Jimmy Doolittle remained one of the most celebrated aviators of the twentieth century. His unique record included command of three air forces—the Twelfth in North Africa, the Fifteenth in Italy, and the Eighth in Britain. He retired a year after V-E Day, a reserve lieutenant general, and returned to Shell Oil. He was the first president of the

Air Force Association and served as a consultant to the U.S. government on scientific research, commercial aviation, and intelligence. Four decades after the war, Congress elevated him to full general, though reportedly some members were uncertain why he received the honor. He died in California in 1993, age ninety-six.

After Italy, Nathan Twining ran the Air Materiel Command, and in 1947 he became head of Alaskan Air Command. Still a three-star, he was preparing to retire in 1950 when the air force vice chief, General Muir Fairchild, died unexpectedly. Twining was promoted to full general and filled out the term, becoming chief of staff in 1953. Four years later he became the first airman named chairman of the Joint Chiefs, holding the position until 1960. He died in 1982, age eighty-four. His younger brother Merrill was a Marine Corps lieutenant general.

Dean C. Strother, chief of XV Fighter Command, rose to four stars and held NATO positions as well as leading North American Air Defense Command. He retired in 1966 and died in 2000.

John D. Ryan, briefly CO of the Second Bomb Group, lost a finger to flak and moved up to Fifth Wing staff. He headed the Strategic Air Command from 1964 to 1967 and was air force chief of staff from 1969 to 1973. In the latter role he was criticized for failing to support General John Lavelle, who conducted "protective reaction strikes" into North Vietnam. Ryan's son Michael also served as chief from 1997 to 2001.

Colonel Arthur Agan, the First Group CO captured in March 1945, became a lieutenant general and retired in 1970 after leading the Aerospace Defense Command.

Among the twenty Mustang aces of the Thirty-first Group, George Loving achieved three stars and retired in 1979 after thirty-six years of commissioned service. His highly readable Mediterranean memoir, *Woodbine Red Leader*, was published in 2003.

Curly Edwinson returned to the States after the Eighty-second Group tangled with Soviet fighters in November 1944. His career was unharmed, and he held numerous other commands, including a P-47 unit prepared to fight the Soviets in earnest during the Berlin Airlift of 1948. When not flying he pursued his passion for skeet shooting and became world champion in 1952. He retired as a brigadier general in 1961 and passed away in 1985.

Some outstanding leaders never advanced far beyond their wartime ranks. They included the popular, puckish Bob Baseler of the Checkertail Clan. He remained a lieutenant colonel until 1952 and retired as a "bird" colonel a decade later. He died of cancer in 1983.

Among the Fifteenth's top fighter aces, Sully Varnell was killed in a P-40 crash in Florida in April 1945, age twenty-three. John Voll retired as a colonel and died in 1987. Herky Green retired in 1964 after thirteen years as a colonel. He wrote a memoir and died in 2006.

Leslie Caplan, the dedicated 449th Group flight surgeon captured in 1944, was awarded the Legion of Merit for his stellar work in captivity. After the war he was treated for tuberculosis and later received a psychology degree in Minneapolis. He died in 1969, only sixty-one, and is buried in Arlington Cemetery.

One of Caplan's POW patients, B-17 gunner Bill Hess, recovered sufficiently from his frostbite to resume civilian life. He went on to serve in the Korean War then pursued a career in the petroleum business in his native Louisiana before retiring to Texas. Hess fought the lingering effects of frostbite—and the VA bureaucracy—for decades. Finally in 2003 he contacted a neurologist who examined him closely. She was appalled: "This has been going on for *how* long?" After a detailed assessment she certified him 40-percent disabled below the knees.

Although he was a bomber crewman, Hess became a world authority on fighter pilots. He wrote or coauthored twenty books on World War II aviation and was secretary-historian of the American Fighter Aces Association. He became close friends with a onetime enemy, Me 262 pilot Franz Stigler.

In recalling the Luftwaffe corporal who fed him and the paternal sergeant who guided him through a potential lynch mob, Hess concluded, "Most people will look out for themselves. But when you have somebody who's as cold and miserable and starving as you are, and he shares his last scrap of food, that is a *friend*."[28]

Ariel Weekes, who bombed the Daimler-Benz tank works in March 1945, looked on wryly when Daimler purchased Chrysler in 1998.

John Mullins, a pilot of the First Fighter Group, completed his tour in time to celebrate his twenty-first birthday at home. In the 1990s he wrote a unit history, *An Escort of P-38s*, and returned to Italy to research the book. Along the way Mullins tried to locate "Sergeant Tony," the youngster the group had adopted.

As Mullins's wife, Phyllis, explained,

> When we went to Italy and the area doing his research, we stayed in a hotel in Foggia where the only one speaking English was the desk clerk. John asked him about Tony Casstriota, did anyone know him? It turned out that he owned a dry goods store right there in town. With much arranging via phone, we arranged to meet Tony at his store. I'm certain he didn't remember John as he was during the war-time ... but when we opened the door of the store, there was Tony *and* his wife all dressed what looked to us as their Sunday best ... along with two of their grandchildren. Tony didn't remember any of the English he knew back in the day, so it wound up that the hotel desk clerk would translate by phone everything spoken between John and Tony.
>
> After we left, John and I agreed the entire time we were together the Casstriotas seemed honored with our visit, and we were glad we'd made the effort.

John Mullins died in 2004.[29]

Three Fifteenth Air Force men became United States senators, all
Democrats: B-24 pilots Lloyd Bentsen of Texas (449th Group) and
George McGovern of South Dakota (455th Bomb Group) and navigator William D. Hathaway of Maine (376th Bomb Group). Hathaway was unseated after one term but McGovern and Bentsen became
professional politicians, and both ran for president. McGovern won
the Democratic Party's nomination in 1972 and lost in a landslide to
the ex-navy man Richard Nixon. Bentsen, as Michael Dukakis's running mate in 1988, uttered one of the most famous political put-
downs of all time when he informed his opponent, Senator Dan
Quayle, that he was "no Jack Kennedy." Bentsen died in 2006 and
McGovern in 2012. At this writing Hathaway is still living.

FRIENDS AND ENEMIES

Aleksandr Koldunov, who tangled with Curly Edwinson's Lightnings, remained active into the Cold War. Twice a Hero of the Soviet
Union, in 1977 he was promoted to marshal of aviation, leading the
air defense command, and wore another hat as deputy defense minister. In 1978 his command shot down the errant Korean Air Lines
flight 007. When the German teenager Mathias Rust landed his
Cessna in Red Square in 1987, humiliating the Soviet defense establishment, Koldunov was forced to resign as chief marshal of aviation.
He died in 1992.

Colonel Gotthard Handrick, the Olympic champion who directed
Vienna's air defense, settled in Hamburg after the war. His family
received food and clothing from his 1936 American pentathlon rival,
later Major General Charles Leonard, and eventually became a sales
representative for Daimler-Benz.

When the war ended, Adolf Galland had barely recovered from
a combat wound and accepted the risk of contacting the Americans
to surrender his command. Widely admired, he died in 1996. His

friend Colonel Johannes Steinhoff, who had lain near death with severe burns from a jet crash, rose to command the postwar Bundes-luftwaffe and was chairman of the NATO military committee upon his retirement in 1974. He wrote two books detailing his wartime service and often attended history symposia in Europe and the United States. He passed away in 1994.

In the 1980s, the former Me 262 pilot Franz Stigler described his "discharge": "I did what any American fighter pilot would have done. I got on my motorcycle with my girlfriend and I went home." He became well known as the Luftwaffe ace who had spared an Eighth Air Force B-17 over the North Sea in December 1943, and he died in 2008.[30]

Constantin Cantacuzino, the Romanian ace who helped organize the POW airlift from Bucharest, remained in the cockpit after his nation switched sides. He added some German aircraft to the nearly forty Russian and American planes he had downed, then resumed his airline career. He came under unwelcome scrutiny from the new Communist regime, however, and decided not to make a return flight from Italy in 1947. He settled in Spain, continuing to impress audiences with his low-level aerobatics, but died following surgery in 1958. He was only fifty-two. Married several times, he produced a daughter, the novelist Oana Orlea, while another wife became the mother of American television star Linda Gray of *Dallas* fame. Cantacuzino was reunited with his American POW conspirator, Colonel James Gunn, at least once after the war. Gunn died in Texas in 1999.

The Hungarian 109 pilot "Mike" Karatsonyi emigrated to America and became friends with his former enemies Bob Goebel and Art Fiedler, who had flown P-51s against the Pumas in 1944.

REFLECTIONS

From the perspective of six or more decades, former Fifteenth airmen—like all veterans—inevitably look astern, trailing slipstreams of memories.

Ralph Anderson, a B-24 group's armorer, was like many Foggia veterans:

> I did not go into towns very often, as they were very smelly as they were primitive and had no sewer systems, so the streets were the sewage lines. I did get to travel some and visited famous places like Rome, Florence, Naples, Leghorn, and Pisa. I was hitch-hiking to Naples and saw Mount Vesuvius erupting ash all over everything. Being twenty years old and not a history student from a small town in Pennsylvania, I did not even know what I was looking at most of the time. Years later I would see something or place and say "Yes, I saw that during the war." My wife and I have traveled in Europe but not back to Italy. I guess I figure I have seen it before but I am sure it's different today.[31]

In contrast to "the joy boys of the Eighth," bomber crews in the Fifteenth did more with less. "Our food was terrible," said one airman. "Our only decent meal was before a mission, and might be chicken. Mostly we got corned beef in blocks and we'd have to cut pieces off the slabs. Sometimes we stole K rations because they were better. Most places were off limits in town because food and water were contaminated. I only made three or four visits [to Amendola] because the place was all torn up. People were selling souvenirs mostly made from crashed airplanes. We were told to avoid the girls—a lot of them had bleached blonde hair because they tried to attract Germans before we got there. Some had blonde headed, blue eyed kids."[32]

The 484th Group in the Forty-ninth Wing had an eye on the far horizon. One veteran wrote of his comrades,

> [T]hey were not fatalists, they knew the power would soon pass into their own hands and had to survive to keep traditional values safe. The people back home were depending

on them. What depressed all airmen was the appearance
of the Me 262 jet powered fighter. With determined vigor
the jets were tearing huge holes in USAAF bomber formations. Luckily the Luftwaffe squadrons were small and the
losses could be tolerated. But! But! Why hadn't the guys
back home come up with something better? The airmen
were determined then and there to do something about this
outrage when they returned home. Today's precision Air
Force is proof.... This retired generation of Pearl Harbor,
its job now almost complete, wants to sit back and write
its memoirs.[33]

A 450th Group ball turret gunner, Hugh Jones, spoke for thousands of combat aircrewmen in 2001 when, commenting on his wartime journal,

The teenage cool sets my teeth on edge at this date, but I
thought I was telling it as it was. There are also several
points I would make now as I look back that I had left out
as I set forth each mission's report.

For example, the bravado was exactly that: I was often
very frightened during the missions, particularly during the
actual bomb run.

The moment after the bombs away call remained a
frightening moment because I was also looking down at
the bomb site from the turret, and I could see not only all
the flak around me, but I also could see the parachutes and
damaged planes that had been hit and were out of control,
some going down in flames, some with parachutes flitting
out, one by one; sometimes with no chutes appearing.[34]

Some fliers, however, found fulfillment in European skies. Fighter
ace George Loving said, "As a twenty-one-year-old P-51 Mustang pilot
assigned to the Thirty-first Fighter Group, I flew fifty combat missions

as a flight, squadron, and group leader escorting formations of hundreds of B-17s and B-24s bounded for targets all across eastern and southern Europe. It was a great adventure."[35]

Another Mustang ace candidly said, "On the day the war ended I sat down and cried, and not because I was glad it was over."

The correspondent Ernie Pyle was the most popular chronicler of the Mediterranean war, writing about fliers as well as GIs. In his 1944 book, *Brave Men*, he wrote, "There was some exhilaration there in Italy, and some fun along with the misery and the sadness, but on the whole it had been bitter. Few of us can ever conjure up any truly fond memories of the Italian campaign. The enemy had been hard, and so had the elements.... There was little solace for those who had suffered, and none at all for those who had died, in trying to rationalize about why things had happened as they did."[36]

Today, the veterans of the "Forgotten Fifteenth," their numbers rapidly dwindling, look back on their experience and know that Pyle's tribute remains as valid as ever.

IN MEMORIAM

As of 2012 about seventy-three thousand Americans were still missing in action from the Second World War, and most of them, of course, will never be found. They lie in long-lost hasty graves, entombed in sunken ships and planes, lost in jungle overgrowth, or simply blasted into nothingness in the era of high explosives.[37]

The common sentiment among survivors is that those who came back should always remember those who didn't. Some take that obligation to extraordinary lengths. Lieutenant John S. McConnon was a 376th Group navigator in August 1944 when his Liberator was shot down over Albania. Four fliers safely bailed out; the others died. The McConnon family in Pittsburgh had little additional information, but with demise of the Soviet Union, travel restrictions eased in the former Communist bloc. John's brother James corresponded with Albanians interested in helping American families, leading to a possible find in 1995. James went to Albania, and three years later U.S. Army MIA searchers recovered three skeletons that were sent to the Central Identification Laboratory in Hawaii. Lieutenant McConnon was identified, as were Major Frank Blakely and Sergeant Wayne Shaffner. In 1999 the McConnon family survivors buried their brother in Oakland, Pennsylvania.[38]

There have been other relentless searches. Staff Sergeant Martin Troy, a thirty-year-old married draftee, was a 460th Bomb Group crewman. He became a B-24 waist gunner and went missing on a June 30, 1944, mission to Hungary. A squadron mate, bombardier Joseph "Jerry" Conlon, recalled that Troy was the only crewman from the lost Liberator not found, and Conlon was determined to bring him home. He made three trips to central Hungary looking for the crash site, and he "pestered the hell out of the U.S. military" to pursue the clues. His persistence was rewarded. In 2007 American military searchers found bones thought to be Martin Troy's. Positive identification came in 2008, and months later Sergeant Troy was buried at Arlington Cemetery in the presence of his ninety-year-old brother.[39]

Not all searches have been conducted by Americans. On December 17, 1944, *Arsenic and Lace* was one of ten 461st Group Liberators lost on an Odertal mission. Lieutenant Gerry Smith's plane was shot down by fighters near Olomuc, now in the Czech Republic. But local residents wanted to honor the memory of their allies and contacted Smith's daughter Claire. In December 2010 the researcher Jirka Cernosek sent the crew's families photos and a video of the monument's dedication.[40]

THEN AND NOW

Today Foggia has far less aviation activity than seventy years ago. Gino Lisa Airport is served by three airlines, mainly from Milan, Turin, and Palermo. They fly Agusta 109 helicopters and Saab 2000 turboprops. The Saab carries fifty-plus passengers at 350 mph or better—a cruise speed seldom attained by World War II fighters. ·

A visit to Foggia conjures up an era that came and went with astonishing speed and violence. In 1941, aerial fleets of hundreds of multi-engine bombers were almost unknown. Four years later they were common in Europe and the Western Pacific. Then, with the end of World War II, air armadas became extinct, never to return.

A handful of the aircraft remain. Of some twelve thousand B-17s produced, only ten were still flying in 2013. Excluding a handful of navy versions, only two of the eighteen thousand B-24s remained airworthy. The Fifteenth's fighters are still represented by roughly 150 flying Mustangs out of fifteen thousand produced and half a dozen of the ten thousand Lightnings built.

✪ ✪ ✪

In the twenty-first century the concept of air power has evolved into "aerospace dominance," including cyberspace. Current operations bear no resemblance to those of the 1940s, when the grandfathers and great-grandfathers of today's airmen penetrated well-defended enemy airspace and manually put gravity bombs on target. The U.S. Air Force's primary missions now are airlift and "remotely-piloted vehicles," firing precision guided weapons controlled by computers continents away. In 2013 the Department of Defense created the Distinguished Warfare Medal for drone pilots, ranking below the Distinguished Flying Cross but, unaccountably, above the Bronze Star for valor and the Purple Heart for combat wounds.[41]

It's a different world today, with new technologies to fight new enemies. When World War II aircrewmen hear about drone operators being studied for signs of stress, the veterans shake their heads. One gunner bomber responded, "Stress? You were nineteen years old. They got you up at 4 a.m. and you might be dead by noon. Don't tell me about stress!"[42]

The armadas that trailed cottony contrails across the European skies represented an enormous investment of people, material, and effort that only Britain and America ever achieved. The Fifteenth's war was fought from the ground up: from the sticky clay of Foggia to battlefields five miles high, from Ploesti to Berlin. In its eighteen months the Fifteenth dominated Europe's southern horizon, smashing the Axis Vulcan forges in a sanguinary effort that remains largely unknown seventy years later.

But let the final word come from the German who perhaps appreciated the Fifteenth's achievement better than any other man. In his memoir, the Nazi armament minister Albert Speer wrote,

> I could see omens of the war's end almost every day in the blue southern sky when, flying provocatively low, the bombers of the American Fifteenth Air Force crossed the Alps from their Italian bases to attack German industrial targets. Not a German fighter plane anywhere in sight; no antiaircraft fire. This scene of total defenselessness produced a greater impression upon me than any reports.[43]

However little the Fifteenth Air Force was honored in its own country, the enemy knew its worth.

ACKNOWLEDGMENTS

My profound gratitude goes to Bill Hess, a lifetime friend and colleague. Our relationship began when I was in high school, only about two years younger than when he flew missions from Italy as a B-17 gunner. Bill has been unstinting in his support for this project, and much of what I learned about the Fifteenth as an institution is due to him.

Other Fifteenth airmen I've enjoyed knowing include the late Colonel Bob Baseler, commander of the 325th "Checkertail" Fighter Group. If there was a more colorful CO in the Mediterranean Theater, I don't know who it was. Additional Fifteenth veterans from the American Fighter Aces Association include Barrie Davis, Art Fielder, Bob Goebel, George Loving, and Tom Maloney.

I was fortunate to become more than casually acquainted with General Jimmy Doolittle in the 1970s and '80s. He led such a richly varied, influential aviation life that command of the Fifteenth Air Force often is reckoned among his lesser accomplishments. As is often the case, in retrospect I wish I had engaged him more often about establishing the Fifteenth, but his perspective was invaluable.

More World War II veterans groups are turning over the controls to children and grandchildren. Via the 449th Bomb Group's "next generation" I was fortunate to establish contact with Laura Caplan, whose flight surgeon father, Major Leslie Caplan, became a revered figure among POWs.

Among the most remarkable people I have ever known was the late General Johannes Steinhoff, who led a Luftwaffe jet unit against the U.S. Strategic Air Forces. Terribly burned in a crash at war's end, he made a full recovery to become West Germany's senior airman in NATO. I had the pleasure to work with him on two symposia, and his perspective was always fresh, astute, and compelling. Thanks to Colin Heaton for putting me in touch with General Steinhoff's daughter Ursula.

In the 1980s I found myself sharing ramp space with Canadian citizen Franz Stigler at Pacific Northwest air shows. His Bf 108 with twenty-eight victory bars on the rudder—testament to his wartime record as a Luftwaffe pilot—always drew a crowd, and Haya was a popular figure at hangar dances.

Another German transplanted to Canada was Oskar Boesch, best known for his sailplane aerobatics performed to classical music. His recollections as a twenty-year-old Focke-Wulf 190 pilot still reverberate in my memory.

The Fifteenth fought five other Axis powers besides Germany: Italy, Hungary, Romania, Bulgaria, and Slovakia. Their role in the southern air campaign, though less than the Luftwaffe's, required coverage for completeness and objectivity. My splendid European sources are cited in the appendix.

Archival support came from Dr. Daniel Haulman and Lynn Gamma of the Air Force Historical Research Agency. When I ran out of my own sources, they and their colleagues answered my pleas promptly and efficiently, providing essential documents for often-obscure subjects. Meanwhile, Terry Aitken and Brett Stolle were equally helpful at the National Museum of the Air Force.

Frequent supporters included Dr. Frank Olynyk, the world authority on aerial victory claims, and longtime colleague Fred Johnsen, who provided numerous photos.

A dip of the wing to my fine agent, Jim Hornfischer, who recognized the value of a "Forgotten Fifteenth" history from the beginning.

Finally, a word to other World War II historians. Over the past eight years, I have logged time's inevitable effect upon the ranks of those who survived the greatest conflict of the twentieth century—or any other. In 2005 one-quarter of the contributors to my study of the First Battle of the Philippine Sea were deceased upon publication. That figure rose to 40 percent with *Whirlwind* in 2010 and passed 50 percent two years later with my history of the aircraft carrier USS *Enterprise*.

Historic memory is perishable—it has a shelf life. As this volume is published, the "Forgotten Fifteenth" was established seventy-one years ago. Its remaining veterans' median age is nearly ninety. In aviation terms, they are rapidly "departing the pattern."

For those intending to record the Second World War, I offer three words:

Do it now.

Barrett Tillman
March 2013

APPENDIX

ABBREVIATIONS

KIA: killed in action

KIFA: killed in flying accident

POW: prisoner of war

ORGANIZATION OF THE FIFTEENTH AIR FORCE
Most dates are wing headquarters under Fifteenth Air Force control. Individual groups often arrived later. Bases are as of April 1945.

5th Bombardment Wing	Foggia
B-17s, November 1, 1943	
2nd Bomb Group	Amendola
97th Bomb Group	Amendola
99th Bomb Group	Tortorella

301st Bomb Group	Lucera
463rd Bomb Group	Celone
483rd Bomb Group	Sterparone

47th Bombardment Wing   Manduria
B-24s, November 1943

98th Bomb Group	Lecce
376th Bomb Group	San Pancrazio
449th Bomb Group	Grottaglie
450th Bomb Group	Manduria

49th Bombardment Wing   Castelluccio
B-24s, 29 December 1943

451st Bomb Group	Castelluccio
461st Bomb Group	Torretta
484th Bomb Group	Torretta

55th Bombardment Wing   Spinazzola
B-24s, March 1944

460th Bomb Group	Spinazzola
464th Bomb Group	Pantanella
465th Bomb Group	Pantanella
485th Bomb Group	Venosa

304th Bombardment Wing   Cerignola
B-24s, December 1943

454th Bomb Group	San Giovanni
455th Bomb Group	San Giovanni
456th Bomb Group	Stornara
459th Bomb Group	Giulia

305th Fighter Wing (Provisional)   Fano
P-38s, September 4, 1944
Subordinate to previously existing 306th Wing

1st Fighter Group	Lesina
14th Fighter Group	Triolo

82nd Fighter Group   Vincenzo

306th Fighter Wing   Mondfolfo?
P-51s, January 15, 1944
Previously included all Fifteenth Air Force fighter groups

31st Fighter Group   Mondolfo
52nd Fighter Group   Piagiolino
325th Fighter Group   Mondolfo
332nd Fighter Group   Ramitelli

5th Photographic Reconnaissance Group Bari
F-4s, F-5s, December 1943

15th Photo Recon Squadron
32nd Photo Recon Squadron
37th Photo Recon Squadron

2641st Special Group   Brindisi
Previously 15th Special Group, December 1944
B-17s, B-24s

859th Bomb Squadron   Rosignano
885th Bomb Squadron   Rosignano

Independent Unit
P-38s, January 1944   Bari
154th Weather Reconnaissance Squadron

BOMB TONNAGE BY COUNTRY

Country	Tonnage	Percent
Italy	90,914	29.3%
Austria	74,211	23.9%
Germany	35,927	11.6%
Romania	26,364	8.5%
Yugoslavia	22,012	7.1%
Hungary	21,933	7.0%
France	19,014	6.1%
Czechoslovakia	10,609	3.4%
Greece	3,226	0.10%
Bulgaria	2,601	0.08%

Poland	2,095	0.06%
Albania	372	0.01%

Total	309,278

BOMB TONNAGE BY TARGETS

Marshalling yards	107,538	34.7%
Petroleum	59,923	19.3%
Airfields, aircraft factories	42,207	13.6%
Railroads, roads, bridges	41,938	13.5%
Support of ground forces	25,657	8.2%
Industrial targets	14,976	4.8%
Harbors and shipping	12,520	4.0%
Unspecified, miscellaneous	4,519	1.4%

Total	309,278

FIFTEENTH AIR FORCE
FIGHTER GROUP AERIAL VICTORIES

325th	P-47s, P-51s	406 from December 1943
31st	P-51s	383 from April 1944
52nd	P-51s	259 from May 1944
14th	P-38s	227 from November 1943
82nd	P-38s	215 from November 1943
1st	P-38s	184 from November 1943
332nd	P-51s	96 from May 1944

SELECTED STATISTICS

Bomber sorties	152,542
Fighter sorties	89,835
Total air victories	3,946
Rounds of ammo	25.1 million
Gallons of gasoline	450 million
Aircraft lost	3,410
Aircraft damaged	14,181
KIA	2,703
MIA	12,359
WIA	2,553

LEADING FIFTEENTH AIR FORCE ACES

Name	Group	Victories	
Capt. John J. Voll	31st	21	
Capt. James S. Varnell Jr.	52nd	17	KIFA US
Maj. Samuel J. Brown	31st	15.5	
Maj. Herschel H. Green	325th	15	+3 12AF
Maj. Robert C. Curtis	52nd	13	+1 12AF
1Lt. James L. Brooks	31st	13	
Capt. Harry A. Parker	325th	13	KIA
1Lt. Michael Brezas	14th	12	POW
1Lt. Norman C. Skogstad	325th	11	
Capt. John R. Goebel	31st	11	
Capt. John B. Lawler	52nd	11	
1Lt. Wayne L. Lowry	325th	11	
1Lt. Robert E. Riddle	52nd	11	
Capt. Walter J. Goehausen Jr.	31st	10	

CONTRIBUTORS

Anderson, Ralph	464th Bomb Group armorer
Boesch, Oscar	Jagdgeschwader 3 pilot
Chalmers, Robert T.	461st Bomb Group pilot
Clemens, Robert C.	463rd Bomb Group navigator
Davis, Barrie S.	325th Fighter Group pilot
Fieldler, Arthur C., Jr.	325th Fighter Group pilot
Goebel, Robert J.	31st Fighter Group pilot (d. 2011)
Heilbrun, Herb	301st Bomb Group pilot
Hess, William N.	97th Bomb Group gunner
Jenkins, Lawrence L.	2nd Bomb Group pilot.
Karr, Robert A.	52nd Fighter Group pilot
Loving, George F., Jr.	31st Fighter Group pilot
Mortensen, Gale	14th Fighter Group pilot
Panas, John N.	461st Bomb Group radar operator
Peters, James S., Sr.	99th Bomb Group gunner
Steinhoff, Johannes	JG 7, JV 44 (d. 1994)
Stigler, Franz	JV 44 (d. 2008)
Sternfels, Robert W.	98th Bomb Group pilot
Wickersham, Charles	2nd Bomb Group pilot

National Museum of the U.S. Air Force
University of North Carolina, Chapel Hill
U.S. Air Force Historical Research Agency
U.S. Embassy in Sofia

Terry Aitken, William H. Allen, Dénes Bernad, Duane and Betty Bohnstedt
(460th Bomb Group Association), Colonel Walter Boyne, Jim Busha, John Bybee,
Laura Caplan, Ed Clendinin (376th Bomb Group Association), Mark Coffee and
Mary Crowley (449th Bomb Group Association), Henry L. deZeng IV, Scott
Douglas, P.M. Fravel, Rick Furr, Hughes Glantzberg (461st Bomb Group Asso-
ciation), Jim Graham, Dr. Richard P. Hallion, Colin Heaton, Jon Jarmon, Frank
Kalinowski, Thomas Lauria, Craig Mackey, Ray Merriam, Holly C. Merrigan,
Mark Morgan, Phyllis Mullins, Snejana V. Laneva, Seth Paridon, John Seward,
Jay Stout, Roy Tebbutt, John L. Tillman, Robert von Maier, Troy White.

A NOTE ON SOURCES

Official records are essential to a book such as this, and numerous unit histories,
operational summaries, and archival assets were consulted. As already noted,
the Air Force Historical Research Agency was a mandatory source and a frequent
resource.

However, officers who served in both the Eighth and Fifteenth Air Forces
noted less emphasis on documentation in the Mediterranean. Speculation held
that by November 1943 the Eighth had a year and a half of experience in administration whereas the Fifteenth had to hit the ground running, with operations
necessarily overriding record keeping.

Of particular aid were the Fifteenth Air Force's study of the Ploesti missions
and the AAF Evaluation Board survey conducted after Romania's capitulation.

The utility of Fifteenth Air Force unit histories varies considerably. By far the
best wing history is the Forty-seventh's, whereas some of the other four bomb
wings produced little or no postwar material. The two fighter wings (one purely
administrative) released little on their own, but individual unit histories generally
are excellent. Some group histories run to multiple volumes, as with the extremely
detailed 449th Bomb Group accounts.

The Fifteenth has a wide presence on the internet, with websites providing
both official and unofficial material. Personal narratives abound, from mechanics to mission planners to aircrews and prisoners of war.

The following links were active as of January 2013. Excepting the 483rd
Bomb Group, every unit of the Fifteenth Air Force is represented, but some have

minimal online presence, especially those without active member associations. Most Fifteenth groups have Wikipedia entries, but the specific unit websites are more inclusive and more reliable.

When in doubt, visit the 15thaf.org site for at least some information on each unit. A few unit designations have been "hijacked" by internet marketers.

Army Air Forces
http://forum.armyairforces.com/.

Aviation Archaeology
http://www.aviationarchaeology.com/src/AFmacrMO.htm.

15th Air Force
http://www.15thaf.org/index.htm.

XV Service Command
http://www.15thaf.org/XV%20SC/.

1st Fighter Group
http://www.1fgww2.org/.
http://raf-112-squadron.org/1stfghonor_roll.html.

2nd Bomb Group
http://www.2ndbombgroup.org/.

5th Photo Recon Group
http://www.15thaf.org/5th_Photo_Recon/.

14th Fighter Group
http://raf-112-squadron.org/14thfghonor_roll42_43.html.

31st Fighter Group
http://raf-112-squadron.org/31stfghonor_roll43_44.html.

52nd Fighter Group
http://raf-112-squadron.org/52ndfghonor_roll42_43.html.

82nd Fighter Group
http://www.82ndfightergroup.com/.

97th Bomb Group
http://www.15thaf.org/5th_BW/97th_BG/97th_BG.html.

98th Bomb Group
http://pyramidiers.com/.

99th Bomb Group
http://www.99bombgroup.org/.

154th Weather Reconnaissance Squadron
http://www.15thaf.org/154th_Weather_Sqdn/.
http://tabacofamily.com/jtabaco/AWRA/0154wrs.html.

301st Bomb Group
http://www.301bg.com/.

325th Fighter Group
http://www.325thfg.org/.

332nd Fighter Group
http://www.332ndfg.org/.

376th Bomb Group
http://www.376hbgva.com/.

449th Bomb Group
http://449th.org/449assoc.php.

450th Bomb Group
http://www.450thbg.com/.

451st Bomb Group
http://www.15thaf.org/49th_BW/451st_BG/index.htm.

454th Bomb Group
http://www.15thaf.org/304th_BW/454th_BG/index.htm.

455th Bomb Group
http://www.455th.org/.

456th Bomb Group
http://www.456thbombgroup.org/.

459th Bomb Group
http://www.459bg.org/.

460th Bomb Group
http://www.15thaf.org/55th_BW/460th_BG/index.htm.

461st Bomb Group
http://www.461st.org/.

463rd Bomb Group
http://www.463rd.org/.

464th Bomb Group
http://www.zplace2b.com/464th/index.htm.

465th Bomb Group
http://www.frankambrose.com/pages/465.html.

483rd Bomb Group
No active website.

484th Bomb Group
http://www.484th.org/.

485th Bomb Group
http://www.485thbg.org/.

859th Bombardment Squadron
http://en.wikipedia.org/wiki/859th_Bombardment_Squadron.

885th Bombardment Squadron
http://en.wikipedia.org/wiki/122d_Fighter_Squadron#World_War_II.

Carpetbaggers
http://harringtonmuseum.org.uk/OtherLinks.htm.

ARTICLES

Churchill, Eugene E. "Weather or Not." *Stars and Stripes* (December 1944).

Gigova, Irina. "Sofia Was Bombed? Bulgaria's Forgotten War with the Allies." *History & Memory* 23, no. 2 (Fall/Winter 2011).

Karatsonyi, Mihaly, and James P. Busha. "Summer of Hell." *Flight Journal* (Winter 2011).

Roe, Tom, with James Bilder. "Flying With the Fifteenth Air Force." *WWII Quarterly* (Summer 2012).

Sauter, Dale. "'So Near Heaven and Surrounded by Hell': The Character and 1942–43 Military Career of WWII Pilot Frank A. Armstrong, Jr." *North Carolina Historical Review* (April 2011).

Seyer, Sean. "The Plan Put Into Practice: USAAF Bombing Doctrine and the Ploesti Campaign." Thesis. University of Missouri, St. Louis. 2009.

Tilghman, Andrew. "New Medal 'Insulting.'" *Army Times* (February 15, 2013).

NOTES

CHAPTER ONE

1. Author interview, Los Angeles, 1976.
2. John W. Huston, *American Airpower Comes of Age: General Henry H. Arnold's World War II Diaries, Volume II* (Fresno: Minerva Group, 2004), 32.
3. Lowell Thomas and Edward Jablonsky, *Doolittle, A Biography* (New York: Doubleday, 1976), 297.
4. James H. Doolittle and Carroll V. Glines, *I Could Never Be So Lucky Again* (New York: Bantam, 1991), 366.
5. W. F. Craven and J. L. Cate, *The Army Air Forces in World War II, Vol. II: Europe—Torch to Pointblank,* August 1942 to December 1943 (Chicago: University of Chicago Press, 1949), 572.
6. Haywood S. Hansell, *The Air Plan That Defeated Hitler* (Stratford: Ayer, 1979), 168.
7. Doolittle and Glines, *I Could Never Be So Lucky Again* (New York: Bantam, 1991), 367.

8. Ibid. The Italian may have been *Regia Aeronautica* chief of staff, General Rino Corso Fougier.

9. Eric Niderost, "World War II: German Raid on Bari," originally published in *World War II* magazine, Historynet.com, June 12, 2006, http://www. historynet.com/world-war-ii-german-raid-on-bari.htm.

10. Doolittle and Glines. *I Could Never Be So Lucky Again* (New York: Bantam, 1991), 269.

11. Craven and Cate, *The Army Air Forces in World War II, Vol. II: Europe— Torch to Pointblank,* August 1942 to December 1943 (Chicago: University of Chicago Press, 1949), 571.

12. Charles E. Sorensen, "Willow Run's Glory Days," *Ann Arbor Observer*, August 3, 2009; see also J. Richard, "Liberator Production Pool," historyofwar.org, December 14, 2007, http://www.historyofwar.org/ articles/weapons_liberator_production_pool.html.

13. "The Willow Run Airport History," yellowairplane.com, http:// yellowairplane.com/Book_Reviews/Warren_Benjamin_Kidder/ WillowRun_Cover.html.

14. Dominic Licata, *Autobiography* (Reno: University of Nevada, 2004), 5.

15. Craven and Cate, *The Army Air Forces in World War II, Vol. VII: The Services Around the World, Washington, D.C., 1945* (Chicago: University of Chicago Press, 1949), 260–61.

16. Herschel H. Green, *Herky!: The Memoirs of a Checkertail Ace* (Atglen, PA: Schiffer, 1996),182.

17. Craven and Cate, *The Army Air Forces in World War II, Vol. VII: Services Around the World, Washington, D.C., 1945* (Chicago: University of Chicago Press, 1949), 261.

18. Ibid.

19. Ford J. Lauer III, "History of the 99th Bombardment Group," 99bombgroup.org, http://www.99bombgroup.org/history.html.

20. Anne Shelton, "Coming Home on a Wing and a Prayer," Anne Shelton.

21. "August 1943 USAAF Missing Air Crew Reports," aviationarchaeology. com, 2004, http://www.aviationarchaeology.com/src/MACRmonthly/ 43AugMACR.htm.

22. Robert F. Dorr, *B-24 Liberator Units of the Fifteenth Air Force* (UK: Osprey, 2000), 41.

23. Craven and Cate, *The Army Air Forces in World War II, Vol. II: Europe— Torch to Pointblank, August 1942 to December 1943* (Chicago: University of Chicago Press, 1949), 582; Craven and Cate, *The Army Air Forces in World War II, Vol. III: Europe: Argument to V-E Day, January 1944 to May 1945* (Chicago: University of Chicago Press, 1949), 25.

24. Charles Richards, *The Second Was First* (Bend: Maverick Publications, 1999), 92–93.

25. Niderost, "World War II: German Raid on Bari," originally published in *World War II* magazine, Historynet.com, June 12, 2006, http://www.historynet.com/world-war-ii-german-raid-on-bari.htm.

26. The Germans grossly overclaimed this time, taking credit for fifty-one kills.

27. John W. Huston, *American Airpower Comes of Age: General Henry H. Arnold's World War II Diaries, Vol. II* (Fresno: Minerva Group, 2004), 71.

28. Ira C. Eaker interview with Hugh Ahmann, Washington, D.C., February 1975.

29. "Honor Roll 1st Fighter Group 1941–APR 45," raf-112-squadron.org, August 24, 2008, http://raf-112-squadron.org/1stfghonor_roll.html.

30. "Honor Roll 14th Fighter Group Jun 1941–Nov 1945," raf-112-squadron.org, August 31, 2008, http://raf-112-squadron.org/14thfghonor_roll42_43.html.

31. Watson to William N. Hess, related to author by Hess, 2011.

32. Undated letter from Colonel Oliver B. Taylor, USAF (Ret), via William N. Hess.

33. Steve Blake with John Stanaway, Adorimini (*"Up and at 'Em!"*): *A History of the 82nd Fighter Group in World War II* (Marceline, MO: Walsworth, 1992), 128.

34. 325th Fighter Group history, http://www.325thfg.org/325thGroup.htm.

35. Copy of undated letter in author's collection.

36. Nico Sgarlato, *Italian Aircraft of World War II* (Warren, MI: Squadron-Signal, 1979).

37. Arthur M. Leadingham, "Escape from Vicenza," 376th Heavy Bomb Group, 2006, http://www.376hbgva.com/memoirs/leadingham.htm.

38. Dale Sauter, "'So Near Heaven and Surrounded by Hell': The Character and 1942–43 Military Career of World War II Pilot Frank A. Armstrong, Jr.," *North Carolina Historical Review* (April 2011): 172.

39. Allan Palmer, "Survey of Battle Casualties, Eighth Air Force, June, July, and August 1944," U.S. Army Medical Department, Office of Medical History, Table 184, http://history.amedd.army.mil/booksdocs/wwii/woundblstcs/chapter9.htm.

40. Jack McKillop, "Combat Chronology of the USAAF," United States Army Air Force, http://www.usaaf.net/chron/index.htm.

41. "Daily Weather History for Foggia," Freemeteo.com, http://freemeteo.com/default.asp?pid=155&la=1&gid=3169070&monthFrom=7&yearFrom=1944&sid=162603.

42. *The Statistical Story of the Fifteenth Air Force*, 28th Statistical Control Unit, 1945, http://www.afhso.af.mil/shared/media/document/AFD-110401-019.pdf.

43. Craven and Cate, *The Army Air Forces in World War II, Vol. II: Europe—Torch to Pointblank, August 1942 to December 1943* (Chicago: University of Chicago Press, 1949), 572.

CHAPTER TWO

1. James H. Doolittle and Carroll V. Glines, *I Could Never Be So Lucky Again* (New York: Bantam, 1991), 372.

2. Brian Hutchins, "General Nathan Twining and the Fifteenth Air Force in WWII," Master's thesis, University of North Texas, May 2008, http://digital.library.unt.edu/ark:/67531/metadc6094/m1/1/high_res_d/thesis.pdf.

3. 14th Fighter Group activities sheet, January 1944, author's collection.

4. Ronald Schaffer, *Wings of Judgment: American Bombing in World War II* (New York: Oxford University Press, 1985), 56.

5. Kenneth P. Werrell, *Who Fears? 301st Bomb Group in War and Peace* (Dallas: Taylor, 1991), 67.

6. 325th Fighter Group press release, January 1944.

7. "456th Bomb Group: Find Out More," encycl.opentopia.com, http://encycl.opentopia.com/term/456th_Bomb_Group.

8. William N. Hess, telecons 2013.

9. "Error led to bombing of Monte Cassino," *Guardian*, April 3, 2000, http://www.guardian.co.uk/world/2000/apr/04/johnezard.

10. Charles W. Richards, *The Second Was First* (Bend, OR: Maverick, 1998), 141.

11. David Hapgood and David Richardson, *Monte Cassino: The Most Controversial Battle of World War II* (Cambridge: Da Capo Press, 2002), 199.

12. Dominic Licata, *Autobiography* (Reno: University of Nevada, 2004), 6.

13. Hapgood and Richardson, *Monte Cassino: The Most Controversial Battle of World War II* (Cambridge: Da Capo Press, 2002), 203.

14. Brian Hutchins, "General Nathan Twining and the Fifteenth Air Force in World War II," Master's thesis, University of North Texas, May 2008, 44.

15. Donald Caldwell and Richard Muller, *The Luftwaffe over Germany: Defense of the Reich* (Barnsley, England: Greenhill Books, 2007), 169.

16. Hans Werner Eulen, *In the Skies of Europe: Air Forces Allied to the Luftwaffe* (UK: Crowood Press, 1998), 79. The First Fighter Group was the only P-38 unit making claims on March 11, but all were German aircraft near Toulon. On the 18th the group claimed two kills and a probable against MC 202s and 109s. Frank Olynyk, MTO aerial victory list, 70.

17. R. F. Downey and D. W. Shepherd, *Maximum Effort: A History of the 449th Bomb Group in World War II* (Panama City: Northfield, 2000), 27–28.

18. Edward Jablonski, *Flying Fortress: The Illustrated Biography of the B-17s and the Men Who Flew Them* (New York: Doubleday, 1965), 233.

19. Downey and Shepherd, *Maximum Effort: A History of the 449th Bomb Group, Book IV* (Panama City: Northfield, 2000), 27.

20. Donald Caldwell, *Day Fighters in Defense of the Reich, 1942–45* (UK: Frontline Books, 2011), 209.

21. Robert F. Dorr, *B-24 Liberator Units of the Fifteenth Air Force* (UK: Osprey), 50.

22. Paul Hadley, *"Grottaglie and Home": A History of the 449th Bomb Group, Book III* (Northfield: Collegiate Press, 1989), 136.

23. Ibid., 5.

24. "Chester Kock," 301st Bombardment Group, http://www.301bg.com/Koch_Chester_K7433_301BG.cfm.

25. Ibid.

26. Caldwell, *Day Fighters in Defense of the Reich, 1942–45* (UK: Frontline Books, 2011), 218.

27. W. F. Craven and J. L. Cate, *The Army Air Forces in World War II, Vol. III: Europe—Argument to V-E Day, January 1944 to May 1945* (Chicago: University of Chicago Press, 1951) http://www.ibiblio.org/hyperwar/AAF/III/AAF-III-2.html. Allied intelligence officers computed damage to factories by the visible destruction of roof area, arriving at fairly precise estimates.

28. "Missing in Action: The Female Work Force in Nazi Germany," 123HelpMe.com, http://www.123HelpMe.com/view.asp?id=33936.

29. Craven and Cate, *The Army Air Forces in World War II, Vol. 3: Europe: Argument to V-E Day, January 1944 to May 1945* (Chicago: University of Chicago Press, 1951), 42.

30. Ibid., 45.

31. Ibid., 43.

32. Reports of Luftwaffe losses in February are contradictory. Attrition might have exceeded 530 in the west, including night fighters. Alan J. Levine,

The Strategic Bombing of Germany, 1940–1945 (Westport: Praeger, 1992), 121.

33. "456th Bomb Group Explained," Everything.Explained.at, http://everything.explained.at/456th_Bomb_Group/.

34. Sedgefield D. Hill, ed., *"The Fight'n" 451st Bombardment Group* (Paducah: Turner, 1990), 21.

35. Brian Hutchins, "General Nathan Twining and the Fifteenth Air Force in World War II," Master's thesis, University of North Texas, May 2008, 38, http://digital.library.unt.edu/ark:/67531/metadc6094/m1/1/high_res_d/thesis.pdf.

36. "Combat Chronology of the USAAF," USAAF, http://www.usaaf.net/chron/index.htm.

37. Robert F. Dorr, *B-24 Liberator Units of the Fifteenth Air Force* (UK: Osprey, 2000), 43.

38. "The 765th at Toretta Field, Italy," liberatorcrew.com, http://liberatorcrew.com/05_765th%20BS.htm.

39. 459th Bomb Group.

40. Kenn C. Rust, *Fifteenth Air Force Story* (Temple City: Historical Aviation Album, 1976), 19.

41. "484th Bomb Group Association," web.archive.org, http://web.archive.org/web/20041130191546/http://members.aol.com/bud484bg/about484.htm.

42. Ronald Schaffer, *Wings of Judgement: American Bombing in World War II* (New York: Oxford University Press, 1988), 56.

CHAPTER THREE

1. Losses to fighters through May 1944: 378 of 700 bombers lost to all causes. Compiled from the *AAF Statistical Digest*, December 1945.

2. Herschel H. Green, *Herky: The Memoirs of a Checkertail Ace* (Atglen, PA: Schiffer, 1996), 78.

3. Taylor of the Fourteenth was age twenty-eight; Agan of the First and McNickle of the Fifty-second were twenty-nine. Today, with higher education requirements, most first-tour jet pilots are twenty-five-year-old first lieutenants.

4. Army Air Forces pay courtesy of Brett Stolle, USAF Museum, email May 2012.

5. Dennis C. Kucera, *In a Now Forgotten Sky: The 31st Fighter Group in WW2* (Stratford: Flying Machines Press, 1997), 235.

6. Charles R. Shrader, *Amicicide: The Problem of Friendly Fire in Modern War* (Fort Leavenworth: U.S. Army Combat Studies Institute, 1982), 105.

7. George Loving, USAF (Ret.), email January 2012.

8.   Barrie Davis emails, January 2012.

9.   Fiedler email, March 2012.

10. Author interview, 1983. A search by the USAF records center at Maxwell Air Force Base produced no specific Fifteenth Air Force document regarding escort policy. Dr. Daniel Haulman email, February 2012.

11. Arthur C. Fielder email, January 2012.

12. *AAF Combat Chronology*, 1944.

13. Denes Bernad and Jiri Rajlich, et al., *Slovakian and Bulgarian Aces of World War 2* (Oxford: Osprey, 2004); Bernad, *Rumanian Aces of World War 2* (Oxford: Osprey, 2003), 74.

14. Hans Werner Neulen, *In the Skies of Europe* (Marlborough, England: Crowood Press, 2000), 167.

15. Tom Ivie and Paul Ludwig, *Spitfires and Yellow Tail Mustangs: The 52nd Fighter Group in World War II* (Crowborough, England: Hikoki, 2005), 103.

16. Irina Gigova, "Sofia Was Bombed? Bulgaria's Forgotten War with the Allies." *History & Memory* 23, no. 2 (Fall/Winter 2011): 140.

17. Ronald Schaffer, *Wings of Judgment: American Bombing in World War II* (New York: Oxford University Press, 1988), 56.

18. "Bombing Sofia," Sofia Echo, http://sofiaecho.com/2011/01/21/1028646_bombing-sofia.

19. Vera Brittain, *One Voice: Pacifist Writings from the Second World War* (London: Continuum Books, 2005), 156; Neulen, *In the Skies of Europe* (Marlborough: Crowood Press, 1998), 168.

20. Schaffer, *Wings of Judgment: American Bombing in World War II* (New York: Oxford University Press, 1985), 56.

21. Bernad, *Rumanian Aces of World War 2* (Oxford: Osprey, 2003), 38.

22. "Flak Towers: Vienna Anti-Aircraft Towers," wien.vienna.com, http://www.wien-vienna.com/flaktowers.php.

23. Alfred Asch, with Hugh R. Graff and Thomas A. Ramey, *The Story of the Four Hundred and Fifty-fifth Bombardment Group (H) WWII: Flight of the Vulgar Vultures* (Appleton, WI: Graphic Communications Center, 1991), 82.

24. Donald Caldwell, *The Luftwaffe Over Germany: Defense of the Reich* (Barnsley, England: Greenhill Books, 2007), 212.

25. Jiri Rajlich et al., *Slovakian and Bulgarian Aces of World War 2* (Oxford: Osprey, 2004), 53–54.

26. Bill L. Disbrow, *On the Edge* (Riverside: Winlock Galey, 2005), 100.

27. Caldwell, *Day Fighters in Defense of the Reich, 1942–45* (Barnsley, England: Frontline Books, 2011), 320.

28. Daily summary, 14th Fighter Group, May 6–7, 1944.

29. Kucera, *In a Now Forgotten Sky: The 31st Fighter Group in World War 2* (Stratford: Flying Machines Press, 1997), 393. Some enlisted men were overseas for three years.

30. Movie comments extracted from Fourteenth Fighter Group diary, May 1944.

31. Steve Blake and John Stanaway. *Adorimini: ("Up and At 'Em!"): A History of the 82nd Fighter Group in World War II* (Marceline: Walsworth, 1992), 177.

32. George G. Loving, *Woodbine Red Leader: A P-51 Mustang Ace in the Mediterranean Theater* (Novato: Presidio Press, 2003), 192.

33. Tom Ivie and Paul Ludwig, *Spitfires and Yellow Tail Mustangs: The 52nd Fighter Group in World War II* (Crowborough: Hikoki, 2005), 132.

34. Robert S. Capps, USAF (Ret.), *Flying Colt: Liberator Pilot in Italy* (Bloomington: Authorhouse, 2004), 408–9.

35. Sedgefield D. Hill, ed., *"The Fight'n" 451st Bombardment Group* (Paducah: Turner, 1990), 124.

36. Derived from Frank Olynyk, *Stars and Bars: A Tribute to the American Fighter Ace 1923–73* (UK: Grub Street, 1995). Of the Fifteenth's seventy-four aces, twenty-six had between three hundred and four hundred hours upon entering combat; five had slightly under three hundred, and the median was over five hundred.

37. Caldwell, *The Luftwaffe Over Germany: Defense of the Reich* (Barnsley: Greenhill Books, 2007), 204.

38. Robert Forsyth, *Luftwaffe Viermot Aces 1942–1945* (Oxford: Osprey, 2011), 13.

39. Steinhoff interview, 1990.

40. Boesch interview, October 1990.

41. Stigler interview, 1985.

42. Forsyth, *Luftwaffe Viermot Aces 1942–1945* (Oxford: Osprey, 2011), 90.

43. Williamson Murray, *Luftwaffe* (Baltimore: Nautical & Aviation Publishing, 1985), 226–27.

CHAPTER FOUR

1.   Pierre l'Espagnol de la Tramerye, *The World Struggle for Oil* (New York: A. A. Knopf, 1924). Berenger was ambassador to the United States from 1926–27.

2.   John G. Bunnell, *Knockout Blow? The Army Air Force's Operations against Ploesti and Balikpapan* (Maxwell AFB: Air University, 2005), 30.

3. Walter J. Boyne, "Tidal Wave," Air Force Magazine 90, no. 12 (December 2007) http://www.airforce-magazine.com/MagazineArchive/Pages/2007/December%202007/1207wave.aspx.

4. Bunnell, *Knockout Blow? The Army Air Force's Operations against Ploesti and Balikpapan* (Maxwell AFB: Air University, 2005), 30.

5. Robert S. Ehlers Jr., *Targeting the Third Reich* (Lawrence: University of Kansas Press, 2009), 253.

6. Jay Stout, *Fortress Ploesti: The Campaign to Destroy Hitler's Oil* (Darby: Casemate, 2003), 100.

7. Army Air Forces Evaluation Board, *Report, Vol. VI: Ploesti* (Mediterranean Theater of Operations, December 15, 1944), 12, 25, 81, 83.

8. "S2 Reports for April 1944," 450th Bomb Group Memorial Association, http://www.450thbg.com/real/s2/1944/april.shtml#Top.

9. Ibid.

10. "S-2 Narrative Report," 450th Bomb Group Memorial Association, http://www.450thbg.com/real/s2/1944/april/5April.shtml.

11. Martin Bowman, *The B-24 Liberator 1939–1945* (Chicago: Rand McNally, 1979), 56.

12. Neil H. Raiford, *Shadow: A Cottontail Bomber Crew in World War II* (Jefferson, NC: McFarland, 2004), 140. Note: the AAF *Combat Chronology* states that the first Fifteenth Air Force pathfinder mission was flown July 9 but that referred to the first use at Ploesti.

13. Dennis Kucera, *In a Now Forgotten Sky: The 31st Fighter Group in World War 2* (Stratford: Flying Machines Press, 1997), 225.

14. Army Air Forces Evaluation Board, *Report, Volume VI: Ploesti* (Mediterranean Theater of Operations, December 15, 1944), 56.

15. Charles Richards, *The Second Was First* (Bend: Maverick, 1999), 266.

16. Robert S. Capps, *Flying Colt: Liberator Pilot in Italy* (Bloomington: Authorhouse, 1997), 282.

17. Ibid.

18. Army Air Forces. *The Air Battle of Ploesti* (n.p., 1945), 20.

19. Barrett Tillman, *Whirlwind: The Air War against Japan* (New York: Simon & Schuster, 2011).

20. Kurtz's daughter, born while he was overseas, became an actress, named for her father's famous airplane.

21. Bunnell, *Knockout Blow? The Army Air Force's Operations against Ploesti and Balikpapan* (Maxwell AFB: Air University, 2005), 39.

22. Blasé and Cassell, *47th Wing History: June 5, 1942, to October 17, 1945* (Fifteenth Air Force, 1945), 40–41.

23. Ford J. Lauer III, "History of the 99th Bombardment Group," 99bombgroup.org, http://www.99bombgroup.org/history.html.

24. Ernest R. McDowell and William N. Hess, *Checkertail Clan: The 325th Fighter Group in North Africa and Italy* (Fallbrook: Aero, 1969), 49.

25. John T. Correll, "The Poltava Debacle," *Air Force Magazine* (March 2011).

26. Edward Jablonski, *Flying Fortress: The Illustrated Biography of the B-17s and the Men Who Flew Them* (New York: Doubleday, 1965), 238.

27. Richard E. Drain et al., *The Diamondbacks: History of the 99th Bomb Group (H)* (Paducah: Turner, 1998), 53.

28. Charles Richards, *Second to None* (Bend: Maverick, 1999), 283.

29. Jay A. Stout, *Fortress Ploesti: The Campaign to Destroy Hitler's Oil* (Havertown: Casemate, 2003), 148.

30. Richards, *The Second Was First* (Bend: Maverick, 2001), 281.

31. John D. Mullins, *An Escort of P-38s: The 1st Fighter Group in World War II* (St. Paul: Phalanx, 1995), 119.

32. "Last Ploesti Refinery Smashed," *Deseret News*, June 10, 1944.

33. Army Air Forces Evaluation Board, *Report, Vol. VI: Ploesti* (Mediterranean Theater of Operations, December 15, 1944), 50.

34. Bunnell, *Knockout Blow? The Army Air Force's Operations against Ploesti and Balikpapan* (Maxwell AFB: Air University, 2005), 42.

35. Robert S. Ehlers, *Targeting the Third Reich* (Lawrence: University Press of Kansas, 2009), 132.

36. Craven and Cate, *Army Air Forces in World War II, Vol. III: Europe— Argument to V-E Day, January 1944 to May 1945* (Chicago: University of Chicago Press, 1951), xiv, http://www.ibiblio.org/hyperwar/AAF/III/index.html.

37. George Crawford, "Three Crawford Brothers: The WWII Memoirs of Three Pilots," 52726.authorworld.com, http://www.52726.authorworld.com/.

38. Blasé and Cassell, *47th Wing History: June 5, 1942, to October 17, 1945* (Fifteenth Air Force, 1945), 45.

39. "Distinguished Unit Citation," 376th Heavy Bomb Group, http://www.376hbgva.com/citations/bratislava.html.

40. Crawford, "Three Crawford Brothers: The WWII Memoirs of Three Pilots," 52726.authorworld.com, http://www.52726.authorworld.com/.

41. John D. Mullins, *An Escort of P-38s: The 1st Fighter Group in World War II* (St. Paul: Phalanx, 1995), 125.

42. Ibid., 126.

43. "The Ultimate Sacrifice," homeofheroes.com, http://www.homeofheroes.com/wings/part2/18_kingsley.html.

44. Ibid.

45. Army Air Forces Evaluation Board, *Report, Volume VI: Ploesti* (Mediterranean Theater of Operations, December 15, 1944), 56.

46. Extracted from *Army Air Forces Statistical Digest* (Washington, D.C.: n.p., December 1945), 256.

47. Army Air Force, *The Air Battle of Ploesti* (n.p., 1945), 75–79.

CHAPTER FIVE

1. Luftwaffe Plans Division report, July 1944, cited in Alfred Price, *Battle Over the Reich: The Strategic Bomber Offensive against Germany, Volume II: 1943–45* (UK: Classic, 2005), 224.

2. Barrett Tillman, "Shot Down or Out of Gas?," *Flight Journal* (August 2006): 50.

3. Ibid., 51.

4. "The Sparta/Wilkins Crew," 376th Heavy Bomb Group, http://www.376hbgva.com/crews/sparta.html.

5. Peter Becker, "The Role of Synthetic Fuel in WW II Germany," *Air University Review* (July–August 1981), http://www.airpower.maxwell.af.mil/airchronicles/aureview/1981/jul-aug/becker.htm.

6. Sedgefield D. Hill, *"The Fight'n" 451st Bombardment Group (H)* (Paducah: Turner, 1990), 114.

7. Barrett Tillman, *Above and Beyond: The Aviation Medals of Honor* (Washington, D.C.: Smithsonian Press, 2002), 113.

8. Hugh N. Jones, "450th Bombardment Group (H)," 450th Bomb Group Memorial Association, http://www.450thbg.com/real/history/history.shtml.

9. Charles E. Francis and Adolph Caso, *The Tuskegee Airmen: The Men Who Changed a Nation* (Wellesley: Branden, 1993), 319.

10. Daniel Haulman, *The Battle of Memmingen, 18 July 1944* (Maxwell AFB: Air Force Historical Research Agency, 2010), 8.

11. John D. Mullins, *An Escort of P-38s: The 1st Fighter Group in World War II* (St. Paul: Phalanx, 1995), 129.

12. Donald Caldwell, *Day Fighters in Defense of the Reich* (UK: Frontline Books, 2012), 334.

13. Walther Dahl, "Rammjager: Das Letzte Aufgebot," library.thing.com, http://www.librarything.com/work/8490553/reviews.

14. John G. Bunnell, *Knockout Blow? The Army Air Force's Operations against Ploesti and Balikpapan* (Maxwell AFB: Air University, June 2005), 44.

15. Luftwaffe returns show that III/SG-77 lost twenty-one aircraft to enemy action in July. Other combat losses that month might have reduced the Americans' actual results, but the Stuka unit only lost twenty-four planes in combat during the previous six months. "Flugzeugbestand und Bewegungsmeldungen," ww2.dk, http://www.ww2.dk/oob/bestand/schlacht/biiisg77.html.

16. Surgeon General, U.S. Army, *Medical Statistics in World War II* (Washington: Historical Unit, U.S. Army Medical Service, 1975), Table 40d.

17. Papers of Lawrence L. Jenkins via John Seward, 2012.

18. Army Air Forces, *The Air Battle of Ploesti* (n.p., 1945), 81.

19. "B17 Pilot 1st Lt. James Jarmon 463rd Bombardment Group," YouTube video of Jarmon's 1985 interview, uploaded by m9078jk3, March 1, 2008, http://www.youtube.com/watch?v=bGOP53TkGtA.

20. "The Ploesti Missions of the 449th Bomb Group," norfield-publishing.com, http://www.norfield-publishing.com/449th/Ploesti/PloestiMissions.html.

21. Steve Blake, *Adorimini ("Up and at 'Em!): A History of the 82nd Fighter Group in World War II* (Marceline, MO: Walsworth, 1992), 198–99.

22. Quentin Richard Petersen, "A Bad Day for QR," Memories Gallery on World War II Living Memorial Page, http://www.seniornet.org/ww2/gallery/memories/quentin/badday.shtml.

23. Army Air Forces, *The Air Battle of Ploesti* (n.p., 1945), 104.

24. Ibid., 67.

25. Jay Stout, *Fortress Ploesti: The Campaign to Destroy Hitler's Oil Supply* (Havertown: Casemate, 2003), 226.

26. Army Air Forces Evaluation Board, *Report, Volume VI: Ploesti* (Mediterranean Theater of Operations, December 15, 1944).

27. Ibid.; Jay Stout, *Fortress Ploesti: The Campaign to Destroy Hitler's Oil Supply* (Havertown: Casemate, 2003).

28. Brian Hutchins, "General Nathan Twining and the Fifteenth Air Force in World War II," Master's thesis, University of North Texas, May 2008, 47. (Recording by Twining in Rome, April 5, 1945.)

29. W. F. Craven and J. L. Cate, *The Army Air Forces in World War II, Vol. III: Europe—Argument to V-E Day, January 1944 to May 1945* (Chicago: University of Chicago Press, 1951), 418, http://www.ibiblio.org/hyperwar/AAF/III/AAF-III-12.html#page424.

30. "Col. Bob Richard's Diary, 1st Fighter Group History."

31. Ibid.

32. Mullins, *An Escort of P-38s: The 1st Fighter Group in World War II* (St. Paul: Phalanx, 1995), 138.

33. *XV FC One Year Escort* (XV Fighter Command: n.p., 1945), 19.

34. Mullins, *An Escort of P-38s: The 1st Fighter Group in World War II* (St. Paul: Phalanx, 1995), 138.

35. "Descent into Hell," Eric Hammel's Books, 1998, http://www. erichammelbooks.com/books/f_aces-in-combat.php.

36. "Col. Bob Richard's Diary, 1st Fighter Group History."

37. Caldwell, *Day Fighters in Defense of the Reich* (Barnsley, England: Frontline Books, 2012), 357–58.

38. Hess interview, May 2011.

39. G. H. Blasé and R. W. Cassel, *47th Wing History, June 5, 1942, to October 17, 1945* (Italy, 1945), 58.

40. John L. Frisbee, "Operation Gunn," *Air Force Magazine* (January 1995).

41. "Constantin M. 'Bâzu' Cantacuzino—The Adventurous Prince," sihss. se, http://www.sihss.se/PrinceCantacuzinobiography.htm.

42. Robert J. Goebel, *Mustang Ace* (Pacifica: Pacifica Press, 19), 206.

43. Daniel Haulman, *Operation Reunion and the Tuskegee Airmen* (Maxwell AFB: Air Force Historical Research Agency, 2012).

44. Charles W. Richards, *Second to None* (Bend: Maverick, 1999), 356.

CHAPTER SIX

1.   E. E. Churchill, "Weather or Not," *Air Force* (December 1944): 62.

2.   Ibid.

3.   William H. Allen email, October 2012.

4.   Francis S. Kalinowski II, *The History of the 154th Weather Reconnaissance Squadron, 1940–1945*, 12.

5.   Frederick W. Gillies, *The Story of a Squadron* (Medford, MA: Privately published, 1946), 124.

6.   Kalinowski II, *History of the 154th Weather Reconnaissance Squadron, 1940–1945*, 12.

7.   Ibid., 13.

8.   Army Air Forces, *The Air Battle of Ploesti* (n.p., 1945), 57.

9.   Ibid., 60.

10. Besides the F-4 and F-5 versions of the P-38, recon variants of other AAF aircraft were the F-3 (A-20), F-6 (P-51), F-7 (B-24), F-9 (B-17), and F-10 (B-25).

11. Gillies, *The Story of a Squadron* (Medford, MA: Privately published, 1946), 92.

12. E. E. Churchill, "Weather or Not," *Air Force* (December 1944): 63.

13. Thomas K. Follis, *He Wore a Pair of Silver Wings* (Bennington: Merriam Press, 2005), 147.

14. "F-5 Lightning Development," 34thprs.org, http://www.34thprs.org/html/aircraft/F5dev.html.

15. *Strategic Photo Reconnaissance: Fifth Recon Group* (n.p.: APO 520, October 1944–March 1945).

16. Follis, *He Wore a Pair of Silver Wings* (Bennington: Merriam Press, 2005), 160.

17. "F-5 Lightning Development," 34thprs.org, http://www.34thprs.org/html/aircraft/F5dev.html.

18. Ibid.

19. The Fifty-second Group history states that the airfield attack was an impromptu decision mandated by poor weather during an escort mission.

20. Attributed to First Lieutenant David Toomey, Third Photo Group, P-38 National Association Facebook page, October 30, 2012.

21. Follis, *He Wore a Pair of Silver Wings* (Bennington: Merriam Press, 2005), 163.

22. *Strategic Photo Reconnaissance: Fifth Recon Group* (n.p.: APO 520, October 1944–March 1945).

23. "Heroism Doesn't Require Death," lowcountrynewspapers.net, September 4, 2006, http://www.lowcountrynewspapers.net/archive/node/98842.

24. *Strategic Photo Reconnaissance: Fifth Recon Group* (n.p.: APO 520, October 1944–March 1945).

25. Philip D. Hart, "Heroes of the Skies: The Yugoslav Detachment," 376hbgva.com, http://www.376hbgva.com/history/yugoslavia/index.html.

26. Ibid.

27. Craven and Cate, *The Army Air Forces in World War II, Vol. III: Europe—Argument to V-E Day, January 1944 to May 1945* (Chicago: University of Chicago Press, 1951), 500–1; Gerald Schwab, *OSS Agents in Hitler's Heartland* (New York: Praeger, 1996), 48.

28. Army Air Forces, *Periodic History, 859th Bombardment Squadron* (USAF Historical Research Agency, December 1944).

29. Ibid.

30. Ibid.

31. Robert W. Fish, ed., *Memories of the 801st/492nd Bombardment Group "Carpetbaggers"* (San Antonio: privately published, 1990), 275.

32. Ibid.

33. Craven and Cate, *The Army Air Forces in World War II, Vol. III: Europe—Argument to V-E Day, January 1944 to May 1945* (Chicago: University of Chicago Press, 1951), 517.

34. Army Air Forces, *Periodic History, 859th Bombardment Squadron* (USAF Historical Research Agency, February 1945).

35. Ibid.
36. Gerald Schwab, *OSS Agents in Hitler's Heartland* (New York: Praeger, 1996), 115.
37. Ibid., 48.
38. William M. Leary, *Fueling the Fires of Resistance: Army Air Forces Special Operations in the Balkans During World War II* (Air Force History & Museums Program, 1995), 27.
39. Adam S. Eterovich, "American Airmen Rescued in Croatia, Bosnia, and Hercegovina by Croatian and Bosnian Partisans in World War II," croatians.com, http://www.croatians.com/MILITARY-AIRMEN-PILOTS. htm.
40. Thomas T. Matteson, Air University Report no. 128, *An Analysis of the Circumstances Surrounding the Rescue and Evacuation of Allied Aircrewmen From Yugoslavia, 1941–1945* (Maxwell AFB: Air War College, April 1977), 26.
41. Ibid., 31.
42. Interview with William N. Hess, September 2012.
43. Adam S. Estrovich, "American Airmen Rescued in Croatia, Bosnia and Hercegovina in World War II," croatians.com, http://www.croatians.com/MILITARY-AIRMEN-PILOTS.htm.
44. Craven and Cate, *The Army Air Forces in World War II, Vol. III: Europe—Argument to V-E Day, January 1944 to May 1945* (Chicago: University of Chicago Press, 1951), 500–1.
45. Dennis Kucera, *In a Now Forgotten Sky: The 31st Fighter Group in WW2* (Stratford: Flying Machines Press, 1997), 271.
46. Tom Rowe with James Bilder, "Flying with the Fifteenth Air Force," *WWII Quarterly* (Summer 2012): 23.
47. Matteson, Air University Report no. 128, *An Analysis of the Circumstances Surrounding the Rescue and Evacuation of Allied Aircrewmen From Yugoslavia, 1941–1945* (Maxwell AFB: Air War College, April 1977), 35.

CHAPTER SEVEN

1. G. H. Blasé and R. W. Cassell, *47th Wing History: June 5, 1942, to October 17, 1945* (Fifteenth Air Force, 1945), 54.
2. Ibid., 55.
3. *Army Air Forces Statistical Digest* (December 1945): 256; Army Air Forces 28th Statistical Control Unit, *The Statistical Story of the Fifteenth Air Force* (n.p., 1945).

4. "Honor Roll Fourteenth Fighter Group Jun 1941—Nov 1945," raf-112-squadron.org, August 31, 2008, http://raf-112-squadron.org/14thfghonor_roll42_43.html.

5. Clayton Kelly Gross interview, 1980.

6. "Bob Clemens, B-17 Navigator," 8th Air Force Historical Society of Minnesota Presentations, https://sites.google.com/site/8thafhsmn/pictures/bob-clemens.

7. After the war Mildred Gillars was tried for treason and remained in prison until 1961. She died in 1988, age eighty-seven. Frank Kurtz retired from active duty in 1960 and died in 1996, age eighty-five.

8. Hess telecons, 2013.

9. Mihaly Karatsonyi and James P. Busha, "Summer of Hell," *Flight Journal* (Winter 2011): 11.

10. Ibid., 14.

11. "The Luftwaffe's Ground-Bound Stealth Fighter," *Flight Journal* (Winter 2013): 90.

12. Edward B. Westermann, *Flak: German Anti-Aircraft Defenses 1914–1945* (Lawrence: University of Kansas Press, 2005), 128–29.

13. Army Air Forces 28th Statistical Control Unit, *The Statistical Story of the Fifteenth Air Force* (n.p., 1945).

14. Horst Boog et al., *Germany and the Second World War, Volume VII: The Strategic Air War* (New York: Oxford University Press, 2006), 321.

15. "In Their Own Words," forum.1cpublishing.eu, http://forum.1cpublishing.eu/showthread.php?t=13591&page=33.

16. "The Curious Case of Martin James Monti," Strategy Page, http://www.strategypage.com/cic/docs/cic304b.asp.

17. "461st Bomb Group History," 461st.org, http://www.461st.org/History/461st%20History/PDFs/oct44.pdf.

18. *Army Air Forces Statistical Digest* (December 1945): 264. Dr. Frank Olynyk's September to December figures, which are specific, show 142 MTO fighter victories, twelve by the Twelfth Air Force.

19. Undated, hand-written account from Lieutenant Lee K. Carr, author's collection.

20. Ibid. The Mustang remained Coulson's only victory.

21. Steve Birdsall, *Log of the Liberators* (New York: Doubleday, 1973), 248–49.

22. Ibid., 249.

23. Steve Blake, *Adorimini: ("Up and at 'Em!"): A History of the 82nd Fighter Group in World War II* (Boise: 82nd Fighter Group Association, 1992), 219.

24. Confidential Message F 57991 from Allied Force Headquarters, Caserta, Italy, to War Department, November 25, 1944, author's copy.

25. Allied Force Headquarters, no. MX 37011, November 13, 1944, 2, author's collection.

26. Gale Mortensen, April 2011.

27. "Pinkus P. Taback—Diary," raf-112-squadron.org, http://raf-112-squadron. org/82nd_fg.html.

28. Dennis C. Kucera, *In a Now Forgotten Sky: The 31st Fighter Group in World War 2* (Stratford: Flying Machines Press, 1997), 338.

29. Ibid.

30. "461st Bomb Group History for December 1944," 41st.org, http:// www.461st.org/History/461st%20History/PDFs/dec44.pdf.

31. Donald Caldwell, *Day Fighters in Defense of the Reich* (UK: Frontline, 2011), 405.

32. Courtesy of John Bybee, May 2012. Also see "December 17th, 1944," homepage.ntlworld.com, http://homepage.ntlworld.com/andrew. etherington/1944/12/17.htm.

33. Contradictory sources state that no German SAMs became operational and that only *Wasserfall* was fired in combat. Since at least two American bomb groups reported encountering missiles, *Wasserfall* is the likely candidate. See the Luftwaffe '46 web site (http://www.luft46.com/missile/ wasserfl.html) and a discussion on Axis History Forum, http://forum. axishistory.com/viewtopic.php?f=49&t=195252&sid=be95270092b9b 520612d87de1a7af6aa&p=1756143#p1756143.

34. Tom Rowe with James Bilder, "Flying with the Fifteenth Air Force," *WWII Quarterly* (Summer 2012): 18.

35. Stephen Ambrose, *The Wild Blue: The Men and Boys Who Flew the B-24s over Germany* (New York: Simon & Schuster, 2001), 111.

36. "B-17's That Flew the Most Missions?," forum.armyairforces.com, http:// forum.armyairforces.com/B1739s-That-Flew-the-Most-Missions-m204741-print.aspx.

37. Vincent Fagan cited in Stephen Ambrose, *The Wild Blue: The Men and Boys Who Flew the B-24s over Germany* (New York: Simon & Schuster, 2001), 169.

38. Ambrose, *The Wild Blue: The Men and Boys Who Flew the B-24s over Germany* (New York: Simon & Schuster, 2001), 174–75.

39. Howard Hawks, dir., *Air Force*, Warner Brothers, 1943, written by Dudley Nichols.

40. *Army Air Force Statistical Digest* (Washington, D.C.: December 1945).

41. Missing Air Crew Report, 464th Bombardment Group, December 2, 1944. http://www.zplace2b.com/464th/macr/10029-464.pdf.

42. "Combat Chronology of the U.S. Army Air Forces: December 1944," USAAF, http://www.usaaf.net/chron/44/dec44.htm.

43. "Merry Christmas 1944 and After," 376th Heavy Bomb Group, http://www.376hbgva.com/memoirs/barton.html.

44. John D. Mullins, *An Escort of P-38s: The 1st Fighter Group in World War II* (St. Paul: Phalanx, 1995), 145.

45. Blake and Stanaway, *Adorimini: ("Up and At 'Em!"): A History of the 82nd Fighter Group in World War II* (Marcelene, MO: Walsworth, 1992), 234.

46. *Army Air Forces Statistical Digest* (Washington, D.C.: December 1945).

CHAPTER EIGHT

1. "Climate Foggia," TuTiempo.net, http://www.tutiempo.net/en/Climate/FOGGIA_GINO_LISA/11-1943/162603.htm.

2. John Mullins, *An Escort of P-38s: The 1st Fighter Group in World War II* (St. Paul: Phalanx, 1995), 147.

3. "The 461st Liberaider," June 2010, http://www.461st.org/Liberaider/PDFs/June%202010.pdf . DOES NOT WORK

4. Steve Blake, *Adorimini ("Up and at 'Em!"): A History of the 82nd Fighter Group in World War II* (Marcelene, MO: Walsworth, 1992), 232.

5. Ibid., 235.

6. Mullins, *An Escort of P-38s: The 1st Fighter Group in World War II* (St. Paul: Phalanx, 1995), 148.

7. Stephen Ambrose, *The Wild Blue: The Men and Boys Who Flew the B-24s over Germany* (New York: Simon & Schuster, 2001), 209–10.

8. Sedgefield D. Hill, *"The Fight'n" 451st Bombardment Group (H)* (Paducah, KY: Turner, 1990), 45.

9. Trevor Constable and Raymond Toliver, *Horrido!: Fighter Aces of the Luftwaffe* (New York: Macmillan, 1968), 259.

10. Robert Forsyth, *Jagdgeschwader 7 "Nowotny"* (Oxford: Osprey, 2008), 43.

11. Charles Richards, *The Second Was First* (Bend: Maverick, 2001), 494.

12. "Clete Roberts interview," Ace 1945, http://www.ace1945.com/cleterobertsinterview.html.

13. Steve Birdsall, *Log of the Liberators* (New York, Doubleday, 1973), 255–56.

14. Ibid., 254.

15. Ibid., 256.

16. "The 2nd Bomb Group's Longest Mission," 2ndbombgroup.org, http://www.2ndbombgroup.org/2ndBombGroup2.htm.

17. Donald Caldwell, *Day Fighters in Defense of the Reich* (Barnsley, England: Frontline, 2012), 456.

18. Daniel Haulman, "A Tale of Two Missions: Memmingen, July 18, 1944 & Berlin, March 24, 1945," The Free Library, http://www.thefreelibrary.com/.

19. "The 2nd Bomb Group's Longest Mission," 2ndbombgroup.org, http://www.2ndbombgroup.org/2ndBombGroup2.htm.

20. "Ariel Weekes, Lead Bombardier 15th AF," 8th Air Force Historical Society of Minnesota, https://sites.google.com/site/8thafhsmn/pictures/ariel-weekes.

21. Haulman, "A Tale of Two Missions: Memmingen, July 18, 1944 & Berlin, March 24, 1945," The Free Library, http://www.thefreelibrary.com/A+tale+of+two+missions%3A+Memmingen,+July+1 8,1944+%26 +Berlin,+March+24, ... -a0245738610.

22. Des Moines, Iowa, *Plain Talk*, May 3, 1945.

23. "'Big Yank'—The William S. Strapko Crew," Warbird Resource Group, http://www.warbirdsresourcegroup.org/URG/bigyank.html.

24. Joe Holley, "Bomber Gunner 'Babe' Broyhill, 83," *Washington Post*, November 28, 2008. http://en.wikipedia.org/wiki/Lincoln_Broyhill.

25. William N. Hess, *German Jets Versus the U.S. Army Air Force* (North Branch, MN: Specialty Press, 1996), 111.

26. Ibid.

27. Many of the details of the March 24, 1945, mission are found in Haulman, "A Tale of Two Missions: Memmingen, July 18, 1944 & Berlin, March 24, 1945," The Free Library, http://www.thefreelibrary.com/A+t ale+of+two+missions%3A+Memmingen,+July+1 8,1944+%26+Berlin, +March+24,...-a0245738610; see also Colin D. Heaton, *The Me 262 Stormbird* (Minneapolis: Zenith, 2012).

28. Stigler, 1983.

29. "Combat Chronology of the US Army Air Forces: April 1945," USAAF, http://www.usaaf.net/chron/45/apr45.htm.

30. Duane L. Bohnstedt, "Poggiorsini," http://www.15thaf.org/55th_BW/460th_BG/Stories/PDFs/Poggiorsini.pdf.

31. 28th Statistical Control Unit, *The Statistical Story of the Fifteenth Air Force*, 1945.

32. "AAF Prisoners of the Japanese," National Museum of the US Air Force, September 29, 2009, http://www.nationalmuseum.af.mil/factsheets/factsheet.asp?id=1471.

33. Alfred Asch, et al., *Flight of the Vulgar Vultures, 1943–1945* (Appleton, WI: Graphic Communications, 1991), 159.

34. Laura Caplan, *Domain of Heroes: The Medical Journal and Story of Dr. Leslie Caplan* (Edina: Jerry's Printing, 2004), ii.

35. Author telecons with Hess, January–February 2013.

36. Mullins, *An Escort of P-38s: the 1st Fighter Group in World War 2* (St. Paul: Phalanx, 1995), 151.

37. John Stanaway, *P-38 Lightning Aces of the ETO/MTO* (Oxford: Osprey,1998), 43.

38. Whitehead is commemorated on a memorial in the Czech Republic. His remains were returned to Indiana after the war. "1/Lt Robert W. Whitehead.," waymarking.com, http://www.waymarking.com/waymarks/WMAAEF_1_Lt_Robert_W_Whitehead.

39. Mullins, *An Escort of P-38s: the 1st Fighter Group in World War 2* (St. Paul: Phalanx, 1995), 156.

40. "Honor Roll 31st Fighter Group 1941–Jul 45," raf-112-squadron.org, September 8, 2008, http://raf-112-squadron.org/31stfghonor_roll43_44.html.; "Honor Roll 52nd Fighter Group 1941–July 45," raf-112-squadron.org, March 25, 2010, http://raf-112-squadron.org/52ndfghonor_roll42_43.html .

41. 28th Statistical Control Unit, *The Statistical Story of the Fifteenth Air Force*, 1945.

42. Ambrose, *The Wild Blue: The Men and Boys Who Flew the B-24s Over Germany* (New York: Simon & Schuster, 2001), 237–38.

43. Alfred Asch, et al., *Flight of the Vulgar Vultures 1943–1945*. (Appleton, WI: Graphic Communications, 1991), 157.

44. Ibid., 158.

45. Details from Duane and Betty Bohnstedt, 460th Bomb Group historians, emails January 2013.

46. Dennis Kucera, *In a Now Forgotten Sky* (Stratford: Flying Machines Press, 1997), 393.

47. Frederick W. Gillies, *The Story of a Squadron* (Medford, MA: privately published, 1946), 112.

48. Charles W. Richards, *The Second Was First* (Bend: Maverick, 1999), 510–11.

49. Kucera, *In a Now Forgotten Sky* (Stratford: Flying Machines Press, 1997), 393–94.

50. Monuments Men Newsletter, No. XXI, May 2010, https://www. monumentsmenfoundation.org/uploads/newsletter_pdf/MMNewsXXIEng. pdf.

51. Gillies, *The Story of a Squadron* (Medford, MA: privately published, 1946), 112.

52. 28th Statistical Control Unit, *The Statistical Story of the Fifteenth Air Force*, 1945.

CHAPTER NINE

1. "Honor Roll 31st Fighter Group 1941–Jul 45," raf-112-squadron.org, September 8, 2008, http://raf-112-squadron.org/31stfghonor_roll43_44. html.

2. Monthly average of continental U.S. losses for January to August 1945, computed from *AAF Statistical Digest*, December 1945.

3. *Diary of John Panas in World War II* (Bronx: Beehive Press, undated), 73–74.

4. Army Air Forces 28th Statistical Control Unit, *The Statistical Story of the Fifteenth Air Force* (n.p., 1945).

5. Army Air Forces, *Periodic History, 859th Bombardment Squadron* (USAF Historical Research Agency, August 1945).

6. Mortensen interview, 2011.

7. Hess telecon, May 2012.

8. Army Air Forces 28th Statistical Control Unit, *The Statistical Story of the Fifteenth Air Force* (n.p., 1945), 21–22.

9. Ibid.

10. U.S. Air Force fact sheets.

11. In June 2011 a Google search showed 495,000 hits for "332nd Fighter Group" versus 486,000 for the 1st, 31st, 52nd, 82nd, and 325th combined. "Tuskegee Airmen" generated nearly one million hits. The 509th Composite Group, which dropped the atom bombs on Japan, yielded 26,500 hits.

12. Emails with pilots of the 31st, 52nd, and 325th Fighter Groups, February 2012. Eighth Air Force bomber losses to enemy fighters dropped from 68 to 35 percent of the combat total. *AAF Statistical Digest*, December 1945.

13. Eighth Air Force dropped 235,000 tons to the Fifteenth's 149,000. Stephen Ambrose, *The Wild Blue: The Men and Boys Who Flew the B-24s over Germany* (New York: Simon & Schuster, 2001), 250.

14. Randall Hansen, *Fire and Fury* (New York: NAL Caliber, 2009), 290.

15. Cargill R. Hall, *Case Studies in Strategic Bombardment* (Washington, D.C.: Air Force History & Museums Program, 1998), 158–59.

16. Williamson Murray and Allan Millett, *Military Innovation in the Interwar Period* (Cambridge: Cambridge University Press, 1998), 46; Williamson Murray, *Strategy for Defeat: The Luftwaffe, 1933–1935* (Maxwell AFD: Air University, 1983), 312.

17. Related by Colonel Walter Boyne, USAF (Ret.), email January 13, 2013.

18. "460 Bombardment Group (H) Stories," 15thaf.org, http://www.15thaf. org/55th_BW/460th_BG/Stories/Stories.htm; Duane L. "Sparky" Bohnstedt, historian of the 460th Bomb Group Association.

19. Sean Seyer, *The Plan Put into Practice: USAAF Bombing Doctrine and the Ploesti Campaign* (St. Louis: University of Missouri, 2009), 82.

20. Army Air Force Evaluation Board, *Report, Volume VI: Ploesti* (Mediterranean Theater of Operations, December 15, 1944), 51–52.

21. Seyer, *The Plan Put into Practice: USAAF Bombing Doctrine and the Ploesti Campaign* (St. Louis: University of Missouri, 2009), 82.

22. Walt W. Rostow, "Recollections on Bombing," University of Texas at Austin, http://www.utexas.edu/opa/pubs/discovery/disc1997v14n2/ disc-recollect.html.

23. William Green, ed., "The Allied Combined Bomber Offensive: Two German Views," *Proceedings of the Second Military History Symposium* (U.S. Air Force Academy, May 1968).

24. Göring interview, May 10, 1945, http://library2.lawschool.cornell.edu/ donovan/pdf/Interrogation_10May45.pdf.

25. Cited in Ambrose, *The Wild Blue: The Men and Boys Who Flew the B-24s over Germany* (New York: Simon & Schuster, 2001), 169.

26. William N. Hess to author, 2011.

27. "Full Text Citations for Award of the Distinguished Service Cross," Home of Heroes, http://www.homeofheroes.com/members/02_DSC/citatons/03_ wwii-dsc/aaf_a.html.

28. Hess to author, 2010.

29. Mrs. Phyllis Mullins emails, July 2012.

30. Stigler, 1983.

31. Ralph Anderson emails, 2012.

32. Bill Hess telecom, December 2012.

33. "War Life," 484th Bombardment Group (H), http://www.484th.org/Life/ Life.htm.

34. "Sgt. Hugh N. Jones," 450th Bob Group Memorial Association, http:// www.450thbg.com/real/biographies/jones/jones.shtml.

35. Email, January 31, 2013.

36. Ernie Pyle, *Brave Men* (New York: Henry Holt, 1944), 293. Pyle was killed in the Okinawa campaign in April 1945.

37. "World War II," dtic.mil, http://www.dtic.mil/dpmo/wwii/.

38. "Killed in 1944, Airman John S. McConnon May Be Coming Home," 376th Heavy Bomb Group, http://www.376hbgva.com/memoirs/mcconnon.htm; Ann Belser, "WWII Aviator from City Will Finally Rest in Peace," *Pittsburgh Post-Gazette* (March 16, 1999).

39. "Martin F. Troy," arlingtoncemetery.net, August 10, 2007, http://www.arlingtoncemetery.net/mftroy.htm.

40. Details courtesy of Dr. Daniel Haulman.

41. Andrew Tilghman, "New Medal 'Insulting,'" *Army Times* (February 15, 2013). The DWM was canceled in April 2013.

42. Hess interview, April 2012.

43. Albert Speer, *Inside the Third Reich* (New York: Simon & Schuster, 1970), 338.

BIBLIOGRAPHY

Ambrose, Stephen E. *The Wild Blue: The Men and Boys Who Flew the B-24s over Germany.* New York: Simon & Schuster, 2001.

Army Air Forces. *The Air Battle of Ploesti.* N.p., 1945.

Army Air Forces. *Periodic History, 859th Bombardment Squadron.* USAF Historical Research Agency, October 1944 to May 1945.

Army Air Forces 28th Statistical Control Unit. *The Statistical Story of the Fifteenth Air Force.* May 20, 1945.

Army Air Forces Evaluation Board. *Report, Vol. VI: Ploesti.* Mediterranean Theater of Operations, December 15, 1944, 50.

Asch, Alfred, with Hugh R. Graff and Thomas A. Ramey. *The Story of the Four Hundred and Fifty-fifth Bombardment Group (H) WWII: Flight of the Vulgar Vultures.* Appleton, WI: Graphic Communications Center, 1991.

Birdsall, Steve. *Log of the Liberators.* New York: Doubleday, 1973.

Blake, Steve, and John Stanaway. *Adorimini ("Up and at 'Em!"): A History of the 82nd Fighter Group in World War II.* Boise: 82nd Fighter Group History, 1992.

Blue, Allan G. *The B-24 Liberator.* New York: Scribners, 1975.

Brittain, Vera. *One Voice: Pacifist Writings from the Second World War*. New York: Continuum Books, 2005.

Caldwell, Donald. *Day Fighters in Defense of the Reich, 1942–45*. UK: Frontline Books, 2011.

———. *The Luftwaffe Over Germany: Defense of the Reich*. UK: Greenhill Books, 2007.

Capps, Robert F. *Flying Colt: Liberator Pilot in Italy*. Bloomington: Author-House, 1997.

Constable, Trevor, and Raymond Toliver. *Horrido! Fighter Aces of the Luftwaffe*. New York: Macmillan, 1968.

Craven, Wesley F., and James L. Cate, eds. *Army Air Forces in World War II, Vol. II: Europe—Torch to Pointblank, August 1942 to December 1943*. Chicago: University of Chicago Press, 1949.

———. *Army Air Forces in World War II, Vol. III: Europe—Argument to V-E Day, January 1944 to May 1945*. Chicago: University of Chicago Press, 1951.

———. *Army Air Forces in World War II, Vol. VII: The Services Around the World, Washington, D.C., 1945*. Chicago: University of Chicago Press, 1958.

Disbrow, Bill L. *On the Edge*. Riverside: Winlock Galey, 2005.

Dorr, Robert F. *B-24 Liberator Units of the Fifteenth Air Force*. UK: Osprey, 2000.

Downey, R. F., and D. W. Shepherd. *Maximum Effort: A History of the 449th Bomb Group, Book IV*. Panama City: Norfield, 2000.

Ehrlers, Robert S. *Targeting the Third Reich*. Lawrence: University of Kansas Press, 2009.

Fish, Robert W., ed. *Memories of the 801st/492nd Bombardment Group "Carpetbaggers."* San Antonio: privately published, 1990.

Follis, Thomas K. *He Wore a Pair of Silver Wings*. Bennington: Merriam Press, 2004.

Forsyth, Robert. *Luftwaffe Viermot Aces, 1942–1945*. UK: Osprey, 2011.

Gillies, Frederick W. *The Story of a Squadron*. Medford, MA: privately published, 1946.

Goebel, Robert J. *Mustang Ace: Memoirs of a P-51 Fighter Pilot*. Pacifica: Pacifica Military History, 2010.

Green, Herschel. *Herky! Memoirs of a Checkertail Ace*. Atglen: Schiffer, 1996.

Hadley, Paul. *"Grottaglie and Home": A History of the 449th Bomb Group, World War II, Book III*. Northfield: Collegiate Press, 1989.

———. *"Maximum Effort": A History of the 449th Bomb Group, World War II, Book IV*. Northfield: Collegiate Press, 2000.

Hall, Cargill. *Case Studies in Strategic Bombardment*. Washington, D.C.: Air Force History & Museums Program, 1998.

Hammell, Eric. *The Road to Big Week: The Struggle for Daylight Air Supremacy over Western Europe*. Pacifica: Pacifica Military History, 2009.

Hansell, Haywood S. *The Air Plan That Defeated Hitler*. Stratford: Ayer, 1979.

Hansen, Randall. *Fire and Fury: The Allied Bombing of Germany, 1942–1945*. New York: New American Library, 2008.

Hapgood, David, and David Richardson. *Monte Cassino: The Most Controversial Battle of World War II*. Cambridge: Da Capo Press, 2002.

Hess, William N. *America's Aces in a Day*. North Branch: Specialty Press, 1996.

———. *German Jets Versus the U.S. Army Air Force*. North Branch: Specialty Press, 1996.

Hill, Sedgefield D., ed. *"The Fight'n" 451st Bombardment Group (H)*. Paducah: Turner, 1990.

Huston, John W. *American Airpower Comes of Age: General Henry H. Arnold's World War II Diaries, Vol. II*. Fresno: Minerva Group, 2004.

Ivie, Tom, and Paul Ludwig. *Spitfires and Yellow Tail Mustangs: The 52nd Fighter Group in World War Two*. East Sussex, UK: Hikoki, 2005.

Jablonski, Edward. *Flying Fortress: The Illustrated Biography of the B-17s and the Men Who Flew Them*. New York: Doubleday, 1965.

Kucera, Dennis C. *In a Now Forgotten Sky: The 31st Fighter Group in WW2*. Stratford: Flying Machines Press, 1997.

Leary, William M. *Fueling the Fires of Resistance: Army Air Forces Special Operations in the Balkans During World War II*. Air Force History & Museums Program, 1995.

Levine, Alan J. *The Strategic Bombing of Germany, 1940–1945*. Westport: Praeger, 1992.

Licata, Dominic. *Autobiography*. Reno: University of Nevada, 2004.

Loving, George G. *Woodbine Red Leader: A P-51 Mustang Ace in the Mediterranean Theater*. Novato: Presidio Press, 2003.

Matteson, Thomas T. *An Analysis of the Circumstances Surrounding the Rescue and Evacuation of Allied Aircrewmen From Yugoslavia, 1941–1945*. Air War College, Air University Report No. 128. Maxwell AFB, April 1977.

McDowell, Ernest R. *Checkertails: The 325th Fighter Group in the Second World War*. Carrollton: Squadron-Signal, 1994.

McDowell, Ernest R., and William N. Hess. *Checkertail Clan: The 325th Fighter Group in North Africa and Italy*. Fallbrook: Aero, 1969.

Mullins, John D. *An Escort of P-38s: The 1st Fighter Group in World War II*. St. Paul: Phalanx, 1995.

Murray, Williamson. *Strategy for Defeat: The Luftwaffe, 1933–1945*. Air University, 1983.

Murray, Williamson, and Allan Millett. *Military Innovation in the Interwar Period*. Cambridge: Cambridge University Press, 1998.

Nalty, Bernard C., with John F. Shiner and George M. Watson. *With Courage: The U.S. Army Air Forces in World War II*. Washington, D.C.: Air Force History & Museums Program, 1994.

Neulen, Hans Werner. *In the Skies of Europe: Air Forces Allied to the Luftwaffe*. UK: Crowood Press, 1998.

Olynyk, Frank. *USAAF (European Theater) Credits for the Destruction of Enemy Aircraft in Air-to-Air Combat, World War 2*. Aurora: privately published, 1987.

Overy, Richard. *Why the Allies Won*. New York: W. W. Norton, 1995.

Panas, John N. *Diary of John Panas in World War II*. Bronx: Beehive Press, undated.

Pindak, Frank F. *Mission No. 263: Second Bombardment Group, Fifteenth Air Force, August 29, 1944*. Denver: L. Dickinson, 1997.

Price, Alfred. *Battle over the Reich: The Strategic Bomber Offensive against Germany, Volume Two: 1943–45*. UK: Classic, 2005.

Pyle, Ernie. *Brave Men*. New York: Henry Holt, 1944.

Raiford, Neil Hunter. *Shadow: A Cottontail Bomber Crew in World War II*. Jefferson, NC: McFarland, 2005.

Rajlich, Jiri, et al. *Slovakian and Bulgarian Aces of World War 2*. UK: Osprey, 2004.

Richards, Charles W. *The Second Was First*. Bend: Maverick, 1999.

Rust, Kenn C. *Fifteenth Air Force Story*. Temple City: Historical Aviation Album, 1976.

Schaffer, Ronald. *Wings of Judgment: American Bombing in World War II*. New York: Oxford University Press, 1985.

Seyer, Sean. *The Plan Put into Practice: USAAF Bombing Doctrine and the Ploesti Campaign*. St. Louis: University of Missouri, 2009.

Sgarlato, Nico. *Italian Aircraft of World War II*. Warren, MI: Squadron-Signal, 1979.

Shepherd, D. William. *Maximum Effort: A History of the 449th Bomb Group in World War II*. Paducah: Turner, 2000.

Shores, Christopher. *Duel for the Sky: Ten Crucial Air Battles of World War II*. UK: Blandford Press, 1985.

Speer, Albert. *Erinnerungen*. Berlin: Propyläen Verlag, 1969.

———. *Inside the Third Reich*. New York: Simon & Schuster, 1970.

Stout, Jay A. *Fortress Ploesti: The Campaign to Destroy Hitler's Oil*. Havertown, PA: Casemate, 2003.

Werrell, Kenneth P. *Who Fears? 301st in War and Peace, 1942–1979*. Dallas: Taylor, 1991.

INDEX

12 O'Clock High, 260

A

A-3, 29, 158
"Able Box," 34–35, 224, 242
Abschüsse, 112
"ace in a day," 34, 223
Adell, Albert, 154
Adriatic coast (Italy), xiv
Adriatic Sea, 14, 33, 42, 45, 102, 213
Aegean Sea, 204–5
Aeronautica Nazionale Repubblicana (ANR), 22, 40–41
Aerospace Defense Command, 262
Africa. *See* North Africa; South Africa
Agan, Arthur C., 223, 262
Aghione, 138

Agusta 109 helicopters, 270–71
Air Crew Recovery Unit (ACRU), 178–81
Air Fleet Two, 39–40. *See also* Luftflotte (Air Fleet) Two
Air Force, 208–9
Air Force Association, 261–62
Air Materiel Command, 249, 262
Air Medals, 165
Air Transport Command, 96, 249
Alaska, 29, 199
Alaskan Air Command, 262
Albania, 174, 269–70, 280
Albuquerque, NM, 187
Aleutian, 260–61
Algeria, 19, 151
Algiers, 5, 159

Alkire, Darr H., 43

Allied Combined Chiefs of Staff, 4

Allies

    bombing of enemy civilians by the, 52–53

    composition of the, 22, 179

    military progress of the, 4, 6, 21, 32, 66–67, 84, 133, 137, 139, 142, 210–11

    Monte Cassino and the, 36

    resources of the, 231

    victory of the, 244

Allison engines, 56, 59, 151

Alps, the, xi–xii, 42, 130, 150, 153, 161, 174, 218, 225, 272

Ambrose, Stephen, 207

Amendola, 59, 110, 143, 243, 267, 277

American Airlines, 50

American Beauty, 202

American Fighter Aces Association, 263, 273

American Revolution, the, 27

Americans

    casualties in World War II, 15, 88, 269–70

    chemical warfare and the, 16

    civilians during World War II, 97

    compared with Europeans, xii, 99–100, 207

    operations in World War II, 2–4, 6, 22, 33, 36, 38, 45–49, 67–68, 71, 78, 87–89, 96, 102, 109, 129, 134–35, 140–41, 145–46, 170, 178, 180–81, 191, 204, 233, 236, 244, 265

    and Soviets, 99, 105, 127, 131

"American summer," 189

American West, xii

Ancona, 13, 181

Anderson, Edwin, 110–11

Anderson, Frederick L., 53

Anderson, Ralph, 267, 281

Andrews, Richard "Dick," 131–32

Angermann (German pilot), 143

Anglo-American forces, 2, 4, 38, 53, 138, 158, 210–11

Antonescu, Ion, 136

Antwerp, 210–11

Anzio, 32, 39

Apollo oil refinery, 106

Archer, Lee, 190

Ardennes Forest, 210

Arkansas National Guard, 151

Arlington Cemetery, 263, 270

Armstrong, Frank, 23

Arnold, Henry "Hap," 3, 5, 7, 17–19, 28–29, 52–53, 68, 261

Aron, William E., 238

Arsenic and Lace, 270

Ashkins, Milton, 222

Asia, 82

"As Time Goes By," 258

Astra Romana, 83, 90, 112, 129–30, 133, 136–37, 155, 257

Atabrine, 108

Athens, 5, 192, 218, 249

Atkinson, John T., 205

Atkinson, Joseph H., 7

Augsburg, 17, 23, 47, 108, 158

Auschwitz, 119, 187, 213

Australia, 251

Austria

    bombing of, 4, 13–14, 39, 42–43, 45, 55, 68, 105, 158, 160, 171, 174, 176–77, 211, 217, 219–24, 241, 250, 254, 279

    geography of, xi, 4

    Germany and, 40

    surrender of, 244, 248

Aviano, 43, 202

Axis
  Allied operations against the, ix–x, 4,
     16, 26, 51, 53, 64, 66, 68, 85, 92,
     101–2, 126, 177, 183, 186, 254,
     272, 274
  casualties among the, 93
  members of the, 31, 53, 66, 68, 83,
     183, 274
  military operations of the, 33, 67, 72,
     86, 109, 112, 127, 131, 136, 191–
     92, 196, 237
  surrender of the, 244
"Axis Sally," 186

B

B-17Ds, 92
B-17 Flying Fortresses, 7
B-17Fs, 35, 140
B-17Gs, 35, 78, 188
B-17s, 7–9, 12–14, 24–26, 28, 33–37,
     41, 44–45, 48, 65, 80, 86, 88, 91, 95,
     97–99, 101–2, 105, 109, 123, 130,
     132, 135, 140, 146, 171, 179, 186–
     88, 205, 208–9, 211, 222, 225–30,
     234, 243, 248, 251, 263, 266, 269,
     271
B-24Gs, 121
B-24Js, 9, 166
B-24s, 7–9, 14, 23, 26, 34–35, 39, 41,
     43, 63, 65–66, 69, 86, 88–89, 94–95,
     102, 106, 112, 116, 118, 120, 122–
     23, 130, 134, 166, 169, 171–73, 176,
     181, 184, 197–98, 204, 216–17, 219,
     221, 225–26, 241–42, 251, 265, 267,
     269–71
B-25 Mitchells, 13
B-25s, 1, 7, 13, 25–26, 31, 249
B-26s, 7, 25–26
B-29s, 92, 187, 251, 261
B-29 Superfortresses, 9
Baetjer, Howard, 61

Baker, Donald, 198
Balkan Air Force, 178, 192, 201
Balkans, the, 4–5, 40, 66, 85, 119, 160,
     171, 175, 177–78, 180, 185, 252,
     254
Baller, Albert, 176
"Bambino Stadium," 6
Bari, 2, 6–7, 14, 16–17, 23, 30, 62, 112,
     126, 145, 151, 155, 159, 166, 173,
     176, 178–79, 181, 184–85, 195,
     209–10, 213, 245
"Barn, the," 74
Baron Pavoncelli, 49
Barton, Bill, 211–12
Baseler, Robert L. "Bob," 20–22, 33–34,
     57–58, 216, 263
Battle of Britain, 39–40, 63, 199, 253
Battle of the Bulge, 211
Bauer, Konrad, 79
Bavaria, 108, 157, 221
"Behind the Rising Sun," 73
Belgium, 80, 210
Belgrade, 68, 116, 185
Benedictine abbey, 35
Benghazi, 84
Bentsen, Lloyd, 265
Berenger, Victor Henri, 81
Bergen, Edgar, 21
Berlin Airlift, 263
Berlin Olympics (1936), 40, 186
Berlin Sleeper III, 135
Bf 109G-6s, 143
Bf 109Gs, 90
Bf 109s, 14, 39, 44, 100–1, 103, 109,
     124, 140, 163, 190, 199, 203
Bf 110s, 39, 43–44, 70
Big Stud, 21, 58
Big Week, 38–39, 46, 48–49, 51, 55, 72,
     91, 125
Big Yank, 228–29

Bishop, Albert, 228
Bizerte, 159
"Black Devil of the Ukraine, The," 117
Black Easter, 67–68
"Black Hammer," 187, 256
Black Sea, 136, 218
Blakely, Frank, 270
Blechhammer, 5, 119, 132–33, 137,
    142–43, 181, 187–88, 190, 204–5,
    210, 213, 217, 255–56
Blechhammer North, 119, 187, 217, 256
Blechhammer South, 119, 187, 217, 256
Bleyer, Julian, 14
Blida, 171–72
Blond Squaw, 105
Blue Force, 197, 219
Blumer, John, 200
Boeing, 7–9, 110–11, 188, 226–27, 251
Boeing Airplane Company, 140
Boesch, Oskar, 79
"boffins," 88
Boise, ID, 65
Bolling Field, 167
Booker, William, 76
Born, Charles F., 15, 29, 168, 195
Bosnia, 178–79
Bratislava, 69, 106, 219
Brave Men, 269
Brazi, 83
Brazil, 249
Breckenridge, TX, 106
Brenner Pass, 4, 240
Brereton, Louis H., 7
Brewer, Arthur, 76
Brewer, Phil, 200
Brezas, Michael "Mike," 238, 252
Brindisi, 172–73, 175
Britain, 7, 12, 17–19, 23, 25, 29–30,
    39–40, 42, 45, 49, 52, 56, 63, 68, 83,
    95, 164, 173, 178, 186, 199, 261,
    272

British Eighth Army, 231
British Isles, the, 25
British Theater, 3
Bronze Stars, 271
Brown, Charles, 76–77, 128
Brown, Roscoe, 229
Brown, Samuel J. "Sam," 70–72, 203,
    252
Broyhill, Lincoln F. "Babe," 228–29
Bruck, 157
Brux, 119, 211, 217, 226, 238
Bucharest, 5, 31, 60, 62, 66, 68, 83, 85,
    88–89, 93, 109, 116, 130–31, 136,
    144–46, 266
Buchner, Hermann, 226
Budapest, 5, 90, 96–97, 137, 153, 187,
    189, 255
Bundesluftwaffe, 266
Bulgaria, Bulgarian, 17, 31, 52–53,
    66–68, 111, 167, 179, 183–84
Bulgarian Air Force. See *Vozdushni
    Voiski*
"Butler's Sister, The," 73
Buzau, 127

C

C-47s, 138, 173, 178–80, 182, 193
C-54s, 218
Cairo, 17, 167–68, 184, 249
Cairo Conference, 17
Calamity Jane, 119–20
"Calamity Jane," 129
California, 251, 262
Campbell, Daniel S., 140
Campina, 81–82
Campoleone, 32
Cantacuzino, Constantin Bâzu, 66, 144–
    46, 266
Caplan, Leslie "Doc," 243–35, 263
Capps, Robert S., 75–76
Carey, Harry, 208

Carlin, Robert, 224

Carlson, Darwin, 210

Caroselli, Philip J., 49

Carpetbaggers, 149, 170–71, 173, 175–77, 241

Casablanca, 167

Castelluccio, 119, 219

Castle Field, CA, 251

Castriota, Antonio "Sergeant Tony," 108, 264

Catch-22, 260

Caucasus, the, 82

Caughlin, William H., 125

Celone, 20, 93

Celone Airfield, 186

Central Identification Laboratory, 270

Cerignola, 181, 240

Cernosek, Jirka, 270

Cervia, 243

Cessna, 265

"Checkerboard" Warhawk Fighter Group, 21

"Checkertails" (Checkertail Clan), 20, 33, 60, 62, 66, 97–98, 100, 109, 123, 190, 195, 199, 203, 217, 223, 226, 251–52, 263. See also Fifteenth Army Air Force: 325th Fighter Group

Chennault, Claire, 261

Chetniks, 177, 179

Chicago, IL, 108, 125, 180

China, 82, 106–7, 261

China-Burma-India Theater, 194, 261

Christmas Day, 20, 23, 168, 211

Chrysler, 264

Churchill, Eugene E., 17, 88, 170, 218

Churchill, Winston, 150

Church, William T., 185

Clark, Forrest, 154

Clark, Mark, 37

Clemens, Robert C., 186

Clifford, Robert V., 157

Co-Belligerent Air Force, 22

Cold War, 265

Coliseum, 173

Collison, James M., 23

Colombia Aquila, 83–84

Colorado Springs, CO, 249

Combined Bomber Offensive (CBO), 4, 23, 38, 258

Command Decision, 259

Command and General Staff College, 28

Committee of Operations Analysts, 256

communism, Communists, 53, 194, 168, 177, 194, 232, 266, 269

Compton, Keith, 14, 167

Concordia Vega, 83, 87, 90–91, 94, 120–21, 130, 155

Conlon, Joseph "Jerry," 270

Consolidated, 9

Consolidated B-24 Liberators, 7

Constanta, 136

ConUS, 249

Cooning, Leon, 188

Corsica, 138, 140–42, 171, 175

"Cottontails," 8, 45, 87–88. See also Fifteenth Army Air Force: 450th Bomb Group

Coughlin, Charles, 193–94

Coulson, Eldon, 196–97

Coulson, Sid, 200

Coventry, 52

Crafton, Charles E., 146

Crawford, Fred, 106–7

Crawford, George, 106–7

Crawford, Raymond, 106

Creditul Minier, 83–84, 122

Crinkley, Robert, 181

Cristea, Gheorghe, 93

Croatia, 193

Cullen, Paul, 243

Cuprija, 144

"Cyclone" engines, 8

Czechoslovakia, 105–6, 119, 143, 172, 176–77, 211, 219, 223, 225–26, 228

Czech Republic, 270

D

D-2, 139

Dacia Romana, 83, 101, 108, 122, 134–35

Dahl, Walther, 126, 204

Daimler-Benz, 225, 264–65

Dakar, 167

Dallas, 266

Danielson, Warren, 239

Daniel, William A. "Billy," 145, 202–3, 229

Danube River, 69, 92, 101, 109, 136

Davis, Benjamin O. "Barrie," Jr., 58, 62, 252

Davis, Robert R., 210

Dayton, OH, 155

D-Day, 38, 85, 94, 101, 104, 138, 140–41, 171, 259

"D-Day South," 137, 139

Deane, John R., 201

Debrecen, 97

de Havilland Mosquitoes, 156, 160

Democratic Party, Democrats, 240, 265

Dessau, 226

Destroyer Wing One, 43

Devers, Jacob, 18, 37, 137, 178

Dinker, William R., 157, 273

Disney, 89

Distinguished Service Cross, 199, 260

Distinguished Unit Citations (DUCs), 44, 46, 106, 156, 175, 230, 260

Distinguished Warfare Medal, 271

Dnieper River, 98

Doboj, 217

Dobran, Ion, 100

Dog Boxes, 35

Doolittle, James Harold "Jimmy," 1–3, 5–7, 13, 15–18, 20, 22–23, 25–30, 33, 38–39, 41, 50, 63, 95, 98, 150–51, 253, 261

Dornier, 34

Douglas, 9

Douglas C-47s, 182

Douhet, Guilio, 51–52

Dresden, 119, 158

Droop Snoot P-38Js, 164

Droop Snoot P-38s, 157

Droop Snoots, 149, 164, 216–17

Drvar, 178

Dryer, Alton "Buddy," 234–36

Dukakis, Michael, 265

Durbin, Deanna, 73

E

"Eager Joe," 129

Eaker, Ira C., 17–18, 27, 33, 37–38, 51, 63, 68, 84–86, 92, 96–98, 104, 133, 136, 138, 178, 261

East Indies, 82

Easy Boxes, 35

Eaton, Robert, 77, 120

Eckert, Clem, 21, 58

Eder, Georg-Peter, 71

Edwinson, Clarence T. "Curly," 199–201, 262

Eggers, Richard, 15–16

Egypt, 166, 184, 194

Ehrler, Heinrich, 226

Eiffel Tower, 173

Eisenhower, Dwight D. "Ike," 3–4, 17–18, 29, 85, 92

Elder, Donald, 15–16

Emery, Leonard H., 60

Emswiler, James E., 164–65

England, 3, 17–19, 27, 29, 199, 259

Epley, David R., 210

Escort of P-38s, An, 264
ETO, 37
Eureka, 171
Europe, 2–3, 25, 29, 38, 40, 78, 81–86,
    95, 137, 150–51, 170–72, 218, 231,
    241, 244, 252, 266–67, 269, 271
Europe Air Shkedra (Scutari), 201
Evans, Bradford E., 36
Evill, Douglas, 85
Experten, 79
Exum, Wyatt, 132

F

F-4s, 159
F-5s, 159, 164, 251,
F-8s, 156
F-15E Strike Eagles, 251
F-51s, 251
Fairchild, Muir, 262
Fascists, 22, 39, 170, 185, 194, 244
FBI, 194
Felder, Bob, 165
Fiats, 109
Fiedler, Arthur, 62, 64, 266
Field, Russell, Jr., 154
Fifteenth Army Air Force, 3–4, 7, 20, 26,
    29, 39, 48, 55, 61, 64, 66–67, 81, 85,
    88, 90, 115, 128, 137, 149–51, 159,
    165–66, 177, 181, 183–84, 189, 192,
    195, 199, 213, 217–18, 223, 225,
    238, 249–53, 265, 272
    5th Bomb Wing, 7, 23, 25, 88, 90,
        93, 97, 109, 120, 122–23, 129–
        30, 134–35, 146, 187, 222, 248,
        262
        2nd Bomb Group, 36, 44, 128,
            249, 262
        97th Bomb Group, 23, 36, 97–98,
            101, 109–10, 135, 143, 146,
            227, 233
        340th Bomb Squadron, 188

99th Bomb Group, 5, 11, 36, 44,
    97, 99, 208
301st Bomb Group, 31, 35–36,
    45, 97, 249
463rd Bomb Group, 92–93, 97,
    100, 124, 130, 135, 186–87,
    227–28, 230
483rd Bomb Group, 97, 124–25,
    217, 222, 230
5th Photographic Reconnaissance
    Group, 159–60, 164–66
    4th Photo Technical Squadron,
        160
    15th Photo Recon Squadron, 160
    32nd Photo Recon Squadron,
        159–160, 163–64
    37th Photo Recon Squadron, 160
15th Special Operations Group, 174–
    75
    859th Bomb Squadron, 172–74,
        176
47th Bomb Wing, 8, 25, 41, 90, 94,
    101, 106, 108, 112, 120–22, 126,
    133–34, 138, 144, 146, 168, 184–
    85
    98th Bomb Group ("Pyramid-
        ers"), 8, 14, 41, 98, 121, 260
    376th Bomb Group ("Liberan-
        dos"), 8, 14, 23, 41, 44, 95,
        106–7, 118, 144, 166–69,
        211, 260, 265, 269
        512th Fighter Squadron, 23,
            167
    449th Bomb Group, 41–43, 46,
        68, 89, 94, 144, 234, 263, 265
    450th Bomb Group ("Cotton-
        tails"), 8, 41, 44–45, 65,
        87–89, 94, 122, 208, 268
        720th Fighter Squadron, 89

49th Bomb Wing, 94, 101, 120, 125, 129, 195, 204, 267
  451st Bomb Group, 49, 76, 94, 119, 212, 219, 241, 260
  461st Bomb Group ("Liberaiders"), 39, 49, 181, 196, 204–6, 216, 248, 270
  484th Bomb Group, 51, 267
55th Bomb Wing, 65, 93, 101, 108, 129, 134
  460th Bomb Group, 232, 242, 256, 270
  464th Bomb Group, 65, 101, 198, 210, 255
  465th Bomb Group, 65, 224
  485th Bomb Group, 65, 205, 248
154th Weather Reconnaissance Squadron, 151–58, 216, 243
304th Bomb Wing, 69–70, 92–93, 109, 129–30, 134, 219
  454th Bomb Group, 43, 56, 69, 134, 144
  455th Bomb Group, 65, 69, 70, 72, 219, 233, 241, 265.
  742nd Squadron, 70
  456th Bomb Group, 49, 69, 75, 91
  459th Bomb Group, 50, 69, 71, 227
305th Fighter Wing, 195
  1st Fighter Group, 59, 107–8, 159, 212, 215, 218, 222, 264
  27th Fighter Squadron, 18, 102–3, 108, 125, 239
  71st Fighter Squadron, 103
  94th Fighter Squadron, 18, 103, 108
14th Fighter Group, 19–20, 30, 40, 44, 72, 88, 105, 127–28, 138, 140, 185, 203, 205, 207, 238–39, 247, 249, 251–52

48th Fighter Squadron, 30
82nd Fighter Group, 20, 34, 44, 71–72, 74, 102–4, 127–28, 131, 192–94, 196, 199–200, 212, 215–17, 226, 251, 260, 262
  95th Fighter Squadron, 20, 23, 196, 217
306th Fighter Wing, 33, 127, 195, 217
  31st Fighter Group, 56, 60–61, 64, 71–72, 90, 94, 116, 125, 127–28, 145, 180, 186, 196, 202, 205, 221, 226, 229, 232, 239, 242, 244, 247, 251–52, 254, 262, 268
  309th Fighter Squadron, 128
  52nd Fighter Group, 56–57, 67, 71, 75, 94, 107, 109, 123–25, 131–32, 195, 205, 226, 229, 240, 251–52
  325th Fighter Group ("Checkertails," "Checkertail Clan," "Clan"), 20–22, 33, 55, 57–58, 60, 62, 64, 66, 97–101, 105, 109, 123, 190, 195, 199, 202–3, 217, 223, 226, 238, 251–52, 263
  318th Fighter Squadron, 100
  319th Fighter Squadron, 105
  332nd Fighter Group (Tuskegee Airmen, "Red Tails"), 56, 58, 123, 125, 190, 226, 228–30, 242, 252–54, 260
  302nd Fighter Squadron, 190
2641st Special Group, 175, 177
  859th Bomb Squadron, 172–74, 176
  885th Bomb Squadron, 171–74, 177

Weather Detachment. *See* Fifteenth Army Air Force: 154th Weather Reconnaissance Squadron

XV Air Service Command, 195, 249

XV Fighter Command, 69, 195, 231, 237, 262

Fifteenth Special Operations Group. *See* Fifteenth Army Air Force: 2641st Special Group

Fighter Division Seven (JG 7). *See* Luftwaffe

Fighter Squadron, 259

Firtree, 155

Flak 18/36/37, 191

Flak 36/37, 191

Flak 38/39, 192

Flak 40, 192

Flak 41, 191

Flakwaffe, 220

Flakwagen, 239

Flame McGoon, 14

Florence, 267

Florida, 263

Florisdorf, 158, 198

Flugzeugabwehrkanone (Flak), 191

Flying Fortresses (Fortresses), 7–9, 15, 32, 34–36, 44, 88, 92–93, 95, 100–1, 105, 108, 110, 121, 124, 130, 135, 140, 142, 146, 187–88, 190, 211, 219, 225, 227, 243, 251

Flying Tigers, 261

Flynn, Errol, 15, 244

Focke-Wulfs (FWs), 43, 48, 60, 64, 77–78, 87, 91, 94, 100, 103, 112, 124, 142, 191, 202, 205, 223, 238–39, 274

Focsani, 101

Foggia, 2–3, 5–7, 10–11, 25, 30, 35, 41, 49, 68–69, 72, 74, 77, 86, 96–97, 104, 108, 119, 132, 139, 142, 145–47, 153, 157, 159, 180, 187, 189, 194, 199, 207, 210–11, 215, 218, 220, 225, 231–32, 237, 242, 244, 247, 249, 259, 264, 267, 270–72

Foggia Eleven, 212

Foggia Main, 11, 215

Foggia Number Three, 74, 215

Follis, Tom, 161

"Fork-tailed Devil," 18. See also *Gabelschwanz Teufel*; P-38 Lightnings

Fox Boxes, 35

France, 4, 13, 17, 29, 32, 38, 52, 57, 85, 105, 119, 137–38, 142, 151, 159–60, 171–77, 206, 210, 244, 252, 259

French Riviera, 137

Friedrichshafen, 123, 125

Fuller, James H., 154

"Funnel," 145

G

Gabelschwanz Teufel, 18. *See also* "Fork-tailed Devil"; P-38 Lightnings

Gable, Clark, 8

Galapagos Islands, 50

Galati, 66, 100–1

Galland, Adolf, 63, 220–21, 230–31, 258, 265

Gent, Thomas J., Jr., 43

Georgia, 240

Germany, Germans, 62–63, 101–2, 134, 139, 186, 194, 254
   aces of, 20, 40
   Allied operations in, 10, 12–13, 15–16, 22, 38–42, 45, 53, 68–69, 139, 144, 151, 167, 170–71, 176–77, 191–92, 197–98, 211, 220–21, 225, 238–40, 250
   American POWs in, 232–36, 238
   Axis powers and, 31, 183, 191
   Balkans and, 175, 185
   Battle of Britain and, 63

bombing of civilians, 52–53
casualties, 48, 63, 80, 142–43, 180,
    200
combat with Americans, xi, 2, 18, 20,
    23, 33, 41–42, 45–47, 69–70,
    92–94, 101–3, 105, 110, 112,
    116–17, 124–25, 129, 156, 167,
    187, 189, 202, 204–7, 223, 238,
    252–53
infrastructure of, 4, 15, 22, 38, 44,
    47–48, 78, 123, 140–42, 158,
    220, 228, 231, 254, 272–73
in Italy, 2, 4, 6, 32, 35–37, 43, 176,
    207, 210–11
military, 4, 12, 77–79, 137, 230, 237
in North Africa, 4
oil supply for, x, 5, 38, 65, 77–78,
    82–85, 92–93, 104–5, 113, 118–
    19, 158, 254–58, 272–73
reconnaissance missions in, 159–65
Romanian declaration of war on,
    135–36, 266
Soviet Union and, 83, 99, 265
surrender of, 242, 244
Yugoslavia and, 166, 178–79, 201
Ghurkas, 38
Giambrone, Bill, 118
Gibraltar, 218
Gillars, Maine, 186
Gilliam, Maurice, 89
Gino Lisa Airport, 270
Gioia del Colle, 49, 76, 176, 215
Giulia, 50, 278
Giurgiu, 101, 109–10, 118
Glantzberg, 50
Goebel, Robert J., 116–17, 226
Gong, Fred, 217
Göring, Hermann, 38, 126, 230, 256,
    258
Gotha, 44
Gothic Line, 115

Graff, Theodore "Ted," 23, 166
Grange, Red, 199
Gray, Linda, 266
Graz, 56, 220
Great War, the, 1, 28, 51–52, 81, 178.
    See also World War I
Greece, 17, 35, 83, 134, 151, 160, 166–
    67, 172, 218, 279
Green, Herschel "Herky," 33–34, 58,
    195, 202, 252, 263, 281
Greenman, John, 241
Gregory, Charles, 248
Grenoble, 138
Gross Tychow, 233–34
Grottaglie, 43, 278
"grounders," 203
Guadalcanal, 28–29
guerrillas, 168, 170, 177, 179–80, 201,
    244
Gunn, James A., III, 134, 144–45, 266
Gustav Line, 2

H

H2S, 88
H2X, 89, 122, 157
Halifaxes, 133
Hamburg, 52, 68–69, 265
Handrick, Gotthard, 40, 44, 69, 142,
    265
Hannibal, xi
Harper, Clair, 228
Hartmann, Erich, 117
Hatch, Herbert "Stub," 103–4
Hawaii, 270
Hawes, Philip R. "Spike," 196
He 162s, 206
Hellcats, 140
Heller, Joseph, 260
Hemingway, Ernest, 259
Heppes, Aladar, 66, 90, 143
Hero of the Soviet Union, 200, 265

Herrausschutz, 45
Hersey, John, 259
Herzegovina, 178
Hess, William N. "Junior" (Bill), 188–89, 233–37, 263
High Command, 21
Hitler, Adolf, 138, 237
  death of, 244
  military strategy of, 82, 211, 221, 230
  oil of, x, 137
  policies of, 47
Hoenshell, Carl, 103
Hoffman, Cullen, 100
Hogg, Roy B., 100
Hollinger, Richard "Stumpy," 212
Holloway, James D., 72
"Hollywood bomber, the." *See* B-17 Flying Fortresses
Holy Land, 249
Holy Synod of Bulgarian Orthodox Church, 52
"Homebound Task Force," 248–49
Hoodecheck, Arthur, 185
Hoosier, 238
Hornet, 1
Houston, TX, 43
Hughes, Howard, 59
Hungary, Hungarians, 62, 66, 70. *See also* Royal Hungarian Air Force
  armed forces of, 70–71, 143, 198–99, 266
  as Axis power, 62, 66, 183, 274
  combat in, 62, 90, 107, 132, 151, 163, 172, 185, 189–90, 201, 203, 205, 220, 223, 238, 270, 274
Huns, the, 52
Huth, Joachim-Friedrich, 39–40, 44

I

IAR 80s, 103, 109

IAR 180s, 88, 109
IARs, 90, 103, 109
Idaho, 65
"Il Duce." *See* Mussolini, Benito
Imperial Japan, 254
Imperial Navy, 82
India, 261. *See also* China-Burma-India Theater
Indianers, xiv
Indians, 38
Innsbruck, xi–xiii, 17, 130, 211, 240
Is Everybody Happy?, 74
Isle of Capri, 75
Italian air force, 6, 153
Italy, Italians, xi, 99, 264, 266–67, 269
  Allied operations in, 2–4, 8, 13, 18, 20–21, 26, 32–33, 36, 42, 45, 53, 55, 76, 93, 106, 113, 128, 151, 167–68, 171–75, 177, 181, 190, 206–7, 218–20, 232, 239–40, 242, 244, 250, 259, 269
  armed forces of, 6, 12, 22, 39–40, 109, 153, 193–94
  as base for the Fifteenth, ix, xi, xiv, 3, 5–7, 14, 16, 22, 25–26, 29–30, 43, 49, 74–75, 101, 105, 108, 131–32, 139, 142, 144–45, 151, 166, 174, 176, 180, 184–85, 189–90, 199, 207, 226, 229–30, 254, 259, 260–62, 269, 272
  German operations in, 20, 39–40, 123, 153, 190
  German surrender of, 176
  photography of, 159–60
  victory flights in, 245
  weather in, 11, 16–17, 25, 29–30, 42, 45, 49, 108, 149, 173, 213, 215
I/ZG76, 70

J

Jack London, 74

Jagdervand (JV) 44. *See under* Luftwaffe

Jagdflieger, 77–78, 80, 225

Jagdfliegerführer Ostmark, 40

Jagdgeschwader (JG). *See under* Luftwaffe

Jagdwaffe. *See under* Luftwaffe

Japan, 1, 73, 82, 92, 96, 254, 260–61

Jarmon, James, 130

Jay, Edward, 71

Jean, Gloria, 73

Jefferson, Thomas W., 242

Jelich, Milosh, 168–69

Jenkins, Larry, 128–29, 281

Jenkins, Robert, 121

Jerries, 125

Jewish, Jews, 107, 176

John Harvey, 16

Johnson, Bruce, 5–7

Johnson, David, 216

Joint Chiefs of Staff, 3, 16, 29, 31, 201, 262

Joint Oil Targets Committee, 129–30

Jones, Bill, 74

Jones, Hugh, 122, 268

Jones, Wilson, 41–42

Junkers, 128, 186, 202

Junkers 52s (J-52s, Ju 52s), 34

Junkers 88s, 16, 106, 140, 202, 236, 238

Kempten, 123

Kennedy, Jack, 265

Kentucky, 33–34

Kepner, William E., 63

Kesselring, Albert, 2, 36–37

King, Ernest J., 218

Kingsley, David R., 110–11, 260

Kirtland Air Base, 187

Kitty Hawk, NC, 173

Klagenfurt, 242

Klemm, Rudolf, 80

Knight's Cross, 39, 79, 230

Knoblock, Bruce D., 188–89

Koch, Chester, 45

Koenig, Hans-Heinrich, 80

Koldunov, Aleksandr, 200, 265

Konsynski, Benjamin, 14

Korea, 94, 251

Korean Air Lines, 265

Korean War, 263

Kovaleski, Edward S., 242

Kraigher, George, 178

Krakow, 128, 189

K rations, 267

Kriefsgefangenen ("Kriegies"), 232–33, 237, 248

Kurtz, Frank A., 92, 186–87

Kyle, Reuben, 184

K

K-17 cameras, 162

K-18 cameras, 162

K-24 cameras, 153

Kameraden, 221–22

Kane, John R. "Killer," 14, 121

Kansas, 199

Karachi, 194

Karatsonyi, Mihaly "Mike," 190, 266

Katschke, Kenneth, 200

Keese, William B., 51

Kelly, Thomas C., 212

L

Lady Be Good, 8

Lake Balaton, 90, 190, 199

Langford, Frances, 74

La Spezia, 13

Latin, 258

Latvia, 96

Lauer, Ford J., 97

Lavelle, John, 262

Lawrence, Charles W., 225, 281

Lay, Beirne, 259

Leadingham, Arthur M., 23

Lecce, 11, 20, 278

Lechner, August, 198

Lee, William L., 195

Legg, Richard A. "Dick," 212

Leghorn, 267

Leigh-Mallory, Trafford, 29

Leipheim, 221

LeMay, Curtis, 8

Leonard, Charles, 265

Leonard, Raymond, 242

Lesina, 206, 278

Lester, Clarence "Lucky," 123–24

Levine, Robert, 56

Lewis, Ted, 74

"Liberaiders," 49. *See also* Fifteenth
Army Air Force: 461st Bomb Group

"Liberandos," 8, 14, 23, 106, 167, 169.
See also Fifteenth Army Air Force:
376th Bomb Group

Liberators (Libs). *See* B-24s

Libya, 84

Licata, Dominic, 36

Lightnings. *See* P-38 Lightnings

Lindemann, Frederick, 88

Linz, 196–97, 212, 224, 241

Little Stud, 58

Litton, William P. "Bill," 127, 131

Lockheed, 18, 21, 164, 203, 206, 212,
231, 237, 239

Lockheed-Vega, 9

Lockney, Ralph, 242, 244

London, 17–18, 74, 84–85, 92, 225,
244, 259

Los Angeles Olympics (1932), 92

Lost City of Atlantis, 256

Louise, the Red Cross lady, 157

Louisiana, 188–89, 263

Loving, George, 61, 262, 268

Loyalists (Italian), 6, 22, 38

"Luft Four." *See* Stalag Luft IV

Luftwaffe, 92, 104, 146, 149, 159, 185,
236–37, 263, 266
  Big Week and, 38–49
  Bulgaria and, 67, 144
  D-Day and, 138
  defense by the, 13, 38, 55, 57, 70–71,
    77, 86, 123, 142, 164–66, 192,
    198, 204–6, 225, 231, 256–57
  fights against the Fifteenth, xiv, 4,
    15–16, 24, 33, 35, 63, 71–72,
    112, 124–27, 153, 219–20, 253
  fights against the Fourteenth, 19
  Frantic and, 105
  fuel shortage and the, 115, 119, 237,
    256–58
  Jagdwaffe, 42, 77, 113
  JG 3, 67, 79, 112, 126
  JG 7, 281
  JG 52, 117
  JG 53, 185
  JG 77s, 185
  JG 300, 204
  JG 301, 67, 112
  JV 44, 230, 281
  leaders of the, 78
  loss rates of the, 80, 192, 268
  Luftflotte (Air Fleet) Two, 39
  organization of the, x
  pilots of the, 20
  POW camps, 233
  raids by the, 16
  reduction in training hours for the,
    77, 255
  Schlachtgeschwader 10, 238
  shortage of men in the, 79
  Staffeln, xiii
  Stuka Wing 77, 128
  Third *Gruppe*, 128
  Thistle aircraft and, 91
  Yugoslavia and, 166–67

Luke, Frank, 18
Lusia, 241
Lyon, 138

M

MacArthur, Douglas, 260
Macchi-Castoldi 205s, 39–40
Macchis, 22, 34, 109
MacCloskey, Monro, 171, 173–74
MacVittie, William R., 157
Madjarevic, Bodgan, 166
Magyar, 90, 190, 238
Maine, 186, 265
Maloney, Thomas E. "Tom," 140–42, 273
Manduria, 45, 65, 85, 94, 132, 278
Manhattan Project, 187
Mann, Farley G., 243
Maquis, 138, 171
Marauders, 37
Mariana Islands, 261
Marine Corps, 28, 159, 262
Marseille, 5, 13, 138, 141
Marshall, George C., 3, 12, 18, 218
"Martin Wiethaupt," 194. *See also* Monti, Martin J.
Massachusetts, 238, 242
Massachusetts Institute of Technology (MIT), 55, 88
Mauldin, Bill, 259
Mauser rifles, 189
Maxwell, Robert W., 175
May Day, 243
Mayer, Egon, 78
Mayer, Frederick, 176
McConnon, James, 269–70
McConnon, John S., 269–70
McCorkle, Charles M., 56
McCorkle, Sandy, 61
McDaniel, Gordon H., 223
McElroy, George, 128

McGovern, George, 208, 240, 265
McGuire, Melvin, 205
McIlheran, R. C., 106
McManus, Leonard M., 173–74, 176
McNichol, George, 20
McQuaid, Frank, 119–20
Me 109s, 62–64, 72, 87, 107, 123–24, 190
Me 110s, 106
Me 163s, 220
Me 210s, 71
Me 262s, 47, 108, 164, 206, 220–22, 225, 227–31, 253, 263, 266, 268
Me 410s, 71
mean point of impact (MPI), 227–28
"Med, the," 259. *See also* Mediterranean Theater
Medals of Honor, 111, 260
Mediterranean Allied Air Forces (MAAF), 18, 27, 201
Mediterranean Theater, 100, 128, 159
   casualties in the, 13
   leaders in the, 2, 18, 27, 40, 133, 137, 178, 273
   as lesser theater, 166, 258–60
   operations in the, 10, 45, 97, 158, 172, 174, 181–82, 192, 202, 210, 242, 250, 255
   polio in the, 128
   strategy for the, 4, 156, 171, 218
Megara Airdrome, 192
Memmingen Airdrome, 123, 125
Memphis Belle, The, 260
Merlin engines, 56, 156, 186
Messerschmitts (Me's), x, xiii
   Budapest and, 90
   factories for, 14, 17, 23, 45, 47, 221
   missions by, 15, 34, 39, 43, 47–48, 57, 60–64, 66, 69–71, 77, 91, 94, 105–6, 108–11, 116–17, 123–24, 133, 142, 145, 153, 158, 163–64,

190, 198, 202, 206, 220, 222, 225, 227–28, 263, 266, 268
resemblance with Mustangs, 60
Messina Strait, 2
MIA, 242, 244, 270, 280
Michael (Romanian king), 136
Mickey Mouse, "Mickey," 89–90, 197–98
Mielec Airdrome, 128
"Mighty Eighth," ix, 18, 41, 95, 105, 258–60. *See also* U.S. Army Air Forces: Eighth Air Force
Mihailovi, Draža, 177–79
Milan, 194, 270
Miller, Edward L., 217
Miller, Harry, 99
Milojevic, Dusan, 167
Minneapolis, MN, 263
Mirgorod, 96, 98–99
Mission 253, 241
Mission 412, 243
Mitchell, Otis, 41–42
Mitchells, 1, 13, 37, 249
Mixson, Marion C., 205
Mohawk, Hiawatha, 105
Mollison, James A., 195, 249
Mondolfo, 244, 279
Monte Cassino, 35–36, 38
Montenegro, 174
Monti, Martin J., 193–94
Moonlight in Vermont, 73
Moosbierbaum, 69, 220
"morale bombing," 4, 22, 51–53, 66
Moravia, 174
Morehead, James B., 139
Morgan, J. L., 118
Morgan, William R., 195
Mormons, 249
Morocco, 249
Morris, Harry, 238

Morrison, George, 118
Morrison, Joe, 103
Mortensen, Gale, 203, 207, 249, 281
Mortimer Snerd, 21
Moscow, 31, 82, 98–99, 136, 183, 200–1
Mosquitoes, "Mossies," 156, 160
Mount Kasereck, 45
Mount Vesuvius, 267
MTAF, 159
Mullins, John, 264
Mullins, Phyllis, 264
Mumford, John D., 66
Munich, xi, xiii, 5, 39, 164, 196–98, 202, 225, 230–31, 238–39, 255
Munn, Marden, 50
Murphy, Audie, 165
Muse, Hugh, 20
Muslim countries, 36
Mussolini, Benito, 6, 22, 40
Mustangs, xiii, 45
design of the, 56–57
overall statistics of the, 251–53, 262
use by the Fifteenth, 56–62, 64, 66–69, 72, 80, 90, 94, 97–98, 100, 105, 107, 109–10, 116–18, 123–32, 139, 145, 151, 156, 164, 186, 195–200, 202–3, 205, 222, 225, 229, 232, 236, 247, 251–53, 262, 268–69, 271

N

Naples, 75, 142, 151, 159, 194, 267
NATO, 262, 266, 274
Nazi Germany, Nazis, 83, 194, 225, 244, 254, 272
Nebraska, 65
Nelson, Robert, 120
Nelson, Roy W., Jr., 29–30, 213
Neuberg, 225
Never a Dull Moment, 74

New Caledonia, 28–29
New Hampshire, 180
New Mexico, 65, 106, 233
New Year's Day, 212, 215
New Year's Eve, 173, 212–13
New Zealand, 38
Nice, 57
Nis, 199–200
Nixon, Richard, 265
Norden bombsight, 110, 216
Normandy, 4, 84, 100, 104, 137
Norris, Roy, 193
North Africa, 11, 18, 22, 25, 36, 98,
    128, 261
    invasion of, 2, 94, 151, 168
North African Coastal Command, 29
North African Strategic Air Force
    (NASAF), 2
North American Air Defense Command,
    262
North American (company), 9, 56–57,
    251
North Sea, 266
North Vietnam, 262
Novak, Alfred, 222
Nové Zámky, 223

O
Oakland, PA, 270
Oberfeldwebel, 236
Obertraubling, 221
Occupation Air Force, 248
O'Connell, Paul B., 242
Odertal, 119, 142, 187, 204–5, 217, 270
Office of Strategic Services (OSS), 170–
    71, 177–79
O'Hare, Edward "Butch," 125
Ohio, 154–55, 202
Ohr, Fred, 94
Oil Plan, 220, 255
"oil triangle," 205

Oklahoma, 141
Olomuc, 270
Operation Anvil-Dragoon, 137
Operation Argument, 38–39, 41, 47–48
Operation Carpetbagger, 170–77
Operation Frantic, 95–97, 101, 105, 131
    Frantic One, 97
    Frantic Three, 127
Operation Frantic Joe. *See* Operation
    Frantic
Operation Freedom, 183–84
Operation Gunn, 145–46
Operation Halyard, 178, 181
Operation Manna, 192
Operation Plunder, 225
Operation Pointblank, 4
Operation Reunion, 146
Operation Strangle, 92
Operation Tidal Wave, 66, 84, 88, 93,
    113, 121
Opissonya, 109–11
Oregon, 28
Oregon National Guard, 110, 159
Orlea, Oana, 266
Oswiecim, 217
Ottomans, 184
Oudna Airfield, 5

P
P-38 Lightnings
    use by the Fifteenth, 18–20, 22,
        38–46, 55, 59–60, 71–73, 87–88,
        102–3, 107–8, 113, 125, 131,
        133, 135, 138–42, 150, 153–60,
        163–64, 190, 193, 196–97, 199–
        203, 206–7, 216, 218, 225–26,
        230–31, 237–40, 251, 256, 264,
        278–80
    P-38Js, 185
    production of, 19, 59
P-39 Airacobras, 151

P-40 Warhawks, 21–22, 33, 58, 252, 263

P-47 Thunderbolts, 22, 33, 39, 56, 58, 60, 138, 252, 263, 280

range of, 21, 55

P-51B, 196

P-51s, 59–61, 64, 66, 90, 97, 109, 123, 143, 151, 163–64, 186, 190, 916–97, 236, 239, 244, 251–52, 268, 279, 280

Allison engine, 56

benefits of, 56–57, 64

cost of, 59, 251

as game changer, 57–58

P-80 Shooting Stars, 206

Pacific Ocean, 271

Pacific Theater, 29, 132, 139, 209, 241–42, 247, 249, 255, 260–61

Padua-Verona, 76, 239, 244

Palermo, 270

Palmer House, 180

Panama Canal Zone, 50, 261

Pan American Airways ("Pan Am"), 178

Panas, John, 216, 248, 281

Panatella, 65

Pantanella, 210, 278

Panther tanks, 230

Panzers, 141

Pape, Nate, 132

Parchim, 222

Paris, 144–45, 173, 259

Parker, Harry, 60–61, 223, 237, 281

Partisans

political opposition to, 177

relationship with Americans, 23, 61, 177–78, 180–81, 199, 222

territory of, 178–81

in World War II, 170, 177–78

Passive Defenses, 93

Pathfinders, 88–89

Pearl Harbor, HI, 82, 120, 166, 268

Pennsylvania, 267, 270

Peterhausen, 41

Petersen, Quentin R., 134

Peters, Jim, Sr., 11

Philco, 88–89

Philippines, the, 92, 251

Phillips, Milford, 135

Phoenix, 83

Photo Joes, 149, 160, 162–63, 165

Piastow, 128

"Pioneer Parachute Company," 232

Piraeus, 35

Pisa, 175, 267

Pittsburgh, PA, 269

Ploesti

bombing of, 8, 14, 66, 68, 76, 84–113, 120–22, 127, 130–36, 144, 185, 187, 255–56

defense of, 68, 85–113, 130, 257

effects of bombing on, 135–37, 256–58

importance of, x, 64, 83–84, 211, 257

location of, 5, 82–83

scouting of, 154–56, 158

Ploesti Marshalling Yard, 87

Poggiorsini, 232

Poland, Poles, 38, 96–97, 119, 187, 280

Poltava, 96, 99–100, 105

Pomigliano, 194

Popesti, 145–46

Popovich, Eli, 178

Portal, Charles, 29, 85

Potomac, 12

Po Valley, 175–76, 240

POW camps, POWs, 244

Americans in, 61, 146, 236, 248, 266, 274

Bucharest airlift, 266

of the Fifteenth, 250, 263
German camps, 233, 236, 248
Italians in, 108
Russians in, 192
Prague, 5, 69, 242
Pranjani, 179
Pratt & Whitneys (P&Ws), 9, 42, 169, 241
preparation for overseas movement (POM), 241
Presbyterians, 107
Presidential Unit Citation, 172
Pribyla, Harry, 43
Princeton University, 61
Protestants, 179
Prufening works, 46
Pucket, Donald, 121, 260
Pucket, Lorene, 121
"Puma" Fighter Group, 90, 143, 189–90, 199, 266
Punitive Expedition, 28
Purple Hearts, 165, 271
Pyle, Ernie, 259, 269
"Pyramiders," 8, 121. See also Fifteenth Army Air Force: 98th Bomb Group
Pyriatin, 96

Q

Quayle, Dan, 265
Quesada, Elwood, 28

R

Ramey, Tom, 233
Ramitelli, 124, 279
Randle, Bill, 231
"rape and rampage," 75
Rapido River, 35–36
Rau, Oscar "Ockie," 199
Rayford, Lee, 123
RDX bombs, 135, 188
Reardon, J. C., 243

"Recce" pilots, 152
Red Air Force, 53, 96
Red Cross, 157, 184, 213, 234
Redeventa, 93
Red Square, 265
"Red Tails," x, 123, 190, 226, 230, 242, 252–54. See also Fifteenth Air Force: 332nd Fighter Group
Red Tails, 260
Regensburg, 5, 12–13, 41, 43, 45–48, 55, 72, 164, 217, 219, 221, 238, 255
Regia Aeronautica, 22
Reich, the. See also Third Reich
bombing of, x, 132, 187, 254
defense of the, 39, 77, 191, 204, 224
industry of the, 47, 68–69, 118–19, 254
Reims, 244
Repubblica Sociale Italiana, 40
Republican Air Force, 40–41
Republicans, 240
Republic P-47 Thunderbolt, 21–22, 33, 49, 55–56, 58, 60, 252, 263, 280
Reschke, Willi, 143
Revi, xiii, 231
Rhine River, 225
Rhone Valley, 172
Rice, Herbert E., 46
Richard, Robert "Bob," 18, 138–39, 142
Rickenbacker, Eddie, 18
Ridenour, Carlyle, H., 8
Riem, 230
Rimini, 13
Ritz Brothers, 74
Ritz Hotel, 259
Rodina, 99
Rolls Royce, 56
Romana Americana, 83, 93–94, 101–3, 108, 112, 122, 126, 133–34, 155
Romania, 57, 131, 146, 199, 206, 274

bombing of, 8, 31, 53, 66, 68, 84, 86–87, 92–93, 100–1, 103–4, 127–28, 133, 137, 254, 256–57, 279

defense of, 66–68, 93, 113, 135

POWs in, 144–45, 184

Russian control of, 185, 188, 257

strategic value of, x, 81–83, 256–57

surrender by, 84, 183, 237

Romanian Air Force

aces of the, 65, 143–45, 266

and the Fifteenth, 66–68, 84, 86, 90, 93–94, 100, 109, 145, 257

losses of the, 109

Ninth Fighter Group, 144

Seventh Fighter Group, 66

Rome, 5, 32, 36, 52, 73, 173, 259, 267

bombing of, 2, 36, 151, 153

capture of, 101, 115

Roosevelt, Elliott, 159

Roosevelt, Franklin Delano, 17, 28, 82, 96, 166, 218, 228, 240

Rosenheim, 240

"Rosie the Riveters," 10

Rosignano, 175–76, 279

Rotterdam, 52

Route Six, 35–36

Rowe, Tom, 180–81

Royal Air Force (RAF), 138

Balkan Air Force, 178, 192

Bomber Command, 39, 254–55

casualties of the, 178

"dicey shows" and, 162

leadership of the, 85

missions by the, 63, 128–29, 133, 155–56, 179, 197, 236, 254–56

morale bombing and, 4, 22, 32, 52, 152

No. 205 Group, 134

Royal Air Force Bomber Command. See under Royal Air Force

Royal Hungarian Air Force, 90, 189. See also Hungary

"R and R," 75

Ruhland, 119, 137, 222, 226

Rush, Hugo P., 94–95, 168, 184

Russia, Russians, 40, 90, 266. See also Soviets; Soviet Union

as ally of the West, 38, 53, 90, 95–97, 135–36, 144, 179, 192, 223, 238

American interactions with, 95–99, 102, 105, 238

Bulgaria and, 183–85

conquest of Germany, 234, 238, 244

Czarist period of, 52

Doolittle raid and, 1

and the Fifteenth, 66, 127, 132, 199–201, 223, 228, 230

German invasion of, 83, 99, 105, 109

Rust, Mathias, 265

Ryan, John D., 262

Ryan, Michael, 262

S

Saab 2000 turboprops, 270–71

Sahara Desert, 8

Saint-Valentine, 224

Salerno, 2, 32

Salsola, 59–60, 74, 108, 215

Salvation Army, 213

Salzburg, 45, 238–39, 243

San Antonio, TX, 236

San Diego, CA, 9

Sandu, Ioan, 109

San Giovanni, 65, 70, 241, 278

San Pancrazio, 166–68, 278

San Severo, 74, 145, 159, 162, 202

Sardinia, 21

Schaffer, Ronald, 52

Schall, Franz, 226, 231

Schallmoser, Eduard, 231
Schambacker, C. O., 106–7
Schlachtgeschwader 10, 238. *See also*
  Luftwaffe
Schleissheim, 39–40
Schlüter, Herbert, 222
Schmidt, Chester, 255
Schultz, Otto, 20
Schwalbe, 220. *See also* Swallow
Schweinfurt, 12, 44
"Schweinfurt II," 13
Scotland, 81
Scroggs, J. F., 131
Second World War, 81, 112, 137, 169,
  191, 244, 269. *See also* World War II
Seldom Available, 242
Serbanescu, Alexandru, 66
Serbia, 167–68, 178–79, 203
Seregelyes Airdrome, 163
Shaffner, Wayne, 270
Shangri-La, 256
Sheetz, Keith W., 164
Shell Oil, 5, 261
Shirley Our Girlie, 98
"shuttle bombing," 96, 101
Siberia, 96
Sicily, 2, 4, 13, 18
Sierra Nevada, xii
Silesia, 119, 205
Silver Star, 132, 165
Skakich, Vojislav, 166–69
Skytrain, 179
Slovakia, Slovaks, 69–71, 183, 274
Slovenia, 168, 180
Sluder, Chester L. "Chet," 57, 98, 100
Smith, Claire, 270
Smith, Gerry, 270
Smith (lieutenant of Thirty-second
  Squadron), 164
Snaith, William G., 122
Snerd, Mortimer, 21

Sofia, Sofians, 5, 31, 52, 67–68, 167,
  183, 282
Sorensen, Charles E., 9
Souhozem, 111
South Africa, 251
Southbridge, MA, 242
South Dakota, 240, 265
South Korea, 251
Soviets. *See also* Russia, Russians
  as ally of the West, 66, 71, 90, 95–96,
    98–99, 101–2, 117, 131, 158,
    199, 257
  attacks against the, 66, 117, 145,
    189–90, 194
  demands of the, 38, 53, 96, 102,
    200–1, 259
  missions flown by the, 83, 90, 135–
    36, 158, 183, 188, 199–201
  post–World War II, 262–63
  Yalta and the, 218, 265, 269
Soviet Union. *See also* Russia, Russians
  Fifteenth's mission to the, 101
  leadership of the, 17
  post–World War II, 269
Spaatz, Carl "Tooey"
  and the Fifteenth Air Force, 3–4, 29,
    38, 45, 85–86, 92, 94, 104
  Göring and, 258
  and other senior officers, 17–18
  relationship with Doolittle, 4
  relationship with Eisenhower, 85
  Stalin and, 95–96
  transfers after V-E Day, 261
Spain, 40, 266
Specht, Gunther, 80
Speer, Albert, 47–48, 221, 258, 272
Spencer, Charles, 34
Spezia, 13, 19
Spinazzola, 232, 278
Spitfires, 56, 200
Spittal, 248

SS *Paul Hamilton*, 159

Stahl, Hermann, 45

Stalag Luft IV ("Luft Four"), 233–34

Stalag XI-B, 236

Stalin, Joseph, 17, 95–96, 136, 183, 218

Standard Petrol, 83

Starbuck, William T., 140

Stars and Stripes, 244

St. Benedict, 36

Steaua Romana, 84, 133–34, 155

Stefonowicz, LeRoy, 241

Steinhoff, Johannes, 78–79, 265–66, 274, 281

Steyr, 42–45, 255

Stigler, Franz, 79, 230, 263, 266, 274, 281

St. Louis, MO, 193

Stornarella, 49

Stoyanov, Stoyan, 66

Strapko, William S., 228

Strategic Air Command (SAC), 249, 262

Stratton, Wilbur, 159–60

Streparone, 228

Strother, Dean, 33, 57, 61, 127, 195, 262

Stud, 21

Stuka Wing 77, 128

Sturmflieger, 205

Sturmstaffel, 79

Sulfur Spa, 138

Sullivan, Michael, 110–11

Superfortresses, 9

Supreme Headquarters, Allied Expeditionary Force, 84

surface-to-air missile (SAM), 205–6

Swallow, 220

Sweden, 48

Swoose, The, 92

Symons, William, 110

T

"tail-end Charlie," 228

"Taps," 228

Taranto, 2

"target checks," 152

Tarrant, Yancey, 127–28

Taylor, Oliver B. "Obie," 19, 128

Taylor, Robert K., 29

Taylor, Yantis H., 195

Tedder, Arthur, 85

Tehran, 17

Tel Aviv, 249

"terror bombing," 52

Terrorflieger, 237

Test Pilot, 8

Teutons, xiii, 148, 191, 235

Texas, xiv, 106–7, 233, 263, 265

Texas Hill Country, 234

Thaxton, Charles, 222

Third Reich, 47. *See also* Reich, the

"Thistle" aircraft, 91

Thorsen, James G., 90

Thousand Plane Raid, The, 259

Thunderbolts, 21, 33–34, 46, 57–58, 60, 251–52

Tiberius, 75–76

Tichy, Ekkehard, 79–80

Tito, Josip Broz, 168, 170, 177–81, 193

TNT, 188

Tokyo, 1, 5, 52, 82

Tone, Franchot, 73

Torremaggiore, 195

Torretta, 39, 51, 287

Tortarella, 11

Toulon, 138

Tovrea, Philip E., 125

Trafton, Fred, 180

Trandafirescu, Virgil, 109

Transport Plan, the, 220

Trinidad, 249

Triolo, 19, 73, 186, 238, 249, 278

Tripoli, 167

Troy, Martin, 270

Tunis, 2, 5

Tunisia, 4–5, 7–14, 20–21, 25, 142, 159, 167

Turbos, 220–21, 227–28, 230

Turin, 270

Tuskegee Airmen, 58, 123, 252–54. *See also* Fifteenth Army Air Force: 332nd Fighter Group

Tuskegee Airmen, 260

Twelve O'Clock High, 259

Twining, Merrill, 262

Twining, Nathan F. "Nate"
    biography of, 27–29, 168
    as leader of the Fifteenth, 27, 29–31, 33–34, 37, 55–56, 65, 84–85, 88, 112, 130, 133, 135, 145, 151, 156, 158–59, 184, 195, 202, 213, 231, 245, 248, 252–53
    military operations conducted under, 32, 37–39, 41, 44, 48–51, 66–67, 84–86, 88–91, 93–94, 102, 104, 108–9, 113, 116, 136–37, 139, 155, 177–79, 185, 189–91, 197–99, 209–10, 216, 218–21, 225, 245
    service after the Fifteenth, 249, 262

Tyrrhenian Sea, 14, 75, 175

U

U-boats, 13, 138

Udine, 20, 33, 123

Ukraine, 117, 132

"Uncle Sugar," 249

Unirea Sperantza, 83, 133, 155

United States, the, 4, 12, 166, 176, 208, 247–49, 261, 266

Untersturmführer, 194

Urton, Tom, 200

U.S. Air Corps Tactical School, 28

U.S. Air Transport Command, 96, 249

U.S. Army, 12, 29, 38, 167–68
    Eighth Army Group, 176
    Fifth Army Group, 37, 101, 176, 231
    Sixth Army Group, 137

U.S. Army Air Forces (AAF), 3, 10, 12–13, 32, 48, 95, 179, 252, 258
    Eighth Air Force, 23, 88, 105, 197, 228, 234, 253–55, 266. *See also* "Mighty Eighth"
        492nd Bomb Group, 171
        801st Bomb Group. *See* Carpetbaggers
        VIII Bomber Command, 34
            859th Fighter Squadron, 172–76, 279
        leadership of the, 27, 29, 33, 51, 63, 97
        missions of the, 12–13, 16–20, 26, 39–41, 44–51, 65, 94–97, 102, 105, 170, 172, 221, 225
        versus other air forces, ix, 25, 34, 49, 195, 197, 258–61, 267, 282
    Eleventh Air Force, 260–61
    Fifteenth Air Force. *See* Fifteenth Army Air Force
    Fifth Air Force, 260
    First Air Force, 261
    Fourteenth Air Force, 261
    Fourth Air Force, 261
    Ninth Air Force, 7, 14, 260
    Seventh Air Force, 260–61
    Sixth Air Force, 261
    Tenth Air Force, 261
        Seventh Bomb Group, 109
    Thirteenth Air Force, 28, 33, 260–61
    Twelfth Air Force, 159, 175, 178, 237, 252, 260
        307th Fighter Squadron, 71
        308th Fighter Squadron, 73
        members of the, 2, 17, 261

missions of the, 4–7, 31–32, 36–37, 138, 180, 192
Thirty-first Fighter Group, 56, 60–61, 71–73, 90, 125–27, 145, 180, 186, 190, 196, 205, 221, 226, 229–30, 232, 239, 242, 244, 247, 251–54, 262, 268, 280–81
transfer to the Fifteenth, 6–7, 20, 56
XII Bomber Command, 7, 29
XII Troop Carrier Command, 178
Twentieth Air Force, 249
Twenty-first Engineer Aviation Regiment, 10
U.S. Army Ground Forces, 29, 248
U.S. Army MIA searchers, 270
U.S. Congress, 262
U.S. Department of Defense, 271
U.S. Department of War, 107, 159
U.S. Eastern Command, 96
U.S. Fifth Army, 37, 101, 176, 231
U.S. Marine Corps, 28, 159, 262
U.S. Military Mission to Moscow, 201
USO, 213, 218
U.S. Sixth Army Group, 137
U.S. Strategic Air Forces in Europe (USSTAF), 3, 29, 95, 178
Utah, xiv, 65

V

V-1 cruise missiles, 220
V-2 ballistic missiles, 220
VII Bomber Command, 34
Valorose (corporal), 73
Varnell, John, 196
Varnell, Sully, 202, 252, 263, 281
Vatican, the, 36
V-E Day, x, 27, 165, 181, 194, 198, 230, 240, 248–49, 260–61
Venosa, 205, 248, 278

Veszprem-Jutas, 90
Vezzano, 90
VHFs (radio sets), 154–56
"Victory Flights," 245
Vienna, 128–29, 187, 205
    as bombing target, 5, 55, 68–69, 76, 137, 142–43, 158, 190–91, 217, 219, 234, 238, 255
    defense of, 40, 69, 137, 142–43, 190–91, 265
Viermots, xiv, 15, 78–80, 126, 142
Villa, Pancho, 28
Vincenza, 23
Virginia, 123, 228
Vis (island), 193
Vladivostok, 243
Volkssturm, 46
Voll, John J., 59, 72, 196, 202, 252, 263, 281
von Richthofen, Wolfram, 40
Voss, Werner, 21
Vozdushni Voiski, 67
Vulgar Vultures, 70, 241. See also Fifteenth Army Air Force: 455th Bomb Group

W

Waco gliders, 193
Walsh, Robert L., 96
War Lover, The, 259
Warm Springs, GA, 240
Warren, Robert H., 95
Warsaw, 52
Washburn College, 199
Washington, D.C., 18, 72, 166–67, 201, 261
Wasserfall, 205–6
Watson, Ralph J. "Doc," 19
Watson, Thomas J., 157
Weather Reconnaissance Detachment, 154, 216, 279

Weekes, Ariel, 227, 264
Wehner, Howard, 228
Wehrmacht, xii, 118–19, 194, 220, 233,
    255–57. *See also* Luftwaffe
Weis (Austria), 211
Weissenberger, Theodor, 222
Wellingtons, 133, 135
Wels (Austria), 212
Wendover, 65
Western Allies, 244. *See also* Allies
Western Europe, 40
West Point, 3, 19, 28–29, 50, 58, 171
Whitehead, Robert W., 238
White, Robbie, 208–9
Whitwell, Joseph, 151
Wiener Neustadt, 14–15, 17, 20, 43, 60,
    92, 166, 205, 255
Willow Run, MI, 9, 65
Wilson, Charles, 132
Wilson, Henry Maitland, 3, 178
Wiltsie, Richard E., 131–32
Wisconsin, 28, 188
Women's Army Corps (WAC), 74
Woodbine Red Leader, 262
World War I, 82. *See also* Great War
    veterans of, 39–40
World War II, 193, 251, 271. *See also*
    Second World War
    Bulgaria and, 67
    casualties of, 109, 165
    end of, 218
    famous troops of, 252, 258
    friendly fire and, 60
    generation, 22
    precision bombing in, 143, 232
    role of oil in, 81–82
    veterans of, ix, 40, 165, 263, 271,
        274
Wray, Robert M. "Bob," 212
"wrench benders," 30, 232
Wright brothers, 9, 173

Wright Field, 155, 206

X

Xenia, 83, 101, 120–21, 130, 133, 135,
    155

Y

Yakovlev, Yaks, 200
Yalta, 218
Yankee Doodle, 97
Yankee Doodle II, 97
Yugos, 149
Yugoslav Detachment, 166–69
Yugoslavia, Yugoslavians
    and Americans, 23, 242
    flight missions and, 89, 100, 102,
        119, 132–33, 144, 151, 160, 167,
        170, 172–75, 177, 180–81, 185,
        199–201, 217, 220, 244, 250, 279
    geography of, 42, 86, 190
    Partisans, 61, 168, 179
Yugoslav Royal Air Force, 166–68

Z

Zadar, 181
Zagreb, 5, 41, 160, 216–17
Zalenak, Pavel, 71
Zara, 181
Zelasko, Thomas, 15–16
Zerstörer, 70–72
Zilistea, 127
Zirkle, Robert, 153
Zurney, Walter, 216–17